Revolutionary Studies

Revolutionary Studies

Essays in Plain Marxism

Paul Le Blanc

Haymarket Books
Chicago, Illinois

Published in 2017 by
Haymarket Books
P.O. Box 180165
Chicago, IL 60618
773-583-7884
www.haymarketbooks.org
info@haymarketbooks.org

ISBN: 978-1-60846-781-5

Trade distribution:
In the US, Consortium Book Sales and Distribution, www.cbsd.com
In Canada, Publishers Group Canada, www.pgcbooks.ca
In the UK, Turnaround Publisher Services, www.turnaround-uk.com
All other countries, Ingram Publisher Services International,
IPS_Intlsales@ingramcontent.com

This book was published with the generous support of Lannan Foundation
and Wallace Action Fund.

Cover design by Rachel Cohen.

Printed in Canada by union labor.

Library of Congress Cataloging-in-Publication data is available.

10 9 8 7 6 5 4 3 2 1

Contents

Author's Note

The previously published essays in this volume have preserved their original citation format. In lieu of endnotes, chapters 2 and 4 contain bibliographic sections.

Introduction

For some people, the word *revolution* is frightening, having the connotation of violence and chaos. For others, it is inspiring, having the connotation of liberation from both tyranny and oppression. It can best be understood as a popular insurgency—mass action on the part of large numbers of people, with the support of even larger numbers of people—to overturn existing and oppressive power structures, creating the basis for different social relationships and different structures of power.

I would argue that violence is not conceptually essential to what a revolution is. The fact remains, however, that most revolutions have involved some degree of violence—which was even the case in relatively "nonviolent" revolutions led by Mohandas Gandhi in India and Nelson Mandela in South Africa. It is especially the case that efforts at counterrevolution, and the often consequent eruption of civil war, can engulf a society in terrible violence. Both the American Revolution of 1775–83 and the even bloodier Second American Revolution (the Civil War, 1861–65) have amply demonstrated this truth. It is documented, for example, in Ray Raphael's *People's History of the American Revolution* and David Williams's *People's History of the Civil War*. Arno Mayer demonstrates the same in his magisterial study *The Furies: Violence and Terror in the French and Russian Revolutions*. At the core of revolution's meaning, however, is not violence but something more fundamental. Whether one is frightened or inspired by revolution, it is important to understand this profound and complex phenomenon.

Revolutions generally involve people's quest for a better world that will allow the realization of the interrelated and interactive triad that defines their humanity—freedom (self-determination), creative labor, genuine community. Revolutions are amazing events with which serious students of society and of politics must engage in order to comprehend adequately the social and political realities they are studying. Revolutions are uncommon happenings, occurring *when masses of common people force their way onto the political stage,*

1

overturning existing power relations, clearing the way for others. Examining this throws light on how history works. At the same time, it is impossible to examine such history without having the intellectual means—theory—to help sort through the complex swirl of causes and effects. Theory and history are the categories around which the present volume is organized.

The ten essays in this volume were written between 2005 and 2016, and most were published or disseminated previously. They are basically divided into two sections, one focused on questions of revolutionary theory, the other focused on revolutionary history.

The first five essays deal with my take on various theoretical aspects of the orientation that has guided many of us seeking to understand, and sometimes to change, the social, economic, and political realities—and the history—that we have been part of. The first essay lays out an approach to Marxism which may strike some as too plain and simple but which has guided my own intellectual and political efforts. The second employs Trotsky's theory of uneven and combined development to sketch out an understanding of the shape and dynamics of European history down through the end of the twentieth century. The third maps out a conceptualization I developed back in the 1980s and '90s—that of a *labor-radical subculture*, which I believe helps explain some of the history of the working class and labor movement, and which I think can be useful in future struggles. This is followed by an essay on *class* and *identities*, both analytical building blocks for those who want to understand reality in ways that can enable them to change it. The fifth essay in this theory section deals with two of my deepest prejudices—(1) the belief in the possibility and desirability of *rule by the people*, democracy, and (2) the belief that this is at the heart of the socialism to which I have committed so much of my life. These are not, however, blind prejudices, and their logic and rightness—I hope—will shine through in what I have written.

The history section of the book was originally more expansive than what is presented here. A reproduction of an article on the momentous Russian Revolutions of 1917, originally composed for the now defunct *Encarta Encyclopedia*, has been dropped in deference to a very substantial volume of mine also being published by Haymarket Books in 2017—*October Song*. The dropped essay can be found as "The Russian Revolutions of 1917" in the online journal *Links: International Journal of Socialist Renewal* (http://links.org.au/russian-revolutions -1917-paul-le-blanc). I urge readers who are interested in the themes explored in this volume to see how I attempt to interweave them in the older article and newer book on revolutionary Russia. Retained here, however, is another essay on why the revolutionary-democratic regime turned into its opposite, to which I have added an additional piece on the heroic Russian revolutionaries who struggled against the bureaucratic-authoritarian betrayal of their revolution. This is followed by reflections on two revolutions in Latin America, the Cuban and the Nicaraguan. For the final chapter, my attention turns to South Africa and the complex evolution of the struggle that brought down the racist apartheid regime (while failing to solve other key problems). Readers might also be interested in another essay considered for this volume but not included, dealing with the fascinating and complex revolutionary struggle in India—which can be found as "India Yesterday: Development and Revolution" (the first part of a three-part series on India's past, present, and future), published in the online journal *Links: International Journal of Socialist Renewal* in 2015 (http://links.org.au/node/4584).

These revolutionary developments call out for a comparative analysis, which perhaps readers will be inspired to initiate on their own, noting common themes and revealing differences. A comparative approach to revolutions—examining similarities and differences, looking for patterns and breaks in patterns—can shed light on what happened (and what might have happened but didn't) in each country. By giving us greater perspective on each revolution, the comparative approach can also give us greater perspective on revolution in general. Such an orientation in regard to the past may even be helpful in orienting us in the present and future, assuming that we don't allow precedents to blind us to possibilities.

Regarding common themes, there are at least five factors that are necessary, as an interactive totality, if there is to be a revolution. Instabilities and dissatisfactions, rooted in the "normal" functioning of society's political economy, are necessary but not sufficient for a revolution to take place. Without a larger political-social-economic calamity that creates a crisis (and crisis in confidence) for the traditional ruling class, undermining its authority and ability to rule, revolution is unlikely; but by itself such a situation does not make revolution inevitable. In other words, it is necessary but not sufficient. The same is true regarding the shared oppressions and exploitations experienced by majority sectors of the population, which form a sense of collectivity and solidarity, sometimes referred to as "class consciousness." No less necessary, and no less insufficient by themselves, are the ideologies and the actual struggles that are capable of animating oppressed social layers. Inseparable from this, of course, are the political groups and organized movements that can give voice to ideologies and edge to struggles. *All of these factors must come into play if there is to be a revolution*, or so it seems to me.

At the same time, each of these factors is advanced or blocked in various ways in one part of the world or another, in one historical moment or another, and this affects in one way or another the fortunes of revolution. There are historical, geographic, and cultural specifics that give a distinctive flavoring to one or another revolutionary struggle, and such specifics also create options in one situation that may not exist in another. Serious scholars, no less than serious revolutionaries, cannot afford to allow the specifics of one historical experience to be congealed into a rigid model to be dogmatically superimposed onto a quite different historical situation. Rather than carping at latter-day revolutionaries for refusing to do just what earlier revolutionaries had done, it is better to embrace and learn from new experiences. This hardly means throwing aside all the positive and negative lessons from the previous experiences, or shrugging off the hard-won insights articulated by revolutionaries of the past. But it does mean honoring the insight that nothing is constant but change, and being open to learning new things from changed situations, enriching both revolutionary theory and our understanding of revolutions. "Theory, my friend, is grey, but ever-green is the tree of life"—or so said the poet Goethe and the revolutionary Lenin.

While my exploration of Russian and Cuban revolutionary experiences took place entirely from afar, both studies have certainly involved a passionate engagement with the stories of the revolutionary activists and the insurgent peoples. I should acknowledge, however, that my life became more intimately intertwined with Nicaragua and South Africa (as was also the case with India). A sustained engagement with people from another country and the experience that comes from being in that country knit into one's personal makeup certain perceptions and emotions that, at least in my case, compelled me to reach out, voraciously, for ever-greater understanding. This gave my writings on these countries a "cast the net broadly" quality, which also left me frustrated over my limited abilities to comprehend and convey all that I might wish. My hope is that these writings will, nonetheless, offer something of value.

In the original conception of this volume, there was also a section on specific people associated with the revolutionary movement—theorists Antonio Gramsci and Georg Lukács, the leftist-turned-reactionary James Burnham, the wonderful poet Dennis Brutus, and the vibrant militant Daniel Bensaïd. Space limitations have forced us to set this aside, but perhaps those essays can appear in a future volume.

Missing from this volume as well is any focused discussion on my native land—although Haymarket has republished my *Short History of the U.S.*

Working Class as well as a volume of essays entitled *Left Americana*, to which interested readers are also encouraged to turn.

The project of understanding the world, and of changing it, is necessarily a collective process. The revolutionary poet Shelley, appealing to the oppressed masses (most of us) in comparison with our oppressors, emphasized that "ye are many, they are few." But these numbers can become a force for positive change only to the extent that more and more of us engage as best we can—with critical minds and creative labor—in efforts pushing forward to a society of the free and the equal, a genuine community in which there will actually be liberty and justice for all. My hope is that these essays will contribute to that.

1.

Explorations in Plain Marxism

The ideas of Karl Marx are often put forward as an invaluable resource for those wishing to understand the world in order to change it for the better. Yet various people who speak as Marxists often insist upon divergent ways of understanding even the most basic concepts associated with Marxism—such as *capitalism* and the *working class*. There are also perplexing divergences regarding such conceptions as *ideology*, *class consciousness*, and the seemingly bizarre concept of *labor aristocracy*. As if this wasn't enough, relatively new concepts—*identity* and *intersectionality*—have been thrown into the mix.

It's almost enough to make activists throw up their hands, shout an expletive or two, and walk away. Of course, one can simply jump into activity to make the world a better place while saying "to hell with all these stupid theories." But this could reduce chances of understanding the world well enough to be able to actually change it positively. Practical action can be most effective if it is guided by certain structures of understanding that correspond to the way the world actually works.

In what follows, controversies among Marxists will be touched on in a manner contributing—I hope—to the development of effective revolutionary socialist perspectives.

C. Wright Mills and Structures of Understanding

For many of us developing intellectually in the English-speaking world during the early 1960s, the radical sociologist C. Wright Mills was an incredibly important influence. While his works—such as *The New Men of Power* (1949), *The Power Elite* (1956), *The Sociological Imagination* (1960)—seem dated in various ways in our own time, their clarity, independence of spirit, and critical edge reward engagement half a century later. My own education as a Marxist was impacted when, in my mid-teens, I pored over his final work, *The Marxists* (1962).

Mills himself was not, strictly speaking, a Marxist. He had little patience with dialectics, was not inclined to fuss with the complexities of *Capital*, and concluded that the working class had—certainly by the 1950s—proved itself incapable of bringing about revolutionary change. Yet his own understanding of the world was structured, in large measure, through his own passionate engagement with the work of Karl Marx. As he put it,

> The history of social thought since the mid-nineteenth century cannot be understood without understanding the ideas of Marx. . . . He contributed to the categories dealt with by virtually all significant social thinkers of our immediate past. . . . Within the classic tradition of sociology, he provides us with the most basic single framework for political and cultural reflection. Marx was not the sole source of this framework, and he did not complete a system that stands closed and finished. He did not solve all of our problems; some of them he did not even know about. Yet to study his work today and then come back to our own concerns is to increase our chances of confronting them with useful ideas and solutions.[1]

The Marxists offered a stimulating discussion of Marxist theory and history, as well as excerpts from a diverse range of thinkers associated in one way or another with Marxism. In his critical presentation, Mills made distinctions between different kinds of Marxists. He was inclined to reject two of these—"vulgar" Marxists, who "seize upon certain ideological features of Marx's political philosophy and identify these parts as the whole," and "sophisticated" Marxists, who are "mainly concerned with Marxism as a model of society and with the theories developed with the aid of this model."[2]

Mills preferred what he termed *plain Marxists*, who "in great travail . . . have confronted the world's problems" and are inclined to be "'open' (as opposed to dogmatic) in their interpretations and uses of Marxism," and who do not shy away from confronting "the unresolved tension in Marx's work—and in history itself: the tension of humanism and determinism, of human freedom and historical necessity."[3] This approach strongly influences the thinking in the present essay.

Underlying Mills's approach is an obvious distinction between (1) the infinitely complex swirl of that vast and amazing Everything commonly referred to as "reality" and (2) the *study* of that reality, involving theoretical constructs, structures of understanding, that we utilize to make sense of reality. It is possible to use different terminologies and different conceptualizations to define the same complex aspects of reality—and nonetheless to come up with insightful and useful understandings of such reality. This outcome is also possible when two self-identified Marxists interpret and develop aspects of Marxist theory in very different ways.

One's analysis is not necessarily invalidated by the utilization of a different way of defining one or another Marxist term. While there may be validity to both approaches, however, one is superior to the other (as Marxism) to the extent that it conforms to *all* of the following criteria: (1) accuracy regarding realities being described, (2) clarity in communicating the understanding of reality, (3) coherence in relation to the totality of Marxist theory, and (4) usefulness in practical efforts to push back against oppression and to advance the cause of socialism.

This is the approach underlying the following discussion of the terms highlighted at the beginning of this essay. The purpose is to help structure our understanding of reality in order to strengthen practical efforts in the struggle for liberation.

Capitalism

Capitalism has been defined by some recent Marxists in a very particular way. For example, in his outstanding study *The American Road to Capitalism*, Charles Post has offered a definition that can be summarized as follows: an economic system in which private owners of the economy—the capitalists (the bourgeoisie)—control the means of production (land, raw materials, tools/technology, etc.) and buy the labor-power of basically propertyless wage workers (the proletariat) in order to produce commodities (products created for the market, by labor-power being turned into actual labor) that are sold at a profit. A similar definition can be found in a number of other Marxist works—for example, *Segmented Work, Divided Workers* by David Gordon, Richard Edwards, and Michael Reich, which succinctly defines capitalism as "a wage labor system of commodity production for profit."[4]

This seems a reasonable description of what happens under capitalism. There is, however, a problem that develops when this definition is applied to history. For example, before the American Civil War (1861–65) a majority of the labor force in the United States was not made up of wage workers. The Southern economy was predominantly agricultural, and the bulk of the Southern agricultural labor force was made up of slaves. Combined with the large number of poor white farmers, the great majority of laborers consisted of those who did not sell their labor-power to capitalists—so by this definition, the Southern economy could not be termed capitalist. For that matter, a majority of the Northern labor force from colonial times down to the Civil War was made up of small farmers, artisans and craftsmen, and small shopkeepers—only a minority were wage workers. By definition, it could be argued, capitalism simply did not exist in the United States until the 1820s or 1840s or 1860s (which is the position of the afore-mentioned volumes).

The problem is that Marx and Engels themselves believed capitalism *did* exist in the United States not only after the Civil War, but before—and not only in the antebellum "free labor" North but also in the slave-labor South. Of course, Marx and Engels were only human and could be wrong—although it seems ironic that those who first developed Marxist theory would be so fundamentally wrong in their understanding of how to apply that theory. The problem deepens when we realize that what was true in the United States was true in most of Europe as well, with the exception of England. This was the case when the two revolutionaries wrote the *Communist Manifesto*, when they were helping to organize the International Workingmen's Association, and when Marx was writing *Capital*. It could be argued their analyses of capitalism represented a forecast of the future rather than a prescription for the present—but this is not how they themselves characterized their work.[5]

An additional complication is posed by the question, if it wasn't capitalism, what form of economy was it? In the slave-plantation South, the dynamics of the economy were different from those of the ancient slave economies, nor did they conform to the dynamics of feudalism. Was it some form of economy that Marx and Engels did not conceptualize? (Post thinks so, presenting it as a theoretically revised variant of what the late historian Eugene Genovese termed "pre-bourgeois civilization.") The same question can be posed regarding the form of economy in the pre–Civil War North and in nineteenth-century Europe. (The above two volumes tag it as a noncapitalist economy of "petty-commodity production.") It is possible to argue that there are better ways of understanding the world than the way Marx and Engels understood it in their day, that they were living—contrary to what they seemed to believe—in a fundamentally *precapitalist* reality. But this suggests a certain incoherence in how this particular definition of capitalism connects with the overall perspectives of Marx and Engels.

On the other hand, the problem may stem from the fact that a reasonable description of *mature capitalism* does not constitute a reasonable definition of capitalism as such. Capitalism involves an incredibly dynamic *process of development*, a process of capital accumulation, transforming the world over and over again. It remains true to its own dynamism by taking on a variety of different forms.

It could be argued that a more useful definition of capitalism (perhaps more consistent, also, with the perspectives of Marx and Engels) would posit four fundamental elements in the capitalist economy, three of which are relatively simple: the economy (means of production combined with labor) is privately owned, it is more or less controlled by the owners (in the sense that they make decisions regarding economic policy), and the guiding principle of economic decision making involves *maximizing* profits for the owners. The fourth element is far more complex: the economy involves *generalized commodity production*—a buying-and-selling economy, or market economy. With generalized commodity production, more and more and more aspects of human needs and human life are drawn into commodity production, into the production of goods and services that are created for the purpose of selling them, in order to maximize the profits of the capitalists over and over and over again. Capitalists are driven to develop technology and the production process to create more and more profits. And more and more people in society are forced to turn their ability to work (their life-energy, their strength, their intelligence, their abilities and skills) into a commodity, selling their labor-power in order to "make a living" (to be able to buy commodities they need in order to live and additional commodities that they want in order to make life more tolerable). This more open way of defining capitalism allows for considerably more diversity in the forms that capitalism takes, and it captures the incredibly fluid, dynamic "all that is solid melts into air" quality of capitalism referred to in the *Communist Manifesto*.

As the Civil War writings of Marx and Engels indicate, it is possible for peculiar variants of capitalism to develop that—for example—make the entire laborer (not just his or her ability to work) into a commodity to be bought and sold, as slaves (not just "wage slaves," as many free laborers dubbed themselves). The different variants of capitalism yield dramatically different social and cultural dynamics, just as they are intertwined with dramatically different economic policy needs (high tariffs versus low tariffs, etc.) as well as consequent dramatic differences in political goals, which combined to culminate in the bloody explosion of 1861–65. Moving back further in economic theory, as Adam Smith's 1776 classic *Wealth of Nations* indicates, capitalism develops and continues to exist before a majority of the labor force is transformed into a wage-earning proletariat. And as Leon Trotsky's theory of uneven and combined development suggests, different modes of production can combine in a variety of peculiar ways to create an unstable economic, cultural, and political mix, often with explosive consequences, especially given capitalism's incredible dynamism. To utilize a relatively simple definition of capitalism, then, does not necessarily whisk away the complications and contradictions with which serious theorists must wrestle.[6]

But we must see capitalism as a complex and dynamically evolving reality, a vast and contradictory process, assuming different forms in different moments of history and in different places on our planet. All this is inseparable from the relentless process of capital accumulation. The diversity of "capitalisms" cannot be defined by a single description. This is particularly true in regard to the shaping and reshaping of the working class, which is always in process, being composed and decomposed and recomposed by the dynamics of the capital accumulation process—over and over again being "pulled apart and pushed together," as Kim Moody once put it. "The shape of the working class in all corners of the world has changed as capitalism itself has altered its geographic, organizational, and technological contours," he noted near the close of the last century. "As old structures of the working class are altered, however, new ones arise."[7]

This brings us to additional Marxist debates about yet another central Marxist category—the *proletariat*, or working class. (Or are these two terms really synonyms?)

The Working Class

Some Marxist theorists have introduced what appear to me to be unnecessary complications in the way the central category *working class* is to be understood. One of the best expositors of Marxism, Hal Draper, makes a distinction between the *proletariat* (which he defines as those whose labor creates surplus-value for capitalists, i.e., those in the private sector of the economy) and a broader *working class* (more simply, those who sell their ability to work). Nicos Poulantzas, in a similar manner but with different labels, makes a distinction between *workers* (those who produce surplus-value for capitalists) and a more inclusive category of those who are *wage-earners* (some of whom do not produce surplus-value and whom he designates as a "new petty bourgeoisie"). Erik Olin Wright, highly critical of Poulantzas, developed the category of *contradictory class locations*, distinguishing between "pure" workers and those who have "mixed locations"—workers who have a significant degree of autonomy over their labor and/or exploited workers who, nonetheless, have control over other workers. Wright sees these as a *blend* of the proletarian and the "petty bourgeois."[8]

All of this is in contrast to the simple, more open definition offered by Frederick Engels in an 1888 footnote to the *Communist Manifesto*: "By bourgeoisie is meant the class of modern capitalists, owners of the means of social production and employers of wage labor. By proletariat, the class of modern wage laborers who, having no means of production of their own, are reduced to selling their labor power in order to live."[9]

It is not clear why Engels's identification of the *class of wage laborers* (working class) with the *proletariat* is inferior to Hal Draper's insistence upon a distinction. Among the problems with Poulantzas's restrictive analysis are (1) the fact that it seems to restrict, in our own time, the working class of advanced capitalist countries to a declining fraction of the labor force (which throws into question a key element of Marxism's strategic orientation), and (2) the fact that historically it would read out of the ranks of the working class most of the leadership and the social base, for example, of the Paris Commune of 1871 (which throws into question the judgment of Marx and Engels, who hailed the Commune as an example of political rule by the revolutionary working class). Even Wright's conceptualization of "mixed-class locations" seems to collide with certain historical realities. For example, through Francis Couvares's incisive study of Pittsburgh's working class from 1877 to 1919, we can see that skilled workers who had both a significant degree of autonomy over their labor and at the same time had a significant degree of control over less-skilled laborers working under them, provided the leadership for the explosive insurgency of 1877 and the momentous Homestead steel strike of 1892.[10]

This is hardly meant to restrict class analysis to the simplicity of Engels's 1888 definition—but keeping the definition simple may enable latter-day Marxist analysts and activists to develop more complex theorizations without violating theoretical coherence, historical accuracy, or the potential for strategic clout. It is here that *identity*, *intersectionality*, and *class consciousness* come in.

Identity and Intersectionality

The driving force in Marx's theoretical work involved a belief in the need for a revolution that could replace capitalism with a new and liberating socialist society. Revolutions involve the active participation of masses of people, the overturn of established ruling groups, and the creation of a new political and social order. How people actually see or identify themselves as they engage in social struggles, and the identities they seek to build on, or to foster, in order to bring about social change, is of central importance for the unfolding of any revolutionary process. The examination of such matters of *identity* is important for those wishing to understand such processes. Among the most potent identities in modern revolutionary movements has been that of class, and we have seen that a belief in the economic role and experience—and the potential power—of the working class was central to Marx's understanding of the revolutionary process.

To a very large extent in the late twentieth century, however, organized labor did not appear to play the militantly class-struggle role Marxists had expected of it—a disappointed expectation (we have noted) that profoundly influenced the thinking of radical intellectuals such as C. Wright Mills. Labor's radical left wing dramatically deteriorated in many capitalist countries in the decades following 1950, with a significant radicalizing reversal in the late 1960s giving way to even more dramatic decline in the century's final decades. This took place even as capitalist reality had increasingly negative impact on various social groups. Under the impact of such realities, over time a specialized concept of *identity* was developed—particularly by theorists influenced by the philosophical current known as post-structuralism—which focuses on the way in which specific social groups have self-identified or have been identified by others, a means for defining relationships with those around them. (Mills had died by this time, but he would have been quick to note similarities between this concept and sociologist Max Weber's notion of *status*).[11]

One can begin an understanding of this conception by reflecting on the fact that each of us is conscious of having many different identities that are important to defining who we are. Among the variety of such identities—some of which seem more vibrant to us than others—are the following (in no particular order): our place within a particular family; our gender; our race and/or ethnicity; our nationality; our age; our religious orientation; our attitude toward specific political ideas; our sexual orientation and preferences; the foods we like; our musical preferences, the clothes we choose to wear, and other cultural inclinations; our favorite hobbies and pastimes; organizations that we happen to belong to; our residential location in a city, a small town, or a rural area; our income level; our particular economic occupation and skill level within that occupation; and *the socioeconomic class we happen to belong to*.

It can be argued that most people are not naturally inclined to "privilege" the final, italicized identity in the previous paragraph. A reasonable question is why—if the critical points made by C. Wright Mills and others are valid—one's class identity, particularly working-class identity, should be privileged. Some have argued that if one is concerned with revolutionary protest and change, an identify focus very different than that of *class* is far more relevant.

One Marxist response could be that the exploitation of a working-class majority by a capitalist minority—and the centrality of the working-class majority to the functioning of society as a whole—creates a social reality and revolutionary potential not duplicated by any of the other identities. This hardly dismisses the central importance of certain other identities—particularly race/ethnicity, gender, sexuality. Liberation struggles of oppressed groups (such as Blacks and women) are absolutely essential for social progress and for human liberation, and independent social movements (respectively controlled by Blacks and women) are indeed needed to advance such struggles.[12]

The fact is, however, that the majority of the people in such mass movements (regardless of how they consciously identify themselves) happen to be part of the working class, that such struggles are objectively in the interests of the working class as a whole, and that such movements and struggles can play a vanguard role in helping to radicalize the working class and lead it forward in the struggle against the capitalist status quo.

Yet the working class reality must be understood not simply as an abstract category but as a process, associated with the ongoing dynamics of capitalism, through which the class is formed and re-formed from a massive body of people who are shaped by a variety of identities, subject to a variety of cultural and historical influences, involving a complex network of relationships and varying elements of consciousness related to these dynamic realities. We are shaped by the simultaneous influences of race, class, gender, sexuality, and more—many of which involve, in our historical context, various distinct and intense forms of oppression. Some activist-theorists have called this complex reality *simultaneity* or *intersectionality*.[13]

In terms of practical revolutionary strategy, the central category of *working class* must be understood in all of its vibrant intersectional diversity, with each struggle by its various component parts understood as a vital and necessary element of the overall class struggle.

Class Consciousness, Ideology, and Labor Aristocracy

A Marxist theorist can insist that a variety of social struggles—against racism, for women's liberation, for gay rights, against war, in defense of the natural environment, in defense of public spaces and services (such as parks, schools, transit systems, health care, libraries), etc.—are really part of the overall class struggle of the proletariat. And such an assertion may arguably be absolutely true. But this does not mean that the working class as a whole, or those who make up the base of the various social struggles (most of whom happen to be part of the working class) will see things that way. This brings us to the vitally important notion, for Marxists, of *class consciousness*.

To discuss this adequately, we must confront another terminological kink within the Marxist tradition having to do with the word *ideology*. Many Marxists, especially those who deeply engage with and base their analysis on early philosophical texts by Marx, give a distinctive definition to *ideology*. For them, it basically adds up to "false consciousness," that is, a set of ideas or belief system covering over the oppressive realities of the status quo, leading the oppressed and exploited and everyone else, in one way or another, to accept and help perpetuate an oppressive and exploitative system. This stands in contrast to a genuinely scientific and true—nonideological—understanding of reality, represented by Marx's thought. There are problems with this approach, one being that it seems a dogmatic assumption that Marxism alone represents the One True System of Understanding Reality (a fatally closed system of thought), thereby gliding over the possibility that Marx himself, and those closest to him (however that is determined), were no less human than the rest of us and therefore may have gotten some important things wrong, may have been deceived, or deceived themselves, into believing false notions. There are other Marxists—most notably Lenin—who have used the term in a more neutral manner. This approach sees an ideology as simply a set of ideas, a belief system, which one utilizes to make sense of reality. That is how I prefer to use the term. An ideology *may* be false (I consider this to be the case with a diverse set of belief systems that include fundamentalist religions, vulgar Marxism, pro-capitalist liberalism, racism, sexism, homophobia, fascism, etc.), but not necessarily. It may yield some valid insights, it may provide a more or less adequate understanding of reality, it may be interpreted and utilized in foolish or invaluable ways, it may be blended fruitfully or chaotically with other ideologies, or it may do something else.[14]

With this neutral usage, Marxism itself represents an ideological perspective. If it is interpreted, developed, and utilized intelligently, and it is communicated clearly, it can play an invaluable role in contributing to the *consciousness* of the working class.

Which brings us to the meaning of the term *class consciousness*. For Marxists, the term does not mean simply whatever happens to be in the mind of a worker. It suggests, instead, (a) understanding that there is a capitalist system that is oppressive and exploitative toward the working class to which one belongs, (b) that it is possible and necessary for workers to join together to advance the interests of themselves and the working class as a whole, (c) that this involves a power struggle with the capitalist class that can be won partially in the short term and definitively in the longer term, and (d) that this struggle leads to an economic, social, and political order that is truly democratic and in which the free development of each person will be the condition for the free development of all. This may seem a tall order, yet such class consciousness has existed on a mass scale many times over the past century and a half.[15]

But this does not happen automatically. History shows that for broad sectors of the working class, due to their location and the objective conditions bearing down on them (living conditions, working conditions, and related experiences and relationships), it is *possible* to develop an accurate understanding of their situation, adding up to the kind of revolutionary class consciousness described above. But it is not the case that workers *always* develop such consciousness. There is often a significant gap between, on the one hand, the "ripeness" of objective conditions (the blatant oppressiveness and destructiveness of capitalism, along with the intensified suffering among the masses of people who are part of the working class) and, on the other hand, the low level of class consciousness among a majority of workers. They may fail to grasp clearly the sources of their misery and what to do to end it. Many workers have an insufficient level of knowledge and revolutionary determination even under the most oppressive conditions. To the extent that class consciousness develops among workers, it does so unevenly. Some come to such insights and beliefs, which they share with others, some of whom are persuaded, and some of whom require more experience before such consciousness makes sense to them. There are some who never develop such consciousness.

This means that bad conditions are not inevitably reflected in an increasingly revolutionary workers' consciousness, that the problems of capitalism do not inevitably turn workers into socialists or revolutionaries. Historically, the first layers of the working class to turn to socialism and labor action—those who assume a vanguard position within the class as a whole—have not been the most oppressed unskilled workers, but rather the less downtrodden skilled workers. At the same time, this relatively "privileged" layer of the working class can become, and historically often has become, an *aristocracy of labor* that follows an utterly opportunistic policy that sacrifices the basic interests of the mass of workers in favor of the temporary interests of a small number of workers.

Before going further, we need to come to terms with another terminological squabble among Marxist theorists, in this case over—*aristocracy of labor*.

In a recent essay, Charles Post challenged the theory of the labor aristocracy. Noting that variants of the theory have been offered by Marx and Engels, by Lenin and Gregory Zinoviev, and more recently by Max Elbaum and Robert Seltzer, he comments that all include two key points: (1) "working-class conservatism is the result of material differences—*relative privileges*—enjoyed by some workers," and (2) "the source of this relative privilege ('the bribe') is a sharing of higher-than-average profits between capitalists and a privileged labor-aristocracy." He argues that the second point appears true in some periods (for example, "during the 1940s, 1950s and 1960s certain branches of industry enjoyed stable, higher-than-average profits and wages," corresponding to conservatized unions in those industries) but that profits then went down in those industries. (He seems to glide over the fact that, subsequently, the unions in question were largely pushed back and in some cases eliminated, partly due to the dynamics of deindustrialization and globalization.) He argues that the first point—regarding the inevitable conservatism of more "privileged" workers—is disproved by the fact that, as we have also emphasized, the better-off skilled workers actually played a vanguard role in trade union and socialist struggles in much of the nineteenth and twentieth centuries.[16]

Among, for example, the skilled metal workers in tsarist Russia, the influence of Lenin's Bolsheviks was quite high. Of course, there were various tendencies, different levels of consciousness, within this stratum. One worker later recalled the early days of the Russian labor movement this way:

> At that time, the difference between metal and textile workers was like the difference between the city and the countryside. . . . Metal workers considered themselves aristocrats among other workers. Their occupations demanded more training and skill, and therefore they looked down on other workers, such as weavers and the like, as an inferior category, as country bumpkins: today he will be at the mill, but tomorrow he will be poking at the earth with his wooden plow.

Naturally, the highest percentage of women workers were among these lowly textile workers, allowing for male chauvinism to blend with the disdain for "bumpkins." Yet later, a militant metal worker would express a different way of thinking: "Only a conscious working person can truly respect a human individual, women, cherish a tender child's soul. We will not learn from anyone but ourselves. We, the conscious working people, have no right to be like the bourgeois." Noting the impulse of many conscious workers to reach out to their less fortunate class brothers and sisters, one observer wrote that "the spiritual process is an active one. Once the voice of the individual has begun to speak in the worker, he can neither sit under a bush . . . nor limit himself to words. . . . The strength of this process is in its dynamism: the upward strata of the proletariat lift up the backward strata to its level." This process was by no means automatic, but rather took years before coming to fruition. Without it, however, there would have been no Russian Revolution. It was this vanguard layer of the working class, as Lenin put it, that would be "capable of assuming power and leading the whole people to socialism, of directing and organizing the new system, of being the teacher, the guide, the leader of all the working and exploited people in organizing their social life without the bourgeoisie and against the bourgeoisie."[17]

In contrast to this were the "opportunist" trends that also existed in the labor movement, which Lenin denounced for training "the members of the workers' party to be the representatives of the better-paid workers, who lose touch with the masses, 'get along' fairly well under capitalism, and sell their birthright for a mess of pottage, renounce their role as revolutionary leaders of the people against the bourgeoisie." An example drawn from US labor history would be the trend among skilled workers within the American Federation of Labor of adopting a narrow "pure and simple" trade unionism that cares for the needs of a small number of organized workers (themselves) while excluding women, immigrants, racial and ethnic minorities, unskilled and unemployed workers, and in general rejects broader social concerns. There is nothing that inevitably pushes this layer in the direction either of opportunist labor aristocracy or principled revolutionary vanguard. What is decisive is the ability of revolutionaries within this layer, as within the entire working class, to organize for the purpose of winning their workmates, and their sisters and brothers in the working class as a whole, over to a revolutionary understanding of what's what and what's needed.[18]

Practical Action Rooted in Theory

Within the tradition of Marxism, the best analysis is grounded in the serious study and understanding of history, economics, and society, and also in the practical experience—instructive mistakes and gains, defeats, and victories—of working-class struggles. Taken as a whole, this constitutes a body of Marxist theory, a way of understanding things. Theory becomes an invaluable guide to practical action. Yet it must remain open to evolving realities, new insights, new tasks. Revolutionary-minded activists, drawing on this rich and open and critical-minded body of thought, can and must reach out to various sectors of today's working class—which in countries such as the United States includes the great majority of people: blue-collar and white-collar workers of various kinds, production workers and service employees in the public and private sectors, proletarianized "professionals" as well as impoverished agricultural laborers, not to mention family members and others dependent on the paychecks of those selling their labor-power, and the substantial ranks of both unemployed and retired workers.

We are many, but our success will be dependent upon a sufficient degree of class consciousness among a substantial number of us. This class consciousness, in our own time, must incorporate insights that reflect the realities associated with notions of *identity* and *intersectionality*. It must be said that this approach is not entirely new. "The Social-Democrat's ideal should not be the trade union secretary, but *the tribune of the people*, who is able to react to every manifestation of tyranny and oppression, no matter where it appears, no matter what stratum or class of the people it affects," Lenin insisted.[19] The struggles we are engaged with encompass the human rights, the elemental democratic rights, of all sectors of our class, all identities within our class. Without the thoroughgoing struggle for such democratic rights, there can be no socialism. Again, Lenin was on the cutting-edge of comprehending such realities:

> The proletariat cannot be victorious except through democracy, i.e., by giving full effect to democracy and by linking with each step of its struggle democratic demands formulated in the most resolute terms. It is absurd to *contrapose* the socialist revolution and the revolutionary struggle against capitalism to a *single* problem of democracy, in this case, the national question. We must *combine* the revolutionary struggle against capitalism with a revolutionary program and tactics on all democratic demands: a republic, a militia, the popular election of officials, equal rights for women, the self-determination of nations, etc. While capitalism exists, these demands—all of them—can only be accomplished as an exception, and even then in an incomplete and distorted form. Basing ourselves on the democracy already achieved, and exposing its incompleteness under capitalism, we demand the overthrow of capitalism, the expropriation of the bourgeoisie, as a necessary basis both for the abolition of the poverty of the masses and for the *complete* and *all-round* institution of *all* democratic reforms. Some of these reforms will be started before the overthrow of the bourgeoisie, others *in the course* of that overthrow, and still others after it. The social revolution is not a single battle, but a period covering a series of battles over all sorts of problems of economic and democratic reform, which are consummated only by the expropriation of the bourgeoisie. It is for the sake of this final aim

that we must formulate *every one* of our democratic demands in a consistently revolutionary way. It is quite conceivable that the workers of some particular country will overthrow the bourgeoisie *before* even a single fundamental democratic reform has been fully achieved. It is, however, quite inconceivable that the proletariat, as a historical class, will be able to defeat the bourgeoisie, unless it is prepared for that by being educated in the spirit of the most consistent and resolutely revolutionary democracy.[20]

This strategic orientation—an uncompromising struggle for thoroughgoing democracy flowing into an unstoppable upsurge toward socialist revolution—becomes effective only when it animates substantial sectors of our class, and this will not happen automatically. Those of us who share this vision must organize ourselves, and join with other like-minded forces to organize struggles through which such revolutionary class consciousness can assume mass proportions. As enough people in the diverse and multifaceted working-class majority become "conscious" workers, organized as a political force capable of bringing about a revolutionary power shift, possibilities will open up for the flowering of a society of the free and the equal.

2.

Uneven and Combined Development and the Sweep of European History (2005)

I t is often rationalized that a European bias in the study of world history makes sense because in modern times that history can best be comprehended as a process of "Westernization"—the growing dominance of capitalism in the global economies of our planet, the gradual and accelerating crystallization of a unified global economy, with the accompanying spread of Western (i.e., European) cultural, social, and political models and norms. While there is a strong element of validity to this, it also can introduce substantial distortions of the historical process.

Before the "rise of the West," driven by the emergence of capitalism and particularly the incredible engine of the Industrial Revolution, the dominant global trend was "Southernization"—the process of extensive diffusion of cultural, economic, social, and political influences from portions of southern Asia and the Middle East (including throughout Europe). In addition, even after the Westernization process began, the dynamics of historical development in the various countries and cultures of the global South have been marked by a sometime relative autonomy that challenges Western conceptualizations. But more, there is an obvious, ongoing, and accelerating impact, influence, and interpenetration of the cultures of the global South on and with those of the West (or North), a global transformative process.

An important conceptual tool for responding to such dynamics is the theory of uneven and combined development formulated by Leon Trotsky as a contribution to the rich body of Marxist analysis. Trotsky's theory will be elaborated and utilized in this essay, and while a European focus is employed here, consistent with the Westernization model, I use it simply as an initial and incomplete effort to suggest the general applicability of Trotsky's theorization, a theorization most consistent with a more rounded account of global history than is provided here.

From the fifteenth through the mid-nineteenth centuries, a fundamental transformation took place in Europe—a transformation based on the shift from one economic system to another, from one mode of production to another, from feudalism to capitalism. The manner in which this shift took place, and the consequences of the shift, set into motion a number of historical dynamics that shaped the modern world and that—among other things—resulted in the major calamities of the twentieth century: the collision of imperialisms, two world wars that sandwiched the Great Depression, the rise and fall of fascism, the haunting specter of Communism, momentous struggles and death camps and labor camps and shattered dreams, and the Cold War threat of nuclear overkill fading into a new global order (accompanied by a carbon-induced tilt in the planet's climate). This essay will trace in broad strokes a general interpretative framework through which, hopefully, we can make better sense of the welter of experiences and the swirl of events that constitute the history of modern Europe.

The Uneven Transition to Capitalism

The concept of the mode of production consists of two interlinked elements: the forces of production and the relations of production. The forces of production, which include such things as raw materials, tools, and sources of energy (taken together, these things are known as the means of production) plus human labor-power, combine in such a way to create the products that make it possible for individuals and society as a whole to survive and develop. These are the productive forces, the means of production (raw materials and technology) plus labor. The relations of production are constituted by the economic ownership of the means of production and control over the labor force—and this can be referred to as the class relations in society.

The old feudal mode of production was primarily agricultural, in which the two principal classes were the powerful warrior stratum, the so-called nobility, and the laboring peasants, who worked the land but were compelled to surrender to the nobles either portions of their labor or the product of their labor over and above what was needed for peasant family subsistence. In return, the nobility was expected to provide protection and assistance to the peasantry. The traditionalist ideology that dominated feudal society involved a vision of divinely created social orders, divided between those who prayed (the clergy), those who fought (the nobility, or feudal lords), and those who worked (the peasants, who were often transformed into serfs—that is, forced to stay on the land under the control of the lords). In this organic view of society, the three social orders (or estates) were mutually supportive and had defined roles, outside of which no one born or appointed to a particular order must step. To do so would be a violation of social stability, of the way things were supposed to be, and of God's will.

A transitional period of several centuries saw the erosion of this system, as international trade created a growing market for products coming from one or another area. More and more, goods were produced not simply for immediate consumption by lords and priests and peasants, but for the purpose of exchange at the marketplace. To facilitate such exchange, a money economy became increasingly important, and the feudal ruling classes became increasingly caught up in it. The notion of property and property rights transformed feudal relations, with the nobles transforming themselves into a landowning aristocracy who came to consider their own private property the lands traditionally occupied by the peasantry.

There was a growing tendency for these aristocrats to exploit their peasants more severely, through feudal dues and rents, in order to accumulate greater wealth and luxuries. This generated peasant rebellions in some cases. In other cases, peasants fled the land. Sometimes peasants were driven out by landowners who sought more profitable uses of the land, such as raising sheep to provide wool for the growing textile trade.

New classes began to emerge, particularly in growing urban areas (or burgs). The burgers—or bourgeois—were largely what came to be known as businessmen, or capitalists. There were those who invested money in trade (or commerce, the activity of the merchants) in order to make a profit, buying products plentiful in one area to sell for a higher price to those in need of them in another area. Some of these merchants were able to accumulate enough money in this way to become financiers—financing various projects undertaken by merchants and aristocrats, making loans at interest. Other merchants of more modest means established small shops, taverns, and inns. Along with these commercial and financial capitalists, there arose a growing stratum of producers—artisans and craftsmen, stratified into apprentices, journeymen, and master-craftsmen—who originally organized into guilds representing various skilled trades.

Less fortunate but increasing in number were unpropertied and unskilled laborers, blurring into the destitute mass of the urban poor. With the passage of time, some capitalists increasingly shifted from a focus in commerce and finance to manufacturing, hiring craftsmen and laborers to produce commodities that would be appropriated by the capitalist and sold at a profit. More and more things became commodities—products to be sold at the marketplace—including human labor-power.

All of this subverted the feudal order. So did the new ideas that began to develop. Individualistic, experimental, scientific, and rationalist orientations came to compete with the traditionalist faith-based and supernatural ideologies. This helped to generate, and was in turn further stimulated by, new developments in knowledge and technology. This trend has been identified with the Age of Reason and the Enlightenment, reflecting a different way of thinking connected with a different way of life. A new mode of production and new ideological perspectives were gaining power.

The feudal order evolved under the impact of all this. Previously, limited communications and transportation systems and the localized nature of the feudal economic units had meant that effective rule could only be exercised over a relatively small area. But remarkable changes in technology and the interconnection of more and more areas by the capitalist marketplace changed this. Not only had it become possible to rule over increasingly large areas, but the needs of capitalist economic development created strong pressures to do so. Certain powerful sections (or factions) of the feudal nobility sought to take advantage of the new possibilities by establishing centralized monarchies, consolidating nation-states under absolutist rule.

In those sections of Europe where such monarchist nation-states took shape, a considerable amount of power was concentrated into the hands of absolutist rulers. But the result was fraught with tensions among different modes of production, among widely differing social classes, among different factions within those classes, and among divergent ideological orientations. All of this was heightened by dramatic complications resulting from the development of the market economy—significant fluctuations in prices, economic rivalry among nations (which generated costly military expenditures and wars), and monetary policies by absolutist rulers that generated debts and taxes at levels that would have been unimaginable in earlier centuries.

Increasingly, rival factions within the aristocracy and within the bourgeoisie sought to enhance their power against each other and against monarchist-absolutism by appealing to and mobilizing the lower middle classes (artisans

and shopkeepers) as well as the urban and even rural poor. This greatly contributed to the ideological ferment—even more so when, in some cases, the newly
politicized masses began to slip away from upper-class influence and develop
even more radical notions of their own. What's more, the growth of towns and
cities, with dynamic urban populations, created centers of social, intellectual, and
revolutionary ferment that would provide leadership for future transformations.

A series of revolutionary upheavals resulted from this profoundly unstable
situation. Revolutions in the Netherlands and England in the 1600s resulted
in a new political and social synthesis in those countries. This culminated in
non-absolutist—limited—monarchies and the triumph of the capitalist mode
of production.

In France, however, the revolutionary explosion of 1789–93 was dramatically more violent and far-reaching. The monarchy sought the implementation
of modest reforms that would ease social tensions in a manner that would help
preserve the power of the monarchy. In contrast, an alliance of aristocrats and
moderate bourgeois elements, with support from the peasantry and the urban
masses, sought to introduce political and social reforms that would ease social
tensions in France while bringing an end to monarchist-absolutism. But the
contradictions in French society were too great, and the resulting social crisis
too severe, to be solved by mild reforms and halfway measures. In the face of
rising expectations and deepening radicalization of the masses, not only was
the authority of the crown overwhelmed, but the new aristocrat/bourgeois
alliance was also swept away. The power of the king was smashed, and a succession of moderately revolutionary leaderships were violently cast aside in
the face of the increasingly revolutionary momentum of the masses. The most
radicalized and politically conscious sections of the masses wanted a thoroughgoing political democracy and a social order in which freedom, equality,
and brotherhood were a living reality.

Although the revolutionary masses of France—covered by the catchall
term "the people"—were uncompromisingly anti-feudal, they were composed
of contradictory class elements, and this made it impossible for a shared consensus to form around a clear program that would bring about a realization of
the most radical of their stated goals. "The people" (that is, peasants, artisans,
shopkeepers, laborers, some capitalist manufacturers, and more) may have been
united in their dissatisfaction with the old order, but they had different conceptions of precisely what would be the virtues of the new order. This, combined
with economic dislocations, civil war, and foreign invasions, paved the way for
confusion and murderous infighting among the revolutionary leaders. In this

context, the radicalizing momentum of the French Revolution was cut short, giving way, from 1794 through 1799, to a succession of rightward-moving and corrupt dictatorships, and finally to the military coup of Napoleon Bonaparte.

Uneven and Combined Development to 1850

The French Revolution is often seen as the high point of *bourgeois-democratic* revolution. This is defined as a revolution that sweeps away the vestiges of the feudal mode of production, clearing the way for the full development of capitalism, replacing monarchist-absolutism with a popular and representative form of government.

In the course of the nineteenth century, the capitalist mode of production triumphed throughout Europe. Yet the transformation in France took place in a manner that was qualitatively different from the form it took throughout the rest of the continent—and if we understand why that was the case, we'll also be able to grasp one of the central keys for explaining the subsequent history of Europe.

There is an obvious and simple law of history that has profoundly important consequences. This is the law of uneven development, which recognizes that different areas and different countries are just that—different. While all of Europe had been dominated by some variety of feudalism, and while all of Europe was affected by the development of the capitalist market, the different regions had their own particular characteristics. For various reasons, technological and cultural and ideological innovations arose first in one area and then had an impact on other areas at different times—leading to uneven development in the history of Europe as a whole.

This leads to another historical law that was expressed most clearly by Russian revolutionary theorist Leon Trotsky in this way: "Unevenness, the most general law of the historic process, reveals itself most sharply and complexly in the destiny of backward countries. Under the whip of external necessity their backward culture is compelled to make leaps. From the universal law of unevenness thus derives another law which, for the lack of a better name, we may call the law of combined development—by which we mean a drawing together of the different stages of the journey, a combining of separate steps, an amalgam of archaic with more contemporary forms."

This law of uneven and combined development guaranteed that the dynamics of the bourgeois-democratic revolution and the transition to a capitalist social order would be quite different in other parts of Europe and in later periods than had been the case in France at the end of the eighteenth century.

The traditional, aristocratic ruling classes of central, eastern, and southern Europe very much felt what Trotsky called "the whip of external necessity." This took several forms. One was the dangerous example of the French Revolution that could potentially become a model for their own discontented classes. Some traditionalists undoubtedly wanted to deal with this through increased repression, pure and simple—favoring reactionary policies that would prevent any changes in the forms and norms of the old social order. There were, however, three other whips of external necessity that thwarted such an easy "solution."

Most important was the Industrial Revolution that was unleashed by the capitalist economic development of western Europe. Such a mighty generator of material wealth and power could hardly be shrugged off. Related to this was the fact that the traditional ruling classes—despite their feudal origins and inclinations—had themselves, for well over a century, been inescapably seduced by and entangled in the world capitalist economy. These two interrelated whips of external necessity (the progress of the Industrial Revolution and the traditional ruling classes' own involvement in the world capitalist economy) made it impossible to return to an earlier feudal golden age. The traditionalists were, instead, compelled to adapt to a profoundly changing social order. A third whip was provided by the French invasions during the Napoleonic wars that spanned the first fifteen years of the nineteenth century.

France's capitalist economy was more efficient and dynamic, unencumbered by semi-feudal restrictions and forged into a cohesive national unit. This was also reflected in the superior military capabilities of Napoleon's armies—in which the inertia of aristocratic privilege had been replaced with sweeping organizational, technological, and tactical innovations combined with performance-based incentives offered to all, regardless of social station. This had two effects. First, Napoleon's forces overran most of Europe and instituted social, economic, and political reforms in those areas, reforms that were designed to facilitate their absorption into a French-dominated social order—Napoleon's French Empire. Second, the traditionalists realized that if they were to successfully cope in the modern world with a challenge such as that posed by Napoleon, then—at least for military reasons—they themselves would have to initiate some "modernization" reforms in their own societies.

An additional impulse for instituting such reforms (or for maintaining some of the Napoleonic reforms even after the ultimate defeat of Bonaparte in 1815) was provided by a desire to defuse the kinds of middle-class and lower-class discontents that had generated the earlier revolutionary explosions in France.

Even with the old ruling classes' grudging adaptation to some aspects of capitalist modernization, however, their determination to maintain as much monarchist power and aristocratic privilege as possible was destined to generate a wave of revolutionary explosions throughout Europe in 1848. But the law of uneven and combined development ensured that these explosions would assume different forms and have different consequences than had been the case during the French Revolution. To understand this, we must grasp the new sociological and ideological realities of the 1840s.

The further development of capitalism—and especially of industrial capitalism—resulted in a growing divergence among the new social classes throughout Europe's cities and towns. What had been simply "the people" in revolutionary France became increasingly the sharply defined, self-conscious, and often openly antagonistic classes of capitalist employers on the one hand and proletarian wage workers on the other. In between was a middle stratum of independent artisans and small shopkeepers, impelled by the dynamics of the capitalist marketplace but also on the verge of being ruined by larger capitalist enterprises. This three-layered class structure in the urban areas—bourgeoisie, petty bourgeoisie, and proletariat—did not form a cohesive revolutionary mass such as had existed in Paris of 1789; rather, it became an uneasy alliance in the struggle against semi-feudal absolutism. In the rural areas there were large landowners and various peasant strata—the former more often than not constituting a backward-looking aristocracy, while the peasant masses (who were a majority of Europeans) were often inclined toward traditionalist values and hostile to urban-capitalist pressures, but also inclined to be revolutionary if this could satisfy their deep hunger for land and dignity.

Three fundamental ideological currents took shape in the first half of the nineteenth century: liberalism, conservatism, and socialism.

Liberalism favored the new capitalist order and sought to eliminate old feudal restrictions and hierarchies, seeking instead to facilitate equal opportunity for all. In its classical form, and throughout most of the nineteenth century, liberalism favored economic policies of laissez-faire, convinced that wealth and progress would be guaranteed if the state put no restrictions on the decisions of the capitalists on how to run the economy. (By the twentieth century the liberal mainstream would come to favor a more active intervention of the state in the economy, presumably to reform and regulate capitalism for its own good.) Committed to freedom of thought and expression, and the separation of church and state, liberalism was inclined toward Enlightenment rationalism as a guide to political reform, favoring the creation of constitutional republics. Throughout much of the nineteenth century, however, a majority of liberals did not favor a democratic republic—fearing that giving propertyless masses the right to vote would create a "tyranny of the majority" that would overturn capitalist property rights. At first, it was only the most radical fringe of this political current that favored moving forward to democracy.

Conservatism accepted the new capitalist order but resisted impulses toward equal opportunity and the upsetting of traditional hierarchies. Often counterposing traditional values and cultural norms to the intellectual innovations of the Enlightenment, it challenged optimistic notions about the possibilities of progress and human betterment—yet its adherents were most concerned about conserving the traditional power relations associated with prevailing monarchs and aristocratic elites. Essentially anti-democratic, it often favored freedom of thought and expression only for the elite, and was inclined to keep the masses in their places through a combination of restrictive and benevolent policies by a more or less authoritarian central government. As parliamentary systems and the right to vote spread through Europe in the nineteenth and early twentieth centuries, of course, forms of conservatism evolved that more or less accepted and adapted to these changes.

Socialism challenged the new capitalist order, wanting to eliminate both the old feudal restrictions and hierarchies and the new capitalist restrictions and hierarchies. It held that equal opportunity would be possible only through the collective ownership of the economy, and that freedom of thought and expression could only be guaranteed by a radical democracy that encompassed not only the politics but also the economic life of society. Some of the earliest theorists of socialism imagined a utopian future whose blueprints they wished to somehow impose on humanity for its own good. By the mid-nineteenth century, however, it became increasingly identified as a goal to be achieved and shaped by society's laboring majority. (At various times, conceptions of communism and anarchism tended to be identified with this broad current.)

Elements from various classes could be found in each political camp, and not surprisingly, many people of various class backgrounds—particularly among the hard-pressed lower classes—identified with no political current at all. The fact remains that, roughly speaking, in nineteenth-century Europe liberalism found its most consistent base among the rising bourgeoisie, conservatism found its most consistent base among the sections of the aristocracy that were adapting to capitalism, and socialism found its most consistent base among the working class. At different times and in different places, elements of the peasantry were drawn to one or another of these basic currents.

Given this sociological and ideological lineup, it may be easier to understand the differences between the bourgeois-democratic revolution of 1789 and that of 1848. In the case of the latter, I will focus on one major example—that of Germany.

If we examine the events of 1789–93 in France, we see—amid an admittedly complex swirl of events—that elements of the rising bourgeoisie helped lead a mass-based movement of the urban and rural poor in smashing the remnants of the old feudal order. Results of the revolutionary triumph included the replacement of monarchy with a constitutional republic; the achievement of national unity, with a form of nationalism strongly tinged with radical-democratic content; and a sweeping land reform that broke the power of the aristocracy, clearing the way for a thoroughgoing development of capitalism.

If we examine the events of 1848–49 in Germany, we see that the dominant elements of the already-existing bourgeoisie, frightened by working-class radicalism, drew back from revolution and sought an alliance with potent remnants of the old feudal order. The results of the defeated revolution included the preservation of a powerful monarchy; the failure to achieve national unity for over two decades; the combined thwarting of democratic political currents and development of a conservative-tinged nationalism; the maintenance of power by a landowning aristocracy; and the entwining of capitalism with traditional elites.

The bourgeois-aristocratic, or liberal-conservative, compromise had a significant impact throughout Europe after 1848, and it profoundly affected the economic, political, and cultural history of that entire region. In the face of this hostile alliance, the first upsurge of self-conscious working-class radicalism (reflected in Karl Marx's small Communist League, for example, and more massively in England's Chartist movement) was smashed and didn't fully recover for about fifteen years. At the same time, the relative political and social stability that resulted facilitated the dramatic economic expansion of industrial capitalism that would set the stage for an even more dramatic working-class upsurge in the future.

Swirling toward 1914

After 1848, the law of uneven and combined development continued to assert pressure on the triumphant conservatives. They felt compelled to carry out "modernizing" reforms that corresponded to the liberal and radical demands—but in a highly distorted form that preserved much of the aristocracy's status and power.

A prime example can be found in the career of Chancellor Otto von Bismarck of Prussia, who initiated policies for more than two decades after the defeat of the 1848 revolution that finally unified different parts of Germany into a powerfully capitalist nation, but as part of a distinctively conservative synthesis. In Prussia—which he guaranteed was Germany's dominant province—the parliament consisted of elected representatives, but the election laws divided the electorate into three groups: the landowning aristocracy, the bourgeoisie, and the laboring population. The votes of the first two sectors were given greater weight than the third, ensuring that the upper classes would get more representatives than the lower classes.

At the same time, the Prussian monarch—the kaiser—exercised far-reaching executive powers over all of Germany. Social reforms beneficial to the working class were adopted, but at the same time there were repressive laws against working-class organizations. Although land reforms were promulgated to relieve peasant discontent, the big landowners' domination of the countryside remained intact. In other words, capitalist development blended with aristocratic privilege, social reforms blended with upper-class paternalism, concessions to the principle of representative government blended with continued authoritarianism, and modernization blended with the policies of repressive bureaucracies committed to maintaining the relationships of power and privilege associated with the old status quo.

This was the pattern throughout much of Europe, although it unfolded with different variations in different countries. In Russia, for example, there had been no bourgeois-democratic upsurge because the indigenous capitalist class and working class did not exist as significant forces until the last years of the nineteenth century; therefore, the conservatism and authoritarianism of the monarchist system—tsarism—were much stronger, and the various modernizing reforms comparatively weaker in Russia.

The triumph of the capitalist mode of production in Europe was an accomplished fact by the middle of the nineteenth century, setting the stage for technological and industrial developments so rapid and so profound that they are sometimes said to constitute a second Industrial Revolution. Communication and transportation systems, levels of industrial production and productivity, the size and proportional increase of urban populations, the level of knowledge and general education, the relative and absolute size of the urban working class, the amount of wealth produced by society—such things increased spectacularly, qualitatively transforming the life-rhythms of European culture.

This naturally increased tensions within European society as a whole, including tensions between different factions of the ruling classes on how to respond to new problems and possibilities. Divergences between conservatives and liberals once again became more pronounced. Both appealed to the masses for support—offering, in return, reforms extending the right to vote and an increasing number of social reforms (which were easier to grant thanks to economic growth).

The consequent resurgence of mass politics in European life, combined with the growing size and productive power of the working class, led to the regeneration of the European labor movement. Mass socialist parties, and mass trade union movements under left-wing leadership, arose and became powerful forces in the political and economic life of Europe. They were able to force the upper classes to implement important economic, social, and political reforms—combating authoritarianism and injustice in society's political life and in capitalism's factories.

At the same time, they inspired millions of working people with a vision of a socialist future, in which the power of the capitalists and landowners would be replaced by the power of the working-class majority. Despite the fact that a majority of these parties gradually embraced the theoretical orientation advanced by Karl Marx and combined into unified international associations (first the International Workingmen's Association, later the Socialist International), divisions opened up among the socialists over how much the revolutionary vision should be compromised for the sake of immediate reforms, and over strategies for attaining socialism. These divisions, and the compromises that spawned them, created a fatal indecisiveness that was to paralyze the socialist movement when the First World War erupted in 1914. The fact remains that, up to that decisive moment, this movement was seen as a powerful challenge to the status quo.

One of the most effective ideological tools utilized by conservatives was nationalism. Nationalism had first been a central component of revolutionary and liberal ideology—linking the ideas of popular sovereignty and national self-determination, celebrating the culture and sense of community of the popular masses.

Conservatives developed forms of nationalism which were designed to blur class differences, accentuating traditionalist cultural elements, glorifying authoritarian symbols, blending patriotism with anti-foreign prejudices and with militarism. They were able to tap into nonrational longings and fears that had been intensified by the dramatic transformations, disruptions, and tensions introduced by the new industrial capitalist order. Liberals and even socialists were affected in some ways by this variation of nationalist ideology that the conservatives developed so skillfully.

If anything, however, this form of intense nationalism was not a source of social stability and cohesion but rather a reflection of the deep tensions and instability that had become part of the core of modern European life. This instability had at least three fundamental sources:

1. The uncompleted nature of the bourgeois-democratic revolution—resulting from the aristocratic/capitalist compromise—created an ongoing antagonism between traditionalist values, expectations, and cultural norms on the one hand, and the newer bourgeois values, practices, and culture on the other. This deep cultural conflict was felt consciously and unconsciously, not only among the upper classes but also within broad sectors of the population.

2. Within the capitalist mode of production, there was a growing contradiction between the forces of production and the relations of production. As we have noted, the awesome development of the forces of production encompassed all of society, bringing about profound and rapid changes in the culture and everyday life of all people in society—but none of this was under their control, because the relations of production involved the private ownership of those productive forces by a small, self-interested minority of capitalists—and even this minority was driven by impersonal market dynamics that were not really under anyone's control. In the experience of the large masses, these immense changes in society were arbitrary, alienating, and threatening.

3. The actual dynamics of the economy contained an additional irrational element. The competition between capitalist firms periodically resulted in overproduction, which would glut the markets, bringing about a collapse in prices and a decline in production and employment—that is, periodic economic depressions. Such problems naturally generated greater tensions and instability.

The development of imperialism provided an economic, political, and even psychological outlet for all of these tensions. The obvious economic outlet was, of course, essential: the continents of Asia, Africa, and Latin America (and even North America and vulnerable portions of Europe) offered vital sources of raw materials, important markets for manufactured goods, and virgin territories for profitable investments. The traditionalist ethos of military glory and authoritarian grandeur also found an outlet, as did popular impulses toward a super-patriotic national chauvinism.

At the same time, imperialism—in addition to being a brutal and oppressive assault on the peoples targeted for exploitation—did not resolve the contradictions of European society but simply led to heightened rivalries between different companies and countries over who would control what areas. Such rivalry, combined with the rising tide of nationalism and militarism, created a framework that generated the eruption of the First World War in August 1914.

Permanent Revolution

The incredible destructiveness of what one Asian scholar, K. M. Panikkar, once referred to as "the European civil war" resulted not only in the slaughter of millions of people but also in a dramatic political and cultural transformation on the European continent. A period combining revolutionary upheaval and counterrevolutionary backlash defined the rest of the twentieth century. One of the focal points of this dialectic was Russia, where the theory of uneven and combined development first came to be articulated. The patterns already discussed were dramatically evident there.

At the summit of Russian society was the tyrannical ruler, the tsar, an absolute monarch. Any opposition to him or to the system over which he ruled could mean arrest, then prison or Siberian exile—or death. Just below him was a powerful layer of hereditary nobles whose wealth and power was secured through the control of Russia's land and the exploitation of the great majority of the Russian people, who were peasants. The condition of even the fairly well-to-do peasants was impoverished, and the great masses of peasants were deprived of adequate land (monopolized by the rich nobles) and lived in terrible and brutalizing destitution. All of this was justified by the religious hierarchy of the Russian Orthodox Church, which glorified the tsar as their "little Father"—a god on earth—and persecuted all who did not accept the doctrines of Russian Orthodoxy. The oppressive second-class status of women received absolute religious justification, as did all policies of the tsarist regime.

The tsars of Russia had conquered many different peoples, and the tsarist empire was known as the "prison-house of nations." At the same time—and most important for Russian development—the tsarist regime felt compelled, under the pressure of competition with other major powers in the world, to modernize aspects of its society—to develop technology and compete in the dynamically growing world market economy. Consequently, it was especially important for the tsars to develop capitalist industry in Russia.

This gave rise to a small but growing capitalist class of industrialists and financiers, a layer of professionals. It also resulted in a rapidly expanding class of wage workers and their families—the proletariat. The labor of this working class created the great wealth that flowed from Russian industrialization, and workers in the factories were exploited intensively—laboring long hours, often in unhealthy and unsafe conditions, pushed hard by factory managers, and paid low wages. It was illegal for workers to organize trade unions to press for improved pay and conditions. In the growing cities, workers and their families lived in crowded and impoverished circumstances.

Such realities as these gave rise to a growing revolutionary movement in which Leon Trotsky became involved. He would become a theorist and leader of the revolutionary movement second in stature only to Vladimir Ilyich Lenin. In the context of the country's intense struggles, Trotsky developed an analysis of the peculiarities of Russian history, which he defined as "uneven and combined development"; from this, he crafted a strategic orientation known as the theory of permanent revolution.

Trotsky's theory linked the struggle for democracy—freedom of expression, equal rights for all, and rule by the people—with the struggle for socialism, a society in which the great majority of people would own and control the economic resources of society to allow for the free development of all. It also linked the struggle for revolution in Russia with the cause of socialist revolution throughout the world. The theory contained three basic points. One held that the revolutionary struggle for democracy in Russia could only be won under the leadership of the working class with the support of the peasant majority. The second point held that this democratic revolution would begin in Russia a transitional period in which all political, social, cultural, and economic relations would continue to be in flux, leading in the direction of socialism. The third point held that this transition would be part of, would help to advance, and would also be furthered by an international revolutionary process.

The first aspect of Trotsky's theory was related to his understanding that the relatively weak capitalist class of Russian businessmen was dependent on the tsarist system, and that the capitalists would be too frightened of the revolutionary masses to lead in the overthrow of tsarist tyranny. The struggle for democracy and human rights could only be advanced consistently and finally won under the leadership of the working class, which was capable of organizing labor unions and political organizations in Russia's cities and towns. Allied with the workers would be the vast peasantry hungry for land, as well as other oppressed social layers—women, oppressed ethnic and national groups, religious minorities, and dissident intellectuals. A victorious worker-led revolution would bring the working class to political power. In other words, democratic revolutions in so-called backward countries such as tsarist Russia must spill over into working-class revolutions.

The second aspect of Trotsky's theory was related to the understanding that the victorious revolutionary working class would not be willing to turn political power over to its capitalist bosses. Instead, they would—with the support of the peasants—consolidate their own rule through democratic councils (known in Russia as *soviets*) and their own people's army. Under working-class rule, there would be dramatic efforts to

- spread education,
- create universal literacy,
- make the benefits of culture available to all,
- provide universal health care to all as a matter of right,
- ensure that decent housing is available for all,
- secure full and equal rights for women and all others oppressed in the old society, and
- include all people in building and developing an economy that would sustain the free development of all.

During this transitional period, the development of society would move beyond the framework of capitalism and in the direction of socialism.

The third aspect of Trotsky's theory was related to his understanding that capitalism is a global system that can only be replaced by socialism on a global scale. It was his conviction that it would not be possible to create a socialist democracy in an economically underdeveloped country such as Russia surrounded by a hostile capitalist world. In fact, a working-class revolution in one country would inevitably generate counterrevolutionary responses in surrounding countries—with efforts to repress the revolution. At the same time, it would inspire the workers and oppressed of countries throughout the world.

The Russian Revolution, as envisioned by Trotsky, would be one of a series of revolutions in country after country throughout the world. This would come about not only because of the example of revolutionary Russia but also especially because of the desire of more and more workers and oppressed people in all countries to end the exploitation and hardship that—Trotsky believed—are the inevitable results of capitalism. The process of socialist revolution can begin within a single country, but socialism can only be created on a global scale.

This outlook was reflected not only in Trotsky's orientation but—by the spring of 1917—also that of the Russian socialist movement's most revolutionary wing, the Bolsheviks, led by Lenin. An immense upsurge of the working class and the peasantry, after sweeping away the tsarist regime, came under Bolshevik sway, culminating in the establishment of a revolutionary workers' government supported by the peasantry.

The combination of the First World War and the Russian Revolution helped to generate revolutionary upheavals on a global scale. The devastating impact of the war not only had disastrous consequences for the populations of Europe (particularly for the continent's working classes), but they also undermined the ability of Europe's "great powers" to maintain their colonial empires. The example of Russia's insurgent workers and peasants inspired masses of people on every continent to struggle more militantly against oppressive realities. The Russian revolutionaries led by Lenin and Trotsky sought to connect with revolutionaries of all countries, establishing the Communist International to aid in the spread of revolutions.

As it turned out, however, the global revolutionary ferment was not able to overcome the resistance of the ruling classes of most countries. Throughout Europe, the ruling powers joined to establish a cordon sanitaire to protect their populations from Bolshevik contagion, and to give massive aid to counterrevolutionary elements in Russia waging a bloody civil war against the Bolsheviks. In some countries, revolutionary uprisings and movements were brutally suppressed; in others, dramatic concessions were made to more moderate (and absolutely anti-revolutionary) sectors of the social democratic labor movement to divert the working class away from the overthrow of capitalism. In some countries, such as Germany, both things happened. The Russian Communists found themselves isolated in a hostile capitalist world. The Russian Revolution's isolation led to bureaucratic, authoritarian, and murderous distortions of Communism in the Soviet Union and (due to the influence of the Stalin regime that arose after Lenin's death) throughout the Communist movements of other countries.

Revolution and Counterrevolution in Interwar Europe

Those who led their countries into the devastation of the First World War utilized an unbridled and murderous "patriotism" that placed militarism into the center of the national ethos. Among the masses of people who were swept into intense political life in the wake of the war, not all were drawn to the banner of Communism or to the more moderate appeals of social democracy.

Interpenetrating elements—ultrapatriotic and militarist forms of nationalism; a glorification of violence, racism, and "benign" tyranny rooted in the maintenance of colonial empires; the searing and brutalizing experience of the world war; long-standing ethnic tensions; deeply rooted patriarchal and authoritarian mores; uneven combinations of horror and fascination and attraction over the challenge that rapid industrialization and modernization posed to traditional values and ways of life—all fed into a political culture that culminated in the crystallization of a new mass political movement that replaced monarchist-absolutism at the extreme right of the political spectrum: fascism.

Fascism involved a strident and militaristic nationalism, employing radical or populist rhetoric, which sought to overcome class conflict (and the threat of left-wing revolution) through a combination of extreme political authoritarianism, a "corporate state" enforcing cooperation between labor and capital, in practice preserving and reinforcing large capitalist corporations while providing at least modest social welfare programs for the masses. Arising first in Italy under the leadership of Benito Mussolini, it assumed various forms. Its German version—the Nazi movement of Adolf Hitler—made the most thoroughgoing racism a centerpiece of ideology and policy. It is noteworthy that this extreme right-wing nationalism evolved in two countries where, on the one hand, the crystallization of nation-states had been delayed until late in the nineteenth century, involving far-reaching compromises and admixtures between modern (capitalist) and traditional (precapitalist) upper classes, and, on the other hand, the working-class Left was particularly strong.

An essential element in the coming of fascism in Italy and Germany was widespread unrest: in both countries, there were mass upsurges arising out of profound political and economic crises. Triumphant revolutions could have resulted, but weaknesses in revolutionary leadership blocked such possibilities. Disappointed hopes among masses of people combined with extreme fears generated among the upper classes and deepening anxieties among sectors of the intermediate "middle classes." This dynamic generated the rising wave of fascism, marked by burgeoning recruits and supporters from sectors of the middle and lower classes and, from sectors of the upper classes, encouragement from sectors of the state (among some conservative politicians, judges, police, etc.) as well as generous material resources.

The relative isolation of Soviet Russia—transformed into the Union of Soviet Socialist Republics (USSR), whose boundaries corresponded to the old Russian empire—contributed decisively to the transformation of Communism into a grotesque blend of dogmatized Marxism and technologically advanced absolutism (drawing from the heritage of tsarism). Under Josef Stalin, a conception of creating "socialism in one country"—the modernization of an industrially backward USSR—both reflected and further contributed to three profound developments:

1. A distancing of the Soviet regime from a commitment to spreading the world socialist revolution, now deemed unnecessary for the triumph of socialism in the USSR (leading to the eventual dissolution of the Communist International).

2. An institutionalization of bureaucratic dictatorship claiming to represent working-class rule and designed to initiate a brutalizing "revolution from above" to overcome economic backwardness through forced collectivization of the land and rapid industrialization.

3. The de-linking of democracy and equality from the meaning of socialism (now redefined narrowly as state ownership and planning-oriented control of the economy).

"Socialism in one country" helped to transform Communist parties of various countries from revolutionary working-class organizations to vehicles meant to advance or resist revolutionary struggles depending on the narrow, nationalistically defined foreign policy needs of the USSR. The revolution from above required the concentration of political, economic, social, and cultural power in a few hands at the expense of the majority of workers and peasants. This concentration of power, advanced by new technologies (and labeled by some as "totalitarianism"), had much in common with developments in Nazi Germany and fascist Italy—with the key difference that capitalism's market economy was replaced by a collectivized "planned economy," and that lip service continued to be paid to democratic, humanistic, and egalitarian ideals repugnant to the likes of Hitler and Mussolini.

The brutality associated with Stalinism was justified by its partisans as a necessary element in dragging "backward Russia" into a modernized existence that would be beneficial to the majority of its laboring population (who were already being offered certain benefits—the right to education, health care and other social services, employment, etc.—previously unavailable). This would, it was argued, eventually become increasingly democratic and would increasingly prove to be a powerful example for peoples around the world. And to many it seemed to represent a practical, compelling alternative to the capitalist status quo and to the fascist "new order." ·

The dramatic economic downturn in the global capitalist economy represented by the Great Depression (1929–39), with massive business failures and unemployment,.generated a sharpening polarization between Left and Right throughout Europe, and an intensified competition between various capitalist nations seeking markets, raw materials, and investment opportunities on a global scale. Related to this, there was a growing militarism requiring large-scale state expenditures that—in the fascist-dominated nations first—revived the economy of one capitalist country after another.

The explosion of the Second World War (1939–45) resulted, to a far greater degree than the First, in an incredible trauma in which different portions of the globe—and different global realities—came together in lethal and profoundly transformative combinations. In a sense, this was several different wars combined. One involved a murderous confrontation between several contending capitalist empires, while another involved a no less murderous confrontation between Nazism and Communism. There was also an ideological confrontation between democratic and egalitarian ideals on one side and idealized dictatorship and racial purity on the other. For many, the war was a defense of their homeland against a ruthless foreign invader. Among the Allies, there were partisans of imperialism and anticolonial revolutionaries, those reaching for a socialist future and those determined to save a capitalist status quo.

The consequences of the war were, of course, devastating for the losers—Germany, Italy, and Japan—and brought extreme discredit to fascism in all its varieties. They also brought discredit to much of the tangled ideological sources of fascism (national and ethnic chauvinism, anti-democratic thought, racism, militarism). Among the victors, the war ushered in disintegration, danger, and a new global power struggle that perceptive partisan Henry Luce foretold would culminate in "the American Century."

Complexities of the Twentieth Century's Last Half

Here it is useful to remind ourselves that what is presented here corresponds to a "Westernization" conceptual model, which needs to be modified by a more complex employment of the "Southernization" conceptualization. Some historians have already begun to emphasize the decisive importance to global development of both past and ongoing cultural, economic, and political influences emanating from Asia, Africa, and Latin America, and more such work needs to be done if we are to have full comprehension of world history. Nonetheless, the process and profound importance to the development of our world of Westernization—which includes the global reach of capitalism and its attendant ideologies, the multiple impacts of scientific and technological developments, spreading struggles for democracy and human rights (and vicious policies designed to thwart such struggles)—is undeniable.

Throughout the nineteenth and twentieth centuries, we find—through a brutal colonialist imperialism as well as an "open door" and "good neighbor" imperialism—the spread and growing predominance of the market economy, with its subordination of more and more aspects of life to the accumulation process and cash nexus, and its crystallization of a very specific socioeconomic class structure throughout Latin America, Asia, Africa, and other capitalistically "underdeveloped" areas (although often intertwined with earlier socioeconomic formations and stratifications). To deal with what were often profoundly invasive, violent, and oppressive realities associated with this economic expansionism, growing sectors of the native population utilized various tools for conceptualization and resistance drawn from Western experience—notions of nationalism, race and ethnicity, democracy, socialism, and so on (although, again, in general these notions were dynamically combined with earlier cultural patterns).

Beginning in the wake of World War II (and in large measure due to its destructive impact on European power), a wave of radical anticolonial and nationalist revolutions challenged and dissolved the European empires through the 1950s, 1960s, and 1970s. This revolutionary wave coincided and in some areas intersected with a powerful surge of Communist expansion.

This Communist expansion in some cases took place through the efforts of indigenous parties that had played central roles in resistance struggles during World War II (China, Yugoslavia, partially in Vietnam and Korea, almost in Greece). To a large extent it came about due to the central role of the USSR in defeating Nazi Germany and rolling back Hitler's legions throughout Eastern Europe—and then placing pro-Soviet regimes in power throughout the region. This was carried out, initially, with the reluctant agreement of its capitalist allies (especially the United States and Britain) in 1943–45, thanks to Stalin's sincere promise to rein in Communist parties in other portions of Europe (particularly in Italy and France, where they had played central roles in the resistance movements and might otherwise have moved to take power). Soon the acquiescence turned into Cold War hostility, particularly as Western European regimes sought to check leftist-influenced anticolonial insurgencies and dominant forces in the United States sought to realize the American Century.

The Cold War of 1946–89 involved a global confrontation—short of total war but marked by multiple smaller wars, diplomatic maneuvering, economic rivalries, coups and countercoups, insurgencies, counter-insurgencies, massive two-way propaganda barrages, espionage, and an arms race involving weapons that could destroy the entire population of the planet several times over. The diminished power of Europe's capitalist democracies forced them to accept US leadership in a "free world" coalition.

It was not necessary for a nation to be free or democratic to be part of the "free world" (some were, in fact, ruled by vicious and unpopular dictatorships)— it was necessary only to be pro-capitalist, anti-Communist, and accepting of US leadership in the Cold War. Within the advanced capitalist democracies of Western Europe, however, the capitalist economic and political forces (fearing potentially revolutionary working-class militancy and the threat of Communism) established far-reaching agreements with the moderate, social-democratic labor movements (both political parties and trade unions) for extensive "welfare state" programs providing substantial benefits through increased incomes, education, health care, housing, social security, unemployment insurance, etc. These countries enjoyed a long wave of prosperity that significantly improved working-class living standards (as was the case, along with an increasingly robust consumerism, throughout the advanced-industrial capitalist world). In exchange for these benefits, the leaderships of these labor movements agreed to help preserve capitalism, and in some cases also to support efforts to maintain colonialism.

Such "welfare state" benefits (minus the robust consumerism) were provided also by the regimes of the Communist bloc, along with the elimination of capitalist enterprises and the establishment of state ownership and control over the economy. Although this was done in the name of the working class and "the people," it was the Communist parties in each of these countries that had a monopoly on political power, maintained according to the bureaucratic-authoritarian Stalinist model. While the new Communist regimes were expected to follow the leadership of the USSR in the Cold War and in other matters, in those countries where Communist parties had taken power with popular support (instead of being placed in power by the USSR), a powerful pull toward independence began to assert itself—first with Yugoslavia, later with China.

A significant number of the newly independent nations emerging from colonialism, particularly those under left-leaning but non-Communist leaders, chose to align themselves neither with the Communist bloc nor with the "free world" of their old colonial oppressors. Both of the Cold War's contending power blocs sought to increase their influence in this sphere, offering economic aid and various alliances designed to bring them closer to one camp or the other. Throughout Asia, Africa, and Latin America, however, there was a powerful desire to find paths of economic development that would nurture at least relative independence and modernization.

An influential model for economic, social, and political development—modernization theory—utilized an interpretation of the historical experience of Western Europe and North America to propose a path for the "less developed" countries. The development of capitalism would generate industrialization, which would generate greater wealth and new variations of social differentiation, in turn breaking down stagnant customs and traditional hierarchies, generating political pluralism, democracy, prosperity—and all the benefits of modernization. Therefore, the solution for Asia, Africa, and Latin America would be for Western capitalist governments to offer economic aid, and especially for Western business corporations to make investments in these regions, leading to greater capitalist economic development, with the consequent modernization payoffs in the social, cultural, and political realms.

Obviously, modernization theory was consistent with the open door/good neighbor variants of economic expansionism advanced by US foreign policy, and also increasingly with the foreign policies of the postcolonialist Western European powers. In fact, it was an ideological and policy-making tool in the Cold War. Related to this was a tendency of the United States and other Western capitalist nations to oppose nationalist, anti-imperialist struggles that threatened the established order—especially if they were in any way tainted with left-wing and especially Communist influences. Often US and Western European policy-makers preferred to support unpopular and anti-democratic regimes when they were challenged by popular insurgencies.

An analysis counterposed to modernization theory (and consistent with the theory of uneven and combined development) took the form of what has become known as dependency theory. According to this analysis, the path of economic development followed by such countries as Britain and the United States in an earlier historical period was no longer open. The advanced capitalist nations were now determined to maintain their dominance in the global economy. Any economic aid they give to so-called underdeveloped countries would not be allowed to make their economies competitive with those of advanced capitalist countries, but rather to make them develop in a manner harmonious with the needs of the advanced capitalist countries—which meant, in a sense, to keep them underdeveloped. Similarly, the investments of business corporations from advanced capitalist countries were not designed to facilitate genuine modernization, but rather to maximize profits for the businesses of the advanced countries. They wished to pump wealth out of the less developed countries, not to contribute to progress or rising living standards for the populations of the underdeveloped regions. Nor would the policies of the advanced capitalist countries' governments or their corporations be designed to promote democracy in Asia, Africa, or Latin America. Genuine democracy could have resulted in "instability" in the form of popular protests against and powerful challenges to the profit-hungry outsiders. This explained why US political and economic interests preferred repressive regimes that would guarantee "stability" and higher profit margins.

Influenced by anti-imperialist perspectives in the late 1950s and 1960s, rebels throughout Asia, Africa, and Latin America initiated revolutionary struggles, challenging traditional elites and also the ostensible modernizers whose policies actually led to imperialist entanglements. In many cases becoming principled opponents of capitalism, they gravitated to variants of Marxist programs and Communist organization. They often tended to view political realities through a prism similar to that of permanent revolution: the democratic struggle (against imperialism, against dictatorship, for human rights and equal rights for all, for land reform, for a decent life for all) could only be secured through the struggles of the laboring masses, whose revolutionary struggle must culminate in their own political power, which would result in socialist-oriented economic development.

Trotsky's theory of permanent revolution, however, anticipated an increasingly successful wave of working-class revolutions, particularly in advance industrial countries, which would give aid to one another as they collectively moved forward to create a world socialist economy. An attempt to create socialism in a single country, or even in a scattering of economically undeveloped countries, could not be successful with such a global revolutionary socialist expansion. In the advanced industrial countries of Western Europe, however, the largely socialist-oriented workers who identified with labor parties and social democratic parties, and even the many workers who were members of Communist parties, were economically relatively well-off and not inclined to make a revolution. In this situation, the USSR and Communist bloc stood as a substitute for international socialist revolution and as the force that could provide for the survival and assistance required for an underdeveloped country to embark on a noncapitalist path of development. One dramatic example of this, beginning in 1959, was the Cuban revolution.

This was problematical in more than one way. The USSR and Communist bloc were prepared to lend support not from principle but from pragmatic and often manipulative considerations in the Cold War power struggle. This meant that under certain circumstances they would be fully prepared to with-hold, reduce, or withdraw support. They might also be inclined to impose re-strictions or conditions consistent with their own narrow foreign policy needs, and to influence revolutionaries of other lands to adopt attitudes, structures, and policies consistent with their own Stalinist traditions.

In the Communist countries, lip service might be paid to democracy, hu-man rights, and control over the economy by the laboring masses, but this was far from the reality. The bureaucratic regimes were increasingly losing what-ever genuine confidence, respect, and support they may have once enjoyed among their own populations. Uprisings of workers, students, and others were violently repressed in East Germany (1953), Hungary (1956), Czechoslovakia (1968), and Poland (1981)—and gradually many dissidents who might have argued for "socialism with a human face" saw no human possibilities at all in this system called "socialism." The centrally and bureaucratically controlled economy—known as the "command economy"—proved increasingly vulnera-ble to mismanagement, not to mention the endemic inequalities and corrup-tions that had been manifest from almost the beginning. Some Communist bloc countries, seeking to avoid economic stagnation and impasse, dabbled with market reforms (which introduced elements of incoherence into their economic reality) and secured substantial loans from Western capitalist banks (which had fatal consequences when a downturn in the global economy made it impossible for them to overcome the accumulation of debts).

The 1960s and 1970s saw ferment, radicalization, and insurgency on a global scale, most dramatically in Asia, Africa, and Latin America—but it also took the form of a youth radicalization embracing not only students but also sections of the working class of the advanced capitalist countries of Western Europe as well as in Eastern Europe. In many cases, the ferment swept past the existing Communist and social democratic organizations and found expression in a pro-liferation and expansion of "far left" groups (although ultimately, the traditional organizations were able to attract much of this youthful ferment). In the West, dissidents mobilized around anti-imperialism, opposition to bureaucratic and alienating structures, anti-racism, feminism, anti-militarism, environmentalism, free speech, and more. And sections of the trade union movement were impacted as well.

In Asia, Africa, and Latin America, there were organizations that de-veloped both the capacity and the will to take political power through revo-lutionary struggle, whereas in Western Europe, those organizations with the capacity to take power (as opposed simply to winning elections in order to run the capitalist state) did not have the will to try. There were many activists, especially among the young, who may have had the will—but they did not have adequate organizations or sufficient mass support. And within the Communist bloc, with the remarkable exception of Poland at certain moments, the repressiveness of the state apparatus seemed too thoroughgoing to allow for more than what seemed to many as ineffectual dissent.

In reflecting on the developments as they stood in the 1980s, one is tempted to play with the formulation "uneven and combined development" by noting that the three very unevenly developed sectors of the world revolution—the advanced capitalist countries, the Communist bloc, and the exploited regions of the global South—while influencing and altering each other in important ways, ultimately failed to combine into a coherent and triumphant challenge to the status quo.

Problems of Permanent Revolution

If treated as a dogma rather than an analytical tool, the theory of permanent revolution stands challenged and discredited by developments of the late twentieth century. A bloc of nations on several continents—for example, Spain, Portugal, Greece, Mexico, Brazil, India, South Korea, Taiwan, Malaysia, Turkey, South Africa, Egypt, Algeria—appeared to be following the path from "backwardness" to modernization (and, more or less, to realization of democratic tasks) without a worker-peasant revolution culminating in a workers' state moving toward socialism.

The fact is that Trotsky explicitly denied that the theory of permanent revolution was a schema or practical recipe equally applicable everywhere, from Paris to Honolulu. It is, above all, an analytical tool that can inform political strategies, but that cannot be valid if it becomes an excuse for not actually studying the specifics and peculiarities of each national and cultural reality. As Trotsky developed it, the theory—far from seeking to establish a closed theoretical-strategic orientation—was part of an open and critical-minded approach to revolutionary analysis and strategy. To make sense of the various "exceptions," it is necessary to determine to what extent they are partial exceptions, and to what extent they may be either exceptions that prove or overturn the "rule" of permanent revolution—a task that goes beyond the present essay.

One could argue, however, that, to the extent that the theory is utilized to provide a strategic orientation, it is consistent with the traditional revolutionary Marxist argument that the full human needs and rights of the working class, of other exploited toilers, and of all oppressed sectors of the population can only be realized through a thoroughgoing democracy, and *that* can solely be achieved when the laboring majority takes political power and establishes full control over the economy. The struggle for democratic demands, if followed all the way, necessary spills over into the struggle for socialism. (This makes the theory relevant not only to underdeveloped regions, but also to advanced capitalist nations.)

In the 1980s, another challenge to the theory seemed to be posed by revolutions in Central America and the Caribbean, particularly the Sandinista revolution in Nicaragua. In this situation, a popular revolution of the partially proletarianized "laboring masses"—led by Marxist-oriented revolutionaries—was mobilized largely as a democratic revolution, culminating in a regime based solidly on mass support, but, instead of moving forward to socialism (taking "the Cuban road"), the Sandinistas doggedly sought to maintain a "mixed economy" with state, cooperative, and private sectors. While some dogmatists accused the Sandinistas of "betraying" the revolution, more realistic analysts noted that—given the dramatic erosion and increasing disintegration of the power of the USSR and Communist bloc during that period—the Cuban road (moving toward the replacement of capitalism with a nationalized planned economy) was not an option for a small nation hoping to survive within the global capitalist economy. Some saw this as a demonstration that Trotsky's theory was invalid.

A careful examination of Trotsky's theory, however, indicates that this particular critique is based on a serious misunderstanding. A central component of the theory of permanent revolution asserts that when a workers' state comes to power, a transitional period opens up that includes the development of precisely such a mixed economy as materialized in revolutionary Nicaragua. The theory's crowning assertion is that such a development can find completion in socialism only as the revolution expands on the international stage, with workers' states coming to power in more and more countries, including industrial advanced countries. Only on a global scale can a socialist economy come into being. The eventual defeat of the Sandinistas (as a force for socialist revolution) was inevitable given the stalemate and defeat of the revolutionary upsurge in Central America, the collapse of the Communist bloc, and the failure of working-class revolutions to triumph in other countries (such as Iran, South Africa, Brazil, etc.).

Setting aside such a specific misunderstanding, and setting aside the elevation of Trotsky's theory to a messianic expression of revolutionary triumphalism, an additional argument could be made in the theory's defense. To the extent that political strategies consistent with the theory of permanent revolution have failed

- to that extent have the movements and struggles of the working class been compromised, eroded, dismantled;
- to that extent has the promise of "the democratic revolution" been compromised, hollowed out, tragically incomplete—despite real gains made in one or another realm of society; and
- to that extent have terrible inequalities persisted, deepened, and contributed to the erosion of the integrity and viability of a particular society (and of the world).

This relates to recent discussions regarding the possibility of eliminating global poverty. In 2000 the United Nations initiated a Millennium Development Goals campaign. This projected the realization of the following eight goals: (1) eradicate extreme poverty and hunger; (2) achieve universal primary education; (3) promote gender equality and empower women; (4) reduce child mortality; (5) improve maternal health; (6) combat HIV/AIDS, malaria, and other diseases; (7) ensure environmental sustainability; and (8) develop a global partnership for development.

The United Nations wants these goals, supported by 190 governments around the world, to be realized by 2015 as an initial step to assuring a decent life for the world's peoples. The goals involve very specific sub-goals and practical policy projections: for example, of the world's 6 billion people, half live on less than $2 per day and 1.3 billion live on less than $1 per day—and the UN's goal is to cut that number of the "most impoverished" in half by 2015.

If these goals can be achieved within the framework of global capitalism, and then progressively advanced upon, a case can be made for the final obsolescence of the theory of permanent revolution. But to the extent that the goals—which, given existing resources, have been shown to be perfectly realizable—prove to be unrealized under the present structures of wealth and power, considerable validity must be granted to at least some variant of Trotsky's theory.

On the other hand, to the extent that a decomposition of the political organizations and capacities for class consciousness and struggle is taking place within the working class and other sectors of the toiling masses, without an accompanying recomposition of the actual or potential power of the laboring majorities of the various countries and cultures of our planet, to that extent will the theory of permanent revolution cease to have practical relevance.

Regardless of any problems related to the theory of permanent revolution, the fact remains that the overarching theory of uneven and combined development can be shown to be valid (that is, to be a useful and illuminating analytical tool) for historians, anthropologists, and other social scientists seeking to understand the developments and complexities of human existence in Europe and beyond.

The Past Flows into the Future

In the past two decades (1985–2005), uneven and combined development has continued to shape the world in which we live.

One of the most dramatic instances has been the decline and collapse of the Communist bloc. The failure of working-class revolution to spread to advanced industrial countries in the years following 1917 and the relative isolation of the USSR (and subsequently that of the bloc of countries under its tutelage) contributed to a fateful combination of, on the one hand, progressive Marxist ideology and goals, and on the other, reactionary and repressive traditions from the pre-revolutionary period. Bureaucratic elites were increasingly prone to draw away from revolutionary principles and goals, internationally and internally, becoming in many ways indistinguishable from other privileged and oppressive elites.

The glowing promise of human liberation was increasingly turned into hypocritical propaganda and bombast. Popular hopes and expectations were increasingly transformed into bitter disappointment, disillusionment, and passive hostility. The increasingly unstoppable interpenetration of the cultures of Eastern and Western Europe contributed mightily to the collapse of popular support or acquiescence, particularly given the growing inability of the command economy—after initial successes in establishing heavy industry and basic social programs—to compete with or resist the incursions of the dynamics of global capitalism.

The corrosive impact of Stalinist traditions and the inadequacies of the command economy had a profound impact beyond the collapse of the USSR and Communist bloc. Particularly as the collapse occurred, rebel regimes of Asia, Africa and Latin America that had been dependent on the Soviet model and on trade and aid from the Communist bloc found themselves increasingly isolated, vulnerable, and in many cases unviable. There was a powerful tendency toward rapid degeneration into some of the worst forms of tyranny, compromise, and corruption. Some joined the ranks of the so-called failed states fragmented by internal divisions, often exacerbated by contending outside economic interests. To a growing extent, multinational corporations from the "developed" North, while distressed over consequent instabilities, no longer faced dilemmas posed by the threat of left-wing insurgencies.

Communism's collapse obviously meant an end, for the most part, of Western Europe's large Communist movement, which increasingly evolved (or collapsed) into the capitalist-friendly reformism long associated with traditional social democratic orientations. At the same time, Western Europe (and other parts of the globe) saw a conservative free market assault on the welfare state and social compact that had been secured in the wake of the Great Depression and World War II: a seemingly unstoppable neoliberal wave of privatization, the dismantling of social programs, the dissolution of unions, the degradation of working-class living standards—accompanied by soaring corporate profits the collapse of labor reformism, and the dramatic decline of social democracy.

Triumphant capitalism unleashed similar dynamics throughout the world, accelerated by new technologies and divisions of labor that—under the banner of globalization—has drawn the diverse cultures and unevenly developed regions of the world into an increasingly intimate if unstable mix.

This has brought an incredibly violent reaction from some sectors of the world, exacerbated by increasingly desperate impoverishment, indignation over violations of national sovereignty, and rage over the pollution of cultural traditions—with a backward-looking religious fundamentalism combining with technologies and other cultural influences from the "advanced" West. It is unlikely that the consequent dialectic of terrorism and counterterrorism will play itself out in the near future.

In opposition to this lethal dialectic, and to the overarching reality of corporate-capitalist globalization, there have been stirrings of a so-called globalization from below. A variety of oppositional forces—fragments of the traditional Left from various regions of different continents blending with vibrant representatives from a variety of new social movements and political formations, also from various regions of different continents—have come together in massive and worldwide global justice mobilizations, in the World Social Forums, and in international campaigns around a number of issues.

In the present historical moment of 2005, we see the continuing dynamic of uneven and combined development. On the one hand, European elites seek a more sweepingly pan-national European Union that might facilitate a sharper contestation with US hegemony—even as their economies and cultures entwine ever more intimately with those of the American Empire. On the other hand, masses of "ordinary" Europeans influence each other across borders with their various struggles to maintain national-cultural identities and decent living standards—saying no to a Europe-wide constitution that would undermine national sovereignty and facilitate the further advance of neoliberal policies.

The past flows into the future in a never-ending swirl and collision of uneven and combined developments.

Bibliographical Essay

There can be no question of providing a comprehensive bibliography here, but a relative handful of titles can suggest some useful sources and what may be fruitful paths for further investigation.

My own general orientation, with some discussion of matters dealt with in this essay, can be found in Paul Le Blanc, *From Marx to Gramsci: A Reader in Revolutionary Marxist Politics* (Chicago: Haymarket Books, 2016), and also in my PhD dissertation, *Workers and Revolution: A Comparative Study of Bolshevik Russia and Sandinist Nicaragua* (University of Pittsburgh, 1989).

Among the key works by Leon Trotsky that have special relevance here are *Permanent Revolution & Results and Prospects* (New York: Pathfinder Press, 1978), *The History of the Russian Revolution* (Chicago: Haymarket Books, 2007), and *The Revolution Betrayed* (New York: Doubleday, 1937). Also see Paul Le Blanc, *Leon Trotsky* (London: Reaktion Books, 2015).

Michael Löwy's *The Politics of Combined and Uneven Development: The Theory of Permanent Revolution* (London: Verso, 1981) is still valuable, as is his fine set of essays, *On Changing the World: Essays in Political Philosophy from Karl Marx to Walter Benjamin* (Chicago: Haymarket Books, 2013). One of the most important interpreters of Trotsky's ideas is Ernest Mandel, among whose many relevant books are *Trotsky as Alternative* (London: Verso, 1995) and *The Meaning of the Second World War* (London: Verso, 1986). Also valuable is Duncan Hallas, *Trotsky's Marxism and Other Essays* (Chicago: Haymarket Books, 2003).

Discussing Trotsky's ideas on uneven and combined development and permanent revolution in the larger frameworks of Marxist economic and philosophical thought are M. C. Howard and J. E. King, *A History of Marxian Economics, 1883–1990*, 2 vols. (Princeton: Princeton University Press, 1992), and John Rees, *The Algebra of Revolution: The Dialectic and the Classical Marxist Tradition* (London: Routledge, 1998).

While not referring to Trotsky's theories, but entirely relevant, is Teodor Shanin, *Late Marx and the Russian Road: Marx and "The Peripheries of Capitalism"* (New York: Monthly Review Press, 1983). Also relevant, and relating to Trotsky's ideas, are two other volumes from Shanin—*Russia as a "Developing Society"* (New Haven, CT: Yale University Press, 1985) and *Russia, 1905–07: Revolution as a Moment of Truth* (New Haven: Yale University Press, 1986).

Discussion on controversies and rival notions of developmental theory can be found in Gilbert Rist, *The History of Development: From Western Origins to Global Faith* (London: Zed Books, 1997). Particularly valuable is Samir

Amin, *Global History: A View from the South* (Capetown, South Africa: Pambazuka Press, 2011). The modernization theory discussed in this essay refers to that presented by Walt Whitman Rostow in *Stages of Economic Growth: A Non-Communist Manifesto* (Cambridge: Cambridge University Press, 1960). The conception of Southernization is introduced in a classic essay by Lynda N. Shaffer, *Southernization* (Washington, DC: American Historical Association, 2002). A sharp critique of Eurocentrism is offered in J. M. Blaut, *Eight Eurocentric Historians* (New York: Guilford Press, 2000).

Studies relevant to issues in this essay are Perry Anderson's *Passages from Antiquity to Feudalism* (London: Verso, 1978) and *Lineages of the Absolutist State* (London: Verso, 1979). Key volumes on transitions from feudalism to capitalism are Rodney Hilton, ed., *The Transition from Feudalism to Capitalism* (London: Verso, 1978), and T. H. Aston and C. H. E. Philpin, eds., *The Brenner Debate: Agrarian Class Structure and Economic Development in Pre-Industrial Europe* (Cambridge: Cambridge University Press, 1985). A sense of evolving mentalities, consciousness, and ideologies in France, during the transition from the "old regime" to the revolutionary transformation and leading to the modern capitalist order, is provided by Robert Darnton's splendid essays in *The Great Cat Massacre and Other Episodes in French Cultural History* (New York: Basic Books, 2009).

There are numerous historical studies that can be useful in considering matters discussed here, among the most obvious being Eric Hobsbawm's four-volume survey—*The Age of Revolution, 1789–1848* (New York: New American Library, 1962), *The Age of Capital, 1848–1875* (New York: New American Library, 1979), *The Age of Empire, 1875–1914* (New York: Vintage Books, 1989), and *The Age of Extremes, 1914–1991* (New York: Vintage Books, 1996).

A relevant survey of intellectual history is provided in George L. Mosse, *The Culture of Western Europe: The Nineteenth and Twentieth Centuries*, 3rd ed. (Boulder: Westview Press, 1988), and suggestive works on social history are provided in George Rudé, *The Crowd in History, 1730–1848* (New York: John Wiley and Sons, 1964) and E. P. Thompson, *The Making of the English Working Class* (New York: Vintage Books, 1966). A blend of political science, anthropology, and history that offers a provocative vision of struggle spanning centuries can be found in James C. Scott, *Domination and the Arts of Resistance: Hidden Transcripts* (New Haven: Yale University Press, 1990).

A pioneering comparative study, quite relevant to this essay, can be found in Barrington Moore Jr., *Social Origins of Dictatorship and Democracy: Lord and Peasant in the Making of the Modern World* (Boston: Beacon Press, 1966). It is in some ways supplemented and in some ways challenged by three outstanding works by Arno J. Mayer, which provide remarkable accounts of European history entirely consistent with uneven and combined development (without referring to it): *The Persistence of the Old Regime: Europe to the Great War* (New York: Pantheon Books, 1981), *Why Did the Heavens Not Darken? The "Final Solution" in History* (New York: Pantheon Books, 1988), and *The Furies: Violence and Terror in the French and Russian Revolutions* (Princeton: Princeton University Press, 2000). Important and relevant volumes making explicit mention of uneven and combined development are David Blackbourn and Geoff Eley, *The Peculiarities of German History: Bourgeois Society and Politics in Nineteenth-Century Germany* (Oxford: Oxford University Press, 1984), and Geoff Eley, *Forging Democracy: The History of the Left in Europe, 1850–2000* (Oxford: Oxford University Press, 2002). Also relevant is Hannah Arendt, *The Origins of Totalitarianism* (New York: Meridian Books, 1960).

Innovative contributions relevant to matters discussed here are provided in the work of anthropologist Carol McAllister—for example, in *Matriliny, Islam and Capitalism: Combined and Uneven Development in the Lives of Negeri Sembilan Women* (University of Pittsburgh, 1987) and "Uneven and Combined Development: Dynamics of Change in Women's Everyday Forms of Resistance in Negeri Sembilan, Malaysia," *Review of Radical Political Economy* 23, nos. 3–4, (1991): 57–98.

An anthropological work relevant to this essay is Peter Worsley, *The Third World* (Chicago: University of Chicago Press, 1964). Even more relevant is Eric R. Wolf, *Europe and the People without History* (Berkeley: University of California Press, 1982), which gives some usefully critical consideration to Trotsky's perspective.

Relevant to final comments in the essay are the following: Manfred B. Steger, *Globalization: A Very Short Introduction* (Oxford: Oxford University Press, 2003), Jeffrey D. Sachs, *The End of Poverty: Economic Possibilities for Our Time* (New York: The Penguin Press, 2005), Walden Bello, *Dilemmas of Domination: The Unmaking of the American Empire* (New York: Metropolitan Books/Henry Holt, 2005), José Corrêa Leite, *The World Social Forum: Strategies of Resistance* (Chicago: Haymarket Books, 2005), and Susan Watkins, "Continental Tremors," *New Left Review* 33 (May–June 2005): 5–21.

3.

Radical Labor Subculture

A Key to Past and Future Insurgencies

L abor radicals have played a key role in the history of the US working-class movement, as in similar movements throughout the world. What are the dynamics that enhance or undermine the effectiveness of these historical actors? The interplay of radical ideologies, broader social and cultural realities, political organizations, social movements, and social change can be illuminated by an analytical concept—*radical labor subculture*. It can be particularly helpful as we seek to make sense of the dramatic divergence of left-wing activists from the actual working-class movement in the 1950s and 1960s, as well as the failures and floundering that afflicted a variety of left-wing currents in the 1970s and 1980s—in stark contrast to more inspiring realities stretching at least from the 1860s through the 1930s (arguably before the American Civil War and after the Second World War). It is also an analytical tool that may be helpful for those who wish to consider future possibilities of class struggle and radicalization.[1]

Culture, Class Conflict, and Subcultures

Culture has been described as a distinguishing characteristic of what it means to be human. Raymond Williams tells us that this term is "one of the two or three most complicated words in the English language."[2] It is worth considering its usage by North American anthropologists—for example, Melville Herskovits described it as "a [conceptual] construct that describes the total body of belief, behavior, sanctions, values, and goals that mark the way of life of any people," adding that "in the final analysis it comprises the things that people have, the things that they do, and what they think." Ruth Benedict referred to it as involving "ideas and standards" people have in common—"learned behavior . . . learned anew from grown people by each new generation." Clyde Kluckhohn and W. H. Kelly elaborated that "culture in general as a descriptive concept means the accumulated treasury of human creation: books, paintings, buildings and the like; the knowledge of ways of adjusting to our surroundings, both human and physical; language, customs, and systems of etiquette, religion, morals."[3] Such things are built up over time—but one must realize that they are created by people to deal with the often changing realities around them. In the face of social and economic transformations, new meanings are given to "traditional" customs, and sometimes dramatic innovations are embraced. Eleanor Leacock indicated how this concept fits into historical materialism by stressing the importance of "analysis that rejects static a-historical views of culture, and transforms the concept into a tool for examining the role of ideology and consciousness in social process." Factors involved in culture, she suggested, include the way people conceptualize and express their relations with each other, which are related to the ties they develop with one another in the course of organizing both the labor of production and daily life—grounded in material conditions and social relations.[4]

Twentieth-century Marxism has offered key insights that allow us to deepen our analysis. For revolutionary Marxists, of course, the conception of *class* is essential for making sense of culture. As Vladimir Ilyich Lenin put it in 1913 (in "Critical Remarks on the National Question"), "There are two nations in every modern nation," and so "there are two national cultures in every national culture"—capitalist and working class. The dominant element in any modern national culture, he argued, was "the national culture of the bourgeoisie," which often intertwined with the even more reactionary orientations of the aristocratic landed proprietors and reactionary elements among the clergy. "Aggressive bourgeois nationalism," he warned, "which drugs the minds of the workers, stultifies and disunites them in order that the bourgeoisie may lead them by the halter—such is the fundamental fact of the times." Against this capitalist-reactionary culture, Lenin counterposed what he called "the international culture of democracy and the world working-class movement," which in turn is grounded in the specific experience of workers in all countries. "The *elements* of democratic and socialist culture are present," he insisted, "if only in rudimentary form, in *every* national culture, since in every nation there are toiling and exploited masses, whose conditions of life inevitably give rise to the ideology of democracy and socialism."[5]

That the complexity of the question is even greater than Lenin suggested was highlighted, ten years later, by Leon Trotsky. "The proletariat is a powerful social unity which manifests its strength fully during the periods of intense revolutionary struggle for the gains of the whole class," Trotsky wrote in *Problems of Everyday Life*. "But within this unity we observe a great variety of types. Between the obtuse illiterate village shepherd and the highly qualified engine driver there lie a great many different states of culture and habits of life." Nor was this simply a problem of "backward Russia," in Trotsky's opinion. "One might say that the richer the history of a country, and at the same time of its working class, the greater within it the accumulation of memories, traditions, habits, the larger number of old groupings—the harder it is to achieve a revolutionary unity of the working class." For Marxists like Lenin and Trotsky, this is one of the problems necessitating the creation of a revolutionary party—to help forge the unity in struggle of a multicultural working class by providing (as Marx and Engels put it in the *Communist Manifesto*) an understanding of "the common interests of the entire proletariat, independently of all nationality" and an "understanding [of] the line of march" that can lead to the triumph of the working-class movement.[6]

But Karl Marx never presumed that it would be possible for would-be revolutionaries to make history just as they pleased. Rather, they would have to make it "under circumstances directly encountered, given and transmitted from the past."[7] They must engage with the kinds of historically determined cultural realities alluded to by the anthropologists and revolutionaries we have been looking at. The specifics of how this actually works have been traced by some of the most perceptive labor historians. The cultural counterposition of capitalists and workers in England, according to E. P. Thompson, can be traced back to eighteenth-century sociocultural tensions of "the gentry" and "the laboring poor." Much of this evolving class divide, he tells us, opened wide in reaction against a "modernizing" capitalism: "We can read much eighteenth-century social history as a succession of confrontations between an innovative market economy and the customary moral economy of the plebs," Thompson tells us. He continues: "In one sense the plebian culture is the people's own; it is a defense against the intrusions of gentry or clergy; it consolidates those customs which serve their interests; the taverns are their own, the fairs are their own, rough music is among their own means of self-regulation." This harmonizes with Lenin's view, as does Thompson's 1963 generalization, which has become a classic statement among Marxist labor historians:

> Class happens when some men [and women], as a result of common experiences (inherited or shared), feel and articulate the identity of their interests as

between themselves, and as against other men whose interests are different from (and usually opposed to) theirs. The class experience is largely determined by the productive relations into which . . . [people] are born—or enter involuntarily. Class-consciousness is the way in which these experiences are handled in cultural terms: embodied in traditions, value-systems, ideas, and institutional forms.[8]

Following in Thompson's footsteps (and also concerning himself with the sort of issues Trotsky pointed to), US labor historian Herbert Gutman observed: "Men and women who sell their labor to an employer bring more to a new or changing work situation than their physical presence. What they bring to a factory depends, in good part, on their culture of origin, and how they behave is shaped by the interaction between that culture and the particular society into which they enter." Surveying the evolving US working class from 1815 to 1919, he noted that it "was constantly altered in its composition by infusions, from within and without the nation, of peasants, farmers, skilled artisans, and casual day laborers who brought into industrial society ways of work and other habits and values not associated with industrial necessities and the industrial ethos." The response to capitalist exploitation and oppression varied: "Some shed these older ways to conform to new imperatives. Others fell victim or fled, moving from place to place. Some sought to extend and adapt older patterns of work and life to a new society. Others challenged the social system through varieties of collective associations."

This last grouping—those involved in organized challenges to the social system—represented what might be called a "vanguard" layer of the working class reflecting a radical labor subculture. According to Gutman, by the middle of the nineteenth century a proletarian recasting of democratic-republican ideology had become an essential element within US working-class culture, adding: "Their beliefs went beyond the redefinition of eighteenth-century republicanism, and sparked and sustained recurrent collective efforts—in the form of trade unions, strikes, cooperatives, a tart labor press, and local politics—to check the increasing power of the industrial capitalist."[9]

The Actuality of Labor-Radical Subculture

In the late 1880s, Karl Marx's bright and perceptive daughter Eleanor, along with her companion Edward Aveling, toured the United States for fifteen weeks, then wrote a fascinating account of *The Working-Class Movement in America*. The book begins with their listing of close to a hundred genuine working-class newspapers published throughout the United States, reflecting and influencing a vibrant subculture. In discussing the objective socioeconomic factors of working-class experience, they noted that the United States, in contrast to Europe, had "no remnants of old systems, no surviving classes that belonged to these"—instead, "the capitalist system came here as a ready-made article, and with all the force of its inherent, uncompromising brutality." The condition of the working class in the United States, they argued, was certainly no better than in England. While the overwhelming majority of the people they met had no idea what socialism was, the Marx-Avelings concluded that there was in fact "the prevalence of what we call unconscious Socialism," since when the actual meaning of socialism was explained (*not* equal division of property, *not* blowing up capitalists with dynamite, *not* anarchy—but social ownership and democratic control of the major economic resources), "in town after town, by hundred upon hundred, declared, 'Well, if that is Socialism, we are Socialists.'" In fact, hundreds of thousands had flocked to the Knights of Labor, which the couple saw as "the first expression by the American working people of their consciousness of themselves as a class." In addition, there were the trade unions associated with the American Federation of Labor (AFL)— as they put it, "the result of many years of evolution" and benefiting from "the practical experience especially of the German[-American] Socialists." The Knights of Labor, the trade unionists, and various labor radicals (including socialists) were joined together, in various cities, in what seemed to be promising labor party efforts that (the two optimists speculated) would "pass through several preliminary stages" that would eventually culminate in the adoption of a socialist program, with "the attainment of supreme political, and then of supreme economic power."[10]

Those familiar with Gutman and other US labor historians are able to identify reasons why the Marx-Aveling forecast was seriously off target. While providing a snapshot of US realities in the late 1880s, the two revolutionary visitors could not adequately factor in enough of the complex and fluid realities, not to mention the dramatic transformations, that would engulf and fragment the US working-class movement. As Lenin warned, disunity of workers along the lines of culture and consciousness (and also the de-radicalizing impact, for some of the more "privileged" skilled workers, of US capitalism's economic upswings) meant that—more than Eleanor Marx anticipated—the bourgeoisie was able to lead many workers "by the halter." One can certainly find brutal ethnic hostility, especially a poisonous racism toward nonwhite peoples, permeating much white working-class life throughout the nineteenth and twentieth centuries. One or another racial or ethnic group was all too often found to be unworthy to belong to one's union and would be excluded from one's workplace—and consequently could be used as a source of scabs during a strike, deepening hatred among workers. There were debilitating fissures along gender lines as well. Sometimes these tainted much of the radical labor subculture—although ultimately, the balance tipped increasingly in a more radical, inclusive direction. This was so particularly as various sections of the ethnically and racially diverse US working class experienced, among themselves, the crystallization of radical-proletarian subcultures and consciousness developing in confrontation to aspects of the bourgeois-dominated "national culture."

The existence of just such a class-conscious layer of the working class is a necessary precondition for creating a genuinely revolutionary party. Workers' class consciousness involves more than whatever notions happen to be in the minds of various members of the working class at any particular moment. It involves an understanding of the insight that was contained in the constitu-tional preamble of the AFL from 1886 to 1955: "A struggle is going on in all the nations of the civilized world, between the oppressors and the oppressed of all countries, a struggle between the capitalist and the laborer, which grows in intensity from year to year, and will work disastrous results to the toiling millions, if they are not combined for mutual protection and benefit."[11] Not all workers have absorbed this insight into their consciousness, but those who have done so can be said to have at least an elementary class consciousness.

Of course, this was a phenomenon by no means restricted to the United States. Several years after the AFL adopted this preamble, a young Marxist named Vladimir Ulyanov was explaining in far-off Russia that "the workers' class consciousness means the workers' understanding that the only way to im-prove their conditions and to achieve their emancipation is to conduct a strug-gle against the capitalist and factory-owner class created by the big factories. Further," he added in the spirit of the *Communist Manifesto*, "the workers of any particular country are identical, that they constitute one class, separate from all the other classes in society. Finally," he concluded, "the class-consciousness of the workers means the workers' understanding that to achieve their aims they have to work to influence the affairs of the state, just as the landlords and cap-italists did, and are continuing to do now."[12]

Such consciousness does not exist automatically in one's brain simply be-cause we happen to sell our labor-power (our ability to work) for wages or a salary. But in the United States, from the period spanning the end of the Civil War in 1865 down through the Depression decade of the 1930s, a vi-brant working-class subculture had developed throughout much of the United States. Often this subculture was more like a network of subcultures with very distinctive ethnic attributes, but these different ethnic currents were at various times connected by left-wing political structures (such as the old Knights of Labor, the Socialist Party of Eugene V. Debs, the Industrial Workers of the World, the Communist Party, various groups of socialist militants, Trotskyists, anarchists, and others) and also, to an extent, by trade union frameworks—culminating in the 1930s in the remarkable Congress of Industrial Organizations (CIO). We see it both reflected in and nourished by such class-struggle battles as the mass uprising of 1877; the eight-hour upsurge of 1886; the Homestead steel strike of 1892; the 1909 uprising of the 30,000 in New York City; the Lawrence textile strike of 1913; the momentous 1919 strike wave; the 1934 general strikes in Minneapolis, Toledo, and San Francisco; the innumerable sit-down strikes of the 1930s; and the nationwide explosion of victorious strikes in 1945–46. Within this context of struggle and organization, inseparable from the radical workers' subculture, flourished the widespread class consciousness that is essential to the creation of a revolutionary party.[13]

If we examine the decade of what has been called Labor's Giant Step—the 1930s—we see a variety of intersecting struggles that were inseparable from, reflected in, and nourished by a broad, amazingly rich and vibrant left-wing subculture. In addition to several significant socialist and communist formations, there was an array of organizations formed around a variety of issues—groups and coalitions for labor rights and democracy, against war and militarism, against racism and fascism, against poverty and unemployment, and others. Related to such things were an incredible number of conferences, educational classes and forums, books and pamphlets, newspapers and magazines, novels and short stories, songs and poems, plays and paintings, picnics and socials, marches and rallies—all blending together to create an expanding and deepening pool of ideas and sensibilities, of human relationships and a sense of solidarity, of insight and understanding. It was, in fact, a subculture (involving, as we've seen, what Herskovits called a "total body of belief, behavior, sanctions, values, and goals") that generated and nourished the kind of consciousness necessary for the sustained struggles that brought about a genuine power shift in US society to the benefit of the working-class majority.[14]

A historical survey of working-class movements in other countries reveals the same reality. Perhaps the best-known example is provided by the German labor movement—which involved such a rich alternative culture in Germany, that sociologist Max Weber referred to it as a "state within a state."[15]

Based on Italian experience, Antonio Gramsci outlined the creation of a working-class "intellectual-moral bloc," as he put it (and which appears to be the same thing as the radical working-class subculture), "which can make politically possible the intellectual progress of the mass and not only of small intellectual groups." While acknowledging the importance of "traditional intellectuals" who had been won to Marxism, Gramsci stressed the importance of developing "organic intellectuals" who were (and remained) part of the working class, and he emphasized the importance of working "incessantly to raise the intellectual level of the every-growing strata of the populace, to give a personality [a 'class consciousness'] to the amorphous mass element," seeking to "stimulate the formation of homogeneous, compact social blocs, which will give birth to their own intellectuals, their own commanders, their own vanguard—who will in turn react upon those blocs in order to develop them."[16]

Trotsky offered a description and theorization in the early 1930s, as he sought to persuade Social Democratic and Communist workers to join together in preventing the imminent Nazi victory in Germany:

> Within the framework of bourgeois democracy and parallel to the incessant struggle against it, the elements of proletarian democracy have formed themselves in the course of many decades: political parties, labor press, trade unions, factory committees, clubs, cooperatives, sports societies, etc. The mission of fascism is not so much to complete the destruction of bourgeois democracy as to crush the first outlines of proletarian democracy. As for our mission, it consists in placing those elements of proletarian democracy, already created, at the foundation of the soviet system of the workers' state. To this end, it is necessary to break the husk of bourgeois democracy and free from it the kernel of workers' democracy. Therein lies the essence of the proletarian revolution.[17]

Of course, one of the highest priorities of the Nazi movement was the thoroughgoing destruction of this subversive counterculture of the German working class, which was quickly and brutally accomplished when Hitler came to power. This is why the Nazis were embraced by Germany's big business interests and initially by the upper classes throughout Europe. It is worth noting how Gramsci described the similar, earlier fascist onslaught on what he saw as radical-labor organizational "links" in 1920s Italy:

> It set out to destroy even that minimum to which the democratic system was reduced in Italy—i.e., the concrete possibility to create an organizational link at the base between workers, and to extend this link gradually until it embraced the great masses in movement. . . . The strength and capacity for struggle of the workers for the most part derive from the existence of these links, even if they are not in themselves apparent. What is involved is the possibility of meeting, of discussing; of giving these meetings and discussions some regularity; of choosing leaders through them; of laying the basis for an elementary organic forma-

tion, a league, a cooperative or a party section. What is involved is the possibility of giving these organic formations a continuous functionality; of making them into the basic framework of an organized movement.... After three years of this kind of [fascist] action, the working class has lost all form and all organicity; it has been reduced to a disconnected, fragmented, scattered mass.[18]

Erosion and Decline of Radical Workers' Subculture

Fascist onslaughts and repression have not been the only means by which such subcultures are destroyed. There was a dramatic break in the continuity of this labor-radical tradition in the United States after 1945, due to the realities that resulted from the Second World War and the social, economic, political, and cultural transformations of the 1950s and 1960s.

Labor-radical Frank Lovell once emphasized that in the history of the twentieth century, "World War II was the great divide, like a chasm caused by an earthquake of unimaginable force." This global holocaust—which really was a convergence of holocausts that destroyed eighty million human beings in both combat and noncombat contexts—was a combination of several wars. Underlying them all was a set of inter-imperialist rivalries between Germany, Britain, France, Italy, Japan, and the United States for global hegemony (which was absolutely won by the United States, setting the stage for what was called the American Century). But also very much coming to the fore was a set of what might be called "people's wars" involving populations of Europe and Asia fighting against the invasion of their homelands by brutal, racist military machines, in some cases also involving anticolonial struggles in Asia and Africa. There was also the massive defense of the Soviet Union (in which more than twenty million people in the USSR died and the back of the Nazi war machine was broken). This, combined with the impending triumph of the Chinese Revolution and the expansion of Soviet dominance in Eastern Europe, set the stage for the decades of Cold War rivalry between the Communist bloc and the so-called Free World coalition led by the United States.[19]

"The war changed the world," Lovell reflects. "It changed almost everything about the world that we had known. It changed class relations among people around the world. And of course it left vast destruction and devastation in its wake." He goes on to make a key point: "But this was the very condition needed for the recovery and expansion of the capitalist system. Capitalism as a world system gained renewed strength from the process of rebuilding." Michael Yates describes the impact of the war on his mother's Western Pennsylvania coal-mining community: "The Second World War brought the mining village out of the Depression. It also helped to assimilate many Italian-Americans into the more conservative American mainstream. After the war, nationalism and anticommunism became much stronger, and individual acquisitiveness began to replace the more communal life of the pre-war era."[20] The reminiscences of Communist stalwart Steve Nelson, who had experience organizing among foreign-born workers, touch on dimensions of the same reality:

> It was a fact of life—the older generation was not pulling the younger into the movement. Increasingly, first and second generations [among the immigrant groups originating from Southern and Eastern Europe] not only spoke different languages but opted for different lifestyles. . . . World War II was a watershed. Sons who went to high school and then served in the armed forces thought in far different terms than their fathers. Daughters who worked in the shipyards and electrical plants were a world away from their mothers' experiences with domestic service and boarders. Industrial workers after the war were no longer pick and shovel men. Machine tenders who enjoyed the security provided by unions with established channels for collective bargaining could not appreciate the chronic insecurity of the pre-CIO era. . . . Participation in the labor movement and especially the war effort . . . eased the process of acceptance [into the "mainstream" of US culture] of the foreign-born and their children.[21]

Essential specifics of workers' occupations and workday experience underwent fundamental changes. Related to this was the transformation of the global economy (and the dominant US role within that economy), as capitalism profitably rebuilt itself after the devastation of war, at the same time bringing about remarkable innovations in economic organization and productivity, and enhanced by a lucrative economic expansionism securing raw materials, markets, and investment opportunities throughout the world. This combined with the victories of unionization and social reforms in the 1930s, which helped fuel not only economic prosperity but an unprecedented upward swing in working-class living standards. There were virtual revolutions in transportation, and in the communication and entertainment industries, plus new lifestyles generated by suburbanization and consumerism. At the same time, the long stretch of Cold War confrontation between the United States and the Soviet Union placed a pervasive and conservatizing anti-communism at the very center of the dominant political culture.

The organizations associated with the labor movement were similarly transformed—impacted by a complex combination of assaults, co-optations, corruptions, and erosions. The communities, culture, and consciousness of the working class became so different from the mid-1940s to the 1960s that only faded shreds of the old radical labor subculture remained.[22] Even in 1953, as he tried to make sense of the decline of radicalism among US workers, the veteran revolutionary socialist James P. Cannon commented:

> It is now sixteen years since the sit-down strikes made the new CIO unions secure by the seniority clause. These sixteen years of union security, and thirteen years of uninterrupted war and postwar prosperity, have wrought a great transformation in the unprivileged workers who made the CIO.... The pioneer militants of the CIO unions are sixteen years older than they were in 1937. They are better off than the ragged and hungry sit-down strikers of 1937; and many of them are sixteen times softer and more conservative. This privileged section of the unions, formerly the backbone of the left wing, is today the main social base of the conservative Reuther bureaucracy [in the United Auto Workers union].[23]

Studying the de-radicalization process of the 1950s and 1960s, sociologist John C. Leggett wrote that "a new middle class arose which included a large number of young people of working class background," noting that many prospering working people had moved out of traditional working-class communities to become homeowners in the suburbs. "The class struggle abated with the end of the post–World War II strikes, although repeated flare-ups between management and workers occurred during and after the Korean War," he added in his description of the same autoworkers discussed by Cannon.

> At the same time, another trend pointed up this harmony. Governmental boards and labor unions often helped minimize class conflict as unions grew more friendly toward companies which were willing to bargain with, and make major concessions to, labor organizations. Prosperity reached almost everyone one. Even working-class minority groups [that is, some African Americans] improved their standard of living and sent sons and daughters into the middle class.[24]

According to Stanley Aronowitz, such realities also involved tendencies, in his words, "toward the replacement of all the traditional forms of proletarian culture and everyday life—which gave working-class communities their coherence and provided the underpinnings for the traditional forms of proletarian class consciousness—with a new, manipulated consumer culture which for convenience's sake we can call mass culture." In 1963, Black autoworker James Boggs commented that "today the working class is so dispersed and transformed by the very nature of the changes in production that it is almost impossible to select out any single bloc of workers as working-class in the old sense." By this "old sense" he meant class-conscious workers. "The working class is growing, as Marx predicted," acknowledged Boggs, "but it is not the old working class which the radicals persist in believing will create the revolution and establish control over production. That old working class is the vanishing herd."[25] As Boggs makes clear, it was hardly the working class that was vanishing—but rather the class consciousness that had been essential to building the labor and socialist movements.

All of this was just fine with the bureaucratic leadership of organized labor. "I believe in free, democratic, competitive capitalism," explained the president of the once-socialist International Ladies' Garment Workers' Union, Sol Chaikin, in 1979. He elaborated that "managers should manage and then workers should sit down with them to collectively bargain for their share of the results of management efficiency and worker productivity." Earlier in the decade George Meany, president of the AFL-CIO, put things this way: "Our members are basically Americans. They basically believe in the American system, and they have a greater stake in the system now than they had fifteen or twenty years ago, because under the system and under our trade union policy, they have become 'middle class.' They have a greater stake."[26]

Such views were not inconsistent with the consciousness prevalent among a majority of union members in the post–World War II decades. When the radical upsurge of the 1960s shifted the political center of gravity leftward—with the massive civil rights struggles, the student and youth insurgencies, the profound opposition to the US war in Vietnam, the early stirrings of a new wave of feminism, and more—it was all far less connected to any genuine working-class movement than had been the case with radical upsurges in the 1880s and '90s, the early 1900s, certainly the 1930s and '40s. This was so even though a majority of the activists came from backgrounds (and were destined for occupations) in which one made one's living by selling an ability to work for a paycheck, which is the classical Marxist definition of what it means to be working class. But the activists tended to see themselves—and were certainly portrayed—as middle class, not as part of a self-conscious working class.

As the thinking of the youthful radicals evolved in socialist and Marxist directions, they found themselves—despite their new-found "proletarian" ideology—in a very different place from the actual organized labor movement of their own time. Marxism itself, initially developed in intimate symbiosis with the actual experiences and struggles of embattled radical workers of earlier times, could not have the same meaning for these young activists, could not be understood in the same vibrant way, as had been the case for working-class activists of the nineteenth and early twentieth centuries. The organizations these young Marxists sought to build, and the way they sought to build those organizations, clearly showed this to be true—although this was generally not self-evident for the activists themselves. This was to have unhappy consequences for the would-be revolutionaries.

Turning once again to Lenin, we find the revolutionary leader explaining in 1920 the successful experience of Russian Bolshevism to less experienced activists. In "*Left-Wing" Communism, an Infantile Disorder*, he noted that there are three necessary conditions for the success of a revolutionary party. First, there must be a "class-consciousness of the proletarian vanguard," a layer of the working class devoted to the goal of working-class revolution. Many from this layer must be part of the organization. Second, there must be an ability of the organization "to link up, maintain the closest contact, and—if you wish—merge, in a certain measure, with the broadest masses of the working people" through real-life struggles. Third, the organization's Marxist strategy and tactics must be seen as being correct by the broad masses "from their own experience." He insisted that "correct revolutionary theory . . . is not a dogma, but assumes final shape only in close connection with the practical activity of a truly mass and truly revolutionary movement." Lenin went on to emphasize: "Without these conditions, discipline in a revolutionary party really capable of being a party of the advanced class, whose mission it is to overthrow the bourgeoisie and transform the whole of society, cannot be achieved." He underscored the point with words that stand as a devastating critique to most would-be US Leninists of the 1980s: "Without these conditions, all attempts to establish discipline inevitably fall flat and end up in phrase mongering and clowning."[27]

New Developments

Historian Warren Van Tine once suggested that the US labor movement has variously been characterized by four different images—"the union as a fraternity, a democracy, an army, and a business." By the 1920s, he tells us, "the concepts of the union as an army and the union as a business were far more prominent and influential," with hierarchy, elitism, and bureaucracy displacing notions of the union as a band of brothers and sisters or as representing rule by the people.[28] This was especially so with the triumph of the dramatically conservatized and corrupted AFL over the idealistic militants of the IWW. In the 1930s, with the rise of the left-wing–influenced CIO, this trend was temporarily reversed. By the 1950s and '60s, as we have seen, the model of "business unionism"—encouraged by the general prosperity and working-class gains—became predominant. But this much-lauded approach, considered at the time to be realistic and mature, would prove woefully inadequate in the face of new challenges that were about to arise.

Through a social compromise forged with big business and big government during and after World War II, the leadership of the organized labor movement in our country embraced the rights of the capitalist elite to control the economy, as well as an essentially imperialist foreign policy, in order to secure "the American Dream" for a majority of the US working class. But by the late 1970s, the most powerful of the capitalists—driven by the profit-maximizing dynamics of their own system—had decided on a different approach. The great revolutionary Rosa Luxemburg once spoke of trade union struggles as "the labor of Sisyphus"—referring to the mythical being who kept rolling an immense boulder up a hill, only to see it roll back down again. That is how capitalism works, and the dynamic reasserted itself with a vengeance.

While the bureaucratic-conservative leadership of organized labor had little interest in maintaining in "their" unions the popular-democratic idealism that had mobilized millions of workers to win the victories of the 1930s and 1940s, it had been these victories that caused important elements among the capitalist power elite to accept a dramatic power shift in the economy. The economic regulations and social programs imposed by a liberal government and the acceptance of organized labor's existence and influence constituted President Franklin D. Roosevelt's New Deal, which (with modifications) was more or less accepted by both the Democratic and Republican parties for three decades. But there had always been a financially powerful conservative faction that refused to accept this. It would spend considerable time, resources, and energies to build what would soon prove to be a triumphant counterattack.

With the electoral sweep of Ronald Reagan in 1980, the once-marginal perspectives of the business conservatives of the late 1940s and 1950s became the new political and economic orthodoxy of the United States in the final decades of the twentieth century. The demolition of the assumptions and programmatic vestiges of the New Deal and of the once-powerful labor movement seemed to have been largely a "mission accomplished" even before George W. Bush took office.[29] Kim Moody's summary cannot be improved upon:

> The industrial centerpieces of the US economy shrank or reorganized, and the cities, towns, and unions based on them went into decline and/or dramatic changes in make-up. The industrial "heartland" became the rust belt. The "industries" that appeared to replace them were low-wage and mostly nonunion. Technology, "deployed with ferocity" in a more competitive world, as one economist put it, eliminated some jobs and intensified others. The loss of union density turned into an absolute loss of union members. The institution of collective bargaining was turned from a phalanx of advance to a line of retreat. The upward trend in real wages of the previous thirty years reversed into a prolonged down-

ward spiral. The decline in economic inequality that began during World War II stopped and inequality accelerated with each decade. The New Deal liberal consensus that had dominated politics for over three decades was drowned in a sea of money and replaced by an aggressive neoliberalism that called itself conservative. The underpinnings of American labor ideology were invalidated, though union leaders clung tenaciously to the old tenets. Greed became good. Business values took center field. What had been national became global. Globalization, in turn, became the reason or excuse for every move against the working-class majority.[30]

The fact that class-conscious layers of the old working class of the 1930s were dramatically fading even by the early 1950s hardly means that the working class as such had evaporated. The working class is bigger than ever, but it is not the same working class that once existed. There has been a combined decomposition and recomposition of the working class, and the old labor-radical subculture is long gone. It, too, needs to be recomposed, and within a very different economic, social, and cultural reality than once existed. But the problems Moody pointed to in 2007 indicate the likelihood of growing working-class discontent—something that, if anything, has been exacerbated by the effects of the recent economic downturn of 2008, not to mention the increasingly unpopular US military interventions in Iraq and Afghanistan. This discontent is reflected in the fact that a powerful right-wing political machine, dominating the national government since 2000, was dislodged by a Black presidential candidate—one who was falsely but widely accused of being a socialist and who certainly utilized quite radical rhetoric in order to win the election, promising fundamental and "meaningful" change. The growing disillusionment over President Obama's failure to deliver on radical and hopeful promises raises the possibility of a deepening mass radicalization.

Implications for Activists

The working-class majority is the sector of the population within which such radicalization is taking root. The fact remains that there is no organized working-class movement that seems able or inclined to provide effective leadership in the present period. The incredible weakness of the labor movement during the first decade of the twenty-first century has been the focus of much comment by knowledgeable left-wing labor analysts, and it is worth turning our attention to what they have to say. They wisely avoid utopian blueprints—the details of struggle must be worked out by those who are engaged in actual struggles. Nonetheless, the kinds of points such commentators make—taken together—seem to push in a direction consistent with the conceptualization of the radical labor subculture.

"The hope for the next upsurge," Kim Moody has written, "is that there is a clearer vision with a wide enough base and an experienced grassroots leadership to push beyond the limits of the ideology, practice, and personnel of business unionism in its old and new forms." Michael Yates has emphasized: "What organized labor lacks is a working-class ideology, a labor-centered way of thinking and acting based upon the understanding that a capitalist society is not and cannot be a just one. What might motivate workers to become part of a movement is the possibility that the current system can be transcended and a new, democratic, egalitarian society built." History suggests, however, that this revitalization will not develop simply within the existing unions, causing Dan Clawson to hope that a "fusion of labor and new social movements might combine the best of both worlds—the energy, imagination, media savvy, and militant symbolic actions of the new social movements with the broad outreach, local chapters, face-to-face majoritarian mobilization, deep commitment, and staying power of the labor movement." In the opinion of Bill Fletcher and Fernando Gapasin, "To bring social justice trade unionism into existence, we must change not only the leadership of existing organized labor but also the relationship between the existing trade union movement and other progressive social forces (for example, workers' centers, independent unions, and progressive social clubs)." They add: "Such change will not happen in the absence of a conscious Left force."[31]

The need for "a conscious Left"—the existence of theoretically grounded, politically committed organizations of socialists—is matched by the need for broader social movements that in various ways will interpenetrate with unions, and by the need (within the linked social movements and union movement) for the spread of a radical vision, a working-class ideology, "a labor-centered way of thinking and acting," with organizers and activists and supporters who are energetic and "media savvy," having a keen sense of imagination and an ability to utilize various forms of symbolism to realize this goal.

These multifaceted, creative, outward-reaching qualities are already in play, and they are influencing the larger culture. There is an increased proliferation of radical books and journals and newsletters, of well-attended left-wing educational conferences, of progressive labor gatherings, of creative performances (including music, poetry slams, plays, art exhibits, independent films and even an occasional big-budget film, even radical television productions such as Howard Zinn's *The People Speak* special). Still in its early stages, this embryonic radical subculture reflects and enhances radicalizing consciousness within the working-class majority. As this develops, it can have a powerful influence on social struggles and left-wing organizing efforts.

By itself, this already-recomposing subculture will not bring about the changes that are needed: not the working-class organizations; not the revitalized union movement; not the coming together of a mass-based, genuinely revolutionary party; not the class-struggle actions that will bring us life-giving reforms in the here and now and create the future possibility of a socialist transformation. But history suggests that it is an integral part of the process. It helps to generate and nourish the class consciousness and the fundamental elements of workers' democracy that experienced Marxists have seen as necessary preconditions for revolutionary transformation. To the extent that Marxist activists understand this process, they will be better able to help advance it. They will also have a greater insight into the tasks and the timing of socialist and working-class organizing.

4.

Class and Identities

In seeking to understand the actualities and possibilities of social protest and revolution, scholars and activists have often sought to comprehend what force would be capable of bringing about fundamental social change. This is related to notions of power, exploitation, and oppression in society. *Revolutions* are generally seen as bringing about, through the active participation of masses of people, the overturn of established ruling groups and the creation of a new political and social order. How people actually see or identify themselves as they engage in social struggles, and the identities they seek to build on, or to foster, in order to bring about social change is of central importance for the unfolding of any revolutionary process. The examination of such matters of *identity* is important for those wishing to understand such processes.

Among the most potent identities in modern revolutionary movements has been that of class. The term *class* has had various meanings, but the modern usage often refers to differences of wealth and power in society. While the notion of class in this sense was highlighted by social theorists of the nineteenth century, most notably by Karl Marx and his co-thinkers, its usage has been traced back to the eighteenth century. Daniel Defoe, commenting on the evolving market economy in Britain, wrote in 1705: "The dearness of wages forms our people into more classes than other nations can show." Referring to similar, though more advanced, developments in 1787, James Madison wrote in *The Federalist* that moneyed and manufacturing interests "grow up of necessity in civilized nations, and divide them into different classes, actuated by different sentiments and views."

In certain stratified precapitalist societies, the modern notion of class may be seen as roughly equivalent to the notions of *social orders* or *ranks* or *estates*. As Raymond Williams has noted, however, "the essential history of the introduction of *class*, as a word which would supersede older names for social divisions, relates to the increasing consciousness that social position is made rather than merely inherited."

Marxist Conceptions and Evolving Realities

The Communist Manifesto (1848), by Marx and coauthor Frederick Engels, has been seen by many as the primary revolutionary text of modern times, and in it the centrality of class is unmistakable. Since the rise of the civilizations that postdate the extended early period of primitive tribal communism, human history has been "a history of class struggle," they tell us. The rise of civilization has been dependent upon the technological development and consequent increase in productivity that results in the production of a socioeconomic surplus, which, in turn, makes it possible for the labor of one person to support himself/herself as well as one or more others. This, in turn, makes possible the rise of the socioeconomic inequality that is essential to the modern concept of *class*.

Marx and Engels assert that since the rise of civilization there have been two primary classes: (a) the exploited majorities whose labor sustains all of society and (b) the powerful minorities whose wealth depends on the exploitation of the majority's labor.

The traditional Marxist schema of successive stages of class society, based on European history, has seen ancient slave-based civilizations (with slaves and slave-owners) superseded by feudal society (with peasant serfs and lords), which in turn has been replaced by capitalism (with the proletariat, or working class, and the bourgeoisie, or capitalist class). Based upon his studies of non-European societies, Marx also advanced the conception of an "Asiatic mode of production." Recent theorists, such as anthropologist Eric Wolf, suggest the more general notion of a "tributary mode of production," which they argue more adequately describes various socioeconomic realities between the erosion of primitive communal society and capitalism.

Marx and Engels suggested, however, that with the rise of capitalism—an incredibly dynamic system based on the powerful, relentless process of capital accumulation, unlike more static forms of previous class society—a new kind of development has taken place, one involving "simplified class antagonisms." Commenting on earlier forms, they asserted: "In ancient Rome we have patricians, knights, plebians, slaves; in the Middle Ages, feudal lords, vassals, guild-masters, journeymen, apprentices, serfs; in almost all of these classes, again, subordinate gradations." Under capitalism, in contrast, "society is more and more splitting up into two great hostile camps, into two great classes directly facing each other: bourgeoisie and proletariat."

The important 1888 footnote to the *Manifesto* by Engels explains: "By bourgeoisie is meant the class of modern capitalists, owners of the means of social production and employers of wage labor. By proletariat, the class of modern wage laborers who, having no means of production of their own, are reduced to selling their labor-power in order to live." It is the class struggle between the working class and the capitalist class, according to Marx and Engels, that will define the trajectory of modern society—culminating in a victory of the working-class majority, leading in turn to a revolutionary transition from capitalism to socialism.

Yet in Marx's own writings, one can find greater complexity than this. In an unfinished chapter for the third volume of *Capital*, Marx wrote: "The owners of mere labor-power, the owners of capital, and the landowners, whose respective sources of income are wages, profit, and rent of land, or in other words, wage laborers, capitalists, and landowners, form the three great classes of modern society based on the capitalist mode of production." He almost immediately added: "Intermediate and transitional strata obscure the class boundaries even in this case." The fact that Marx's analysis here remained only an initial fragment prevents us from following his thought further. Surveying the vast body of Marx's writings, Edward Reiss has offered the following compilation of classes under capitalism:

- The big landowners, aristocracy, nobility, can be seen as a residual class from feudalism, increasingly supplanted by the bourgeoisie.
- The bourgeoisie, owners of the factories (means of production), the transport system (means of distribution), and the big shops (means of exchange). Marx distinguishes between industrial capitalists (for example mill-owners) and finance capitalists (the "bankocracy").
- The petty bourgeoisie: small-scale businesses, shopkeepers, etc. In times of boom, they aspire to the bourgeoisie. In recession, they shift towards the proletariat.
- The proletariat: those who have nothing to sell but their labor-power. The worker "belongs not to this or that capitalist, but to the capitalist class, and it is his business to dispose of himself, that is to find a purchaser within this capitalist class."

- The lumpen proletariat: "the 'dangerous class,' the social scum, that passively rotting mass thrown off by the lowest layers of the old society.' This is what is now called the under-class: criminals, beggars etc."

Nor is this complete. Missing from the list are the majority of laborers for most of the world (including Europe) when Marx wrote—the peasantry. In the *Communist Manifesto*, peasants are lumped together with other social strata destined to pass out of existence: "The lower strata of the middle class— the small trades people, shopkeepers, and retired tradesmen generally, the handicraftsmen and peasants—all these gradually sink into the proletariat." Yet this is a category deserving greater attention.

As Teodor Shanin (himself operating within a broadly Marxist framework) has insisted, peasants must be seen "as a class, i.e., as a social entity based on a community of economic interests, shaped by conflict with other classes, expressed in typical patterns of cognition and political consciousness and capable of united political action on a national level."

From the standpoint of many social scientists, peasants cannot be equated simply with people who are engaged in agriculture (such as existed among many of the tribes of Native American peoples, or "Indians," before they were overwhelmed by European and US conquest). Nor are they like small-scale farmers engaged in commercial agriculture, treating their land as small business enterprises producing primarily for the market in order to maximize profits (which would make them "petty bourgeois"). According to Shanin, "The peasantry consists of small agricultural producers who, with the help of simple equipment and the labor of their families, produce mainly for their own consumption and for the fulfillment of obligations of political and economic power" (whether these be feudal lords, powerful monarchies, priestly castes, absolutist states, capitalistic landowners, or merchants or banks).

In social organization, culture, and mentality, they are noncapitalist. As Hal Draper has noted, the common English translation of the *Manifesto* that seems to refer pejoratively to "the idiocy of rural life" (*dem Idiotismus des Landlebein*) is better understood as "the seclusion and ignorance of rural life," referring descriptively to the fact that "the peasant population stood outside modern civilization within a nation."

This "awkward class" (as Shanin has labeled it) has been the majority of the world's laborers throughout much of human history. Far from being "petty bourgeois," it has the potential for being profoundly hostile to capitalist economic development. In fact, Marx and Engels—as well as Russian revolutionaries associated with the Bolshevik wing of the Marxist movement, and later the Communist International, such as Lenin, Trotsky, Bukharin—saw the peasants as essential allies of the working class in anticapitalist struggles in countries with substantial agricultural economies. This conception of a worker-peasant alliance, and of peasants as a revolutionary class, was also taken up, often with dramatic emphasis and adaptation, by revolutionaries throughout Asia, Latin America, and Africa.

The Working Class

The fact remains that the analytical generalization made by the young Marx and Engels in the *Communist Manifesto* has seemingly been borne out over the past century and a half—the peasantry has increasingly given way, on the one hand, to commercial farming interests that are part of the capitalist class (with the smaller farmers being wiped out, more and more, by large-scale "agribusiness") and, on the other hand, to absorption into the working class—either being converted into an agricultural proletariat or being driven into the labor forces of urban areas. A complication in economically "underdeveloped" areas has involved the question of the extent to which ex-peasants become relatively low-pay wage laborers in industrial/service enterprises and the extent to which they become part of an "informal economy" of part-time workers/part-time petty entrepreneurs. But the decline of the peasantry and growth of the proletariat appears to be a fact of life as capitalism has continued to develop.

In Marxist terms, the working class (or proletariat) is commonly seen as that sector of society that subsists (makes its living) by selling its labor-power (ability to work). Capitalist employers purchase this labor-power as a commodity along with other commodities (raw materials, tools) in order to produce commodities of greater value to sell at a higher price than was originally invested. The wages or salaries paid to the workers allow them to support themselves and their families. But the amount of actual labor squeezed out of the workers necessarily produces more value than the capitalist originally invested—which is the basis both for exploitation and profits. The working class is commonly seen as consisting not only of those workers who are drawn into this relationship but also of family members who are dependent on the worker's income, as well as workers not actually working because they are unemployed (including those suffering from long-term structural unemployment) or retired.

The importance of the working class for Marx and Engels seems to consist in a combination of factors:

1. The working class is in the process of becoming the majority class in capitalist society.
2. The working class provides the creative energy, the labor, that is essential for sustaining all of society.
3. The working class is an essential ingredient in the functioning of the capitalist system (through the exploitation of its labor, which is the source of capitalist profits), yet its role transcends the framework of capitalism.
4. Regardless of differences in the conditions of various groups of workers at various times, all workers experience the capitalist labor process as essentially exploitative, degrading, and authoritarian.
5. The relative compactness, socialization, and education of the working class has facilitated efforts to organize it as an effective force for economic, social, and political change (through protest movements, trade unions, political parties, and sometimes revolutionary struggles).
6. The negative impact of capitalism on the working class—an impact which has fluctuated but periodically intensified—creates a class-wide interest to replace capitalism with a less socially destructive, less oppressive, more humane, and more democratic economic system.

The orientation implied by this class-struggle perspective of Marxism was powerfully influential in labor movements, social protests, and revolutionary struggles throughout the world, especially from the period of 1850 to 1950. In the final half of the twentieth century, however, a number of complications developed that raised questions about the Marxist orientation to the working class.

Complications, Intermediate Layers, Recomposition

Regarding the anticipated "simplification" of the class structure into a growing confrontation between shrinking bourgeoisie and swelling proletariat predicted by the *Communist Manifesto*, radical sociologist C. Wright Mills commented, in the early 1960s: "In the course of capitalism's history, the class structure has not been simplified . . . into two classes. On the contrary, the opposite trend has been general—and the more 'advanced' the capitalism, the more complex and diversified has the stratification become." In fact, "the wage workers in advanced capitalist countries have leveled off as a proportion of the labor force" and "the intermediary or middle classes have not dwindled away" but have been increased by "salaried professionals, managers, office workers and sales personnel" into a growing non-proletarian strata, the upper managerial levels of which "have joined the property owners and with them constitute a corporate rich of a sort Marx did not know."

So committed a Marxist theorist as Ralph Miliband has similarly acknowledged that a substantial segment of this "white collar" sector constitutes an "army of 'foremen' and 'overseers' of every description" that stands as a genuine "intermediate" layer "quite distinct from the bourgeoisie on the one hand and from the working class on the other." Yet it can be argued that the central thrust of Mills's point about a declining proletariat and rising "middle class" has not been borne out as realities continued to evolve. Instead, there seems to have been a recomposition rather than a dwindling of the working class. By far the larger segment of the "white collar" work force has been, according to perceptive analyst Harry Braverman, "enlarged into a mass of working-class employment, and in the process divested of all its privileges and intermediate characteristics." As Miliband's study of classes under modern capitalism concludes, "The vast aggregate of people in advanced capitalist societies, amounting to something like two-thirds to three-quarters of their population, . . . constitute the working class: industrial workers, clerical, distributive, and service workers, skilled and unskilled, young and old, white and black and brown, men and women." This includes others not working for wages or salaries—non-employed partners, spouses, family members (some of these future workers), as well as sick, unemployed, and retired workers; he adds that there is also much overlap between the most destitute segments of the working class and the so-called under-class, which also accounts for a significant percentage of the population.

Past critics of Marx (including Mills) also commented on the relative affluence of substantial working-class sectors in the advanced capitalist countries, which was a striking feature of the decades following World War II, particularly from 1950 to 1980, resulting in an obvious decline in revolutionary inclinations among workers with access to a proliferation of consumer goods.

Yet this was actually reversed with the global expansion of capital (associated with a much-heralded "globalization," and in part fueled by the collapse of Communism). While global working-class occupations doubled between 1975 and 1995 to a total of 2.5 billion, the developing technologies and job mobility (in the words of sociologist Ronaldo Munck) have had quite a negative impact on "the industrial workers of the old smokestack industries" in the advanced capitalist countries, yielding declining wage levels combined with sweeping neoliberal/neoconservative cuts in social programs that had been the norm in the earlier post–World War II decades.

The situation at the dawn of the twenty-first century seemed in some ways to reinforce much of the *Communist Manifesto*'s relevance, despite the "long detour" of those previous decades. "Class struggle has certainly changed its format and its modalities since the early days of capitalism but there is nothing to indicate that struggle has vacated the contemporary workplace," Munck asserts. Some analysts of late twentieth/early twenty-first-century labor have emphasized that the negative impacts of "globalization" will compel active forces seeking change, within the working-class majority, to look for radical alternatives. "If a convincing, democratic version of socialism as the rule of the working class can be put forth in the context of the real struggles and organizations of the working class," in the words of veteran analyst Kim Moody, "it has a chance to take on a material force it has lacked for decades." He added (in 1997): "Perhaps to a greater extent than in most of the twentieth century, the opportunity for this idea and movement to spread globally is also more inherent in today's capitalist world than at any time in the past seventy years."

And yet the fact that the working classes of most countries throughout most of the twentieth century had, by and large, not seemed to be in a position or even a mind-set to carry out the kind of proletarian revolution projected by the *Manifesto* gave credence to other critical observations and alternative orientations.

Some social scientists have followed C. Wright Mills in considering contributions of such non-Marxist theorists of the early twentieth century as Max Weber, the twentieth century's foremost sociologist, in exploring the problems that seem to be associated with the Marxist approach. As Lewis Coser observes, "Much of Weber's work . . . can best be understood as a continued interchange with the ideas of Karl Marx." While agreeing that economically determined classes were essential components of modern capitalist societies, Weber also emphasized the importance of what he labeled "status groups"—or might be termed strong *group identities*—constituting communities that might be based on lifestyles, a sense of "honor," social esteem, or prestige. He commented that "class distinctions are linked in the most varied ways with status distinctions," sometimes crossing class lines, sometimes fragmenting class cohesion. Coser remarks that often status-consciousness is manifest among people "who are fearful of losing their status or who bridle at not having been accorded a status they think is their due." He has suggested that Weber's twofold classification of social stratification—based on concepts similar to Marx's notion of class but also on the notion of status—"lays the groundwork for an understanding of pluralistic forms of social conflict in modern society and helps to explain . . . why

Marx's exclusively class-centered scheme failed to predict correctly the shape of things to come."

Consciousness and Class

Interesting disputes have arisen among Marxists over the role of consciousness in defining the term *class*. In his magisterial history *The Making of the English Working Class* (1963), E. P. Thompson emphasized that "the notion of class entails the notion of historical relationship" that "happens when some men, as a result of common experiences (inherited or shared), feel and articulate the identity of their interests as between themselves, and as against other men whose interests are different from (and usually opposed to) theirs. The class experience is largely determined by the productive relations into which men are born—or enter involuntarily. Class consciousness is the way in which these experiences are handled in cultural terms: embodied in traditions, value-systems, ideas, and institutional forms." He added: "There is today an ever-present temptation to suppose that class is a thing. This was not Marx's meaning, in his own historical writing, yet the error vitiates much latter-day 'Marxist' writing. 'It,' the working class, is assumed to have a real existence, which can be defined almost mathematically—so many men who stand in a certain relation to the means of production." He dismissed this as "the crude notion of class."

In his highly acclaimed *Karl Marx's Theory of History* (1978), G. A. Cohen went out of his way to challenge Thompson's comments. He insisted that the appropriate way of understanding the concept "defines class with reference to the position of its members in the economic structure, their effective rights and duties within it. A person's class is established by nothing but his objective place in the network of ownership relations, however difficult it may be to identify such places neatly." He stressed that the person's "consciousness, culture, and politics do not enter the *definition* of his class position. Indeed, these exclusions are required to protect the substantive character of the Marxian thesis that class position strongly conditions consciousness, culture, and politics."

There is, however, a strong tendency within the Marxist tradition inclining in the direction suggested by Thompson. "*A class is born in the class struggle,*" argued Ernst Fischer and Franz Marek in their exposition of Marx's thought. "Only through such struggle does it develop into a social and historical force." A key aspect of Marx's conception of class involves its dual character, what might be called an objective dimension and a subjective dimension, the distinction between what he called "a class-in-itself" and "a class-for-itself." The first means "the actual role a social grouping plays in the economy and in society," the second means "the consciousness members of that group have regarding their common situation, their common interests and struggles." From this standpoint, Marx scholar David McLellan has stressed, for Marx "a class only existed when it was conscious of itself as such, and this always implied common hostility to another social group." He quotes Marx's comments on the French peasantry in *The Eighteenth Brumaire of Louis Bonaparte* (1852):

> In so far as millions of families live under economic conditions of existence that separate their mode of life, their interests and their culture from those of the other classes and put them in hostile opposition to the latter, they form a class. In so far as there is merely a local interconnection among those small-holding peasants and the identity of their interests begets no community, no national bond, and no political organization among them, they do not form a class. They are consequently incapable of enforcing their class interest in their own name.

One could add (as have some critics of Marxism) that the US working class, "in the Marxist sense," has ceased to exist because most of its prospective "members" see themselves not as "proletarian" but instead as "middle class" (neither rich nor poor, but in the middle).

In response to this, Cohen points out that Marx himself, in the very same work cited by McLellan, writes that these peasant smallholders "were the most numerous *class* of French society." He comments: "It is precisely because a class need not be conscious of itself that the phrase 'class-in-itself' was introduced." Whether or not one accepts Cohen's lucid reasoning, however, his dispute with Thompson highlights a problematical development that arose during the twentieth century.

There was, in fact, a vibrant correspondence between the perspectives of the *Communist Manifesto*'s program for the working class and the actual development of the European labor movement in the late nineteenth century. Its shared priorities were to engage in militant struggles for reforms, build increasingly strong trade unions, and build political parties of the working class that would project a socialist future. But there were also countervailing tendencies, as Marx and Engels more than once emphasized.

Others in the Marxist tradition also gave attention to this matter. For example, V. I. Lenin in *What Is to Be Done?* and Rosa Luxemburg in *The Mass Strike, the Political Party and the Trade Unions* each stressed a sharp distinction between a narrow "trade union consciousness" and a more expansive class consciousness as two very different mind-sets that could lead workers into either a reconciliation with capitalism or into a revolutionary confrontation with it, and both thinkers during World War I emphasized the negative effects of a form of consciousness that Lenin labeled "social-patriotism" that drew workers to support and even sacrifice their lives to imperialism. Lenin, referring to characterizations by Engels of elements within the late nineteenth-century British working class, advanced a general notion of "labor aristocracy" to define a layer of more privileged workers (generally more highly skilled and more highly paid) inclined to separate themselves from the masses of less fortunate workers and to make their peace with the capitalist system—which could be seen as conceptually similar to Weber's conception of *status*.

Georg Lukács contributed substantially to analyses of these and similar matters in his 1923 classic *History and Class Consciousness*, an exposition of Marxism that was profoundly influenced by the philosopher G. W. F. Hegel, sociologists Georg Simmel and Max Weber, and especially the revolutionary theorizations of Lenin—particularly in the essays "Class Consciousness" and "Reification and the Consciousness of the Proletariat." The term "false consciousness" gained currency among many Marxists in discussions about how some workers are drawn to outlooks and practices—including racism and various forms of chauvinism, support for conservative or reactionary political figures, selfish materialism or self-destructive behaviors, etc.—that were inconsistent with the insights and the working-class trajectory projected by Marx.

At the same time, a far-reaching critique of Marxism found powerful articulation in the twentieth century, based on the observation—expressed, for example, by sympathetic critic C. Wright Mills—that "wage-workers in advanced capitalism . . . have not become the agency for any revolutionary change of epoch," but rather "to a very considerable extent they have been incorporated into nationalist capitalism—economically, politically, and psychologically. So incorporated, they constitute within capitalism a dependent rather than an independent variable. The same is true of labor unions and labor parties." He acknowledged "basic class conflicts of interest" but insisted "there is little class struggle." According to Mills, Marx's analysis captured realities of capitalism as it existed in the Victorian era (1837–1901) but missed crucial developments that became manifest afterward: "We must accuse him of dying, his work unfinished, in 1883." The thrust of this argument found expression in numerous critiques, at various times, from the 1940s through the 1990s, perhaps most dramatically expressed in André Gorz's phrase of the 1980s, "Farewell to the Working Class."

While radical labor analyst Sheila Cohen has similarly noted "the lack of awareness of most workers, most of the time, of their collective class interests," she has also pointed out that the impact of capitalist exploitation as well as inevitable shifts in the dynamic capitalist economy preclude "uninterrupted acceptance of the status quo." Time after time, workers have been pushed into struggles—by the very nature of capitalism—that have periodically resulted in the expansion of radicalized class consciousness.

Identity

To a very large extent in the late twentieth century, however, organized labor did not appear to play the militantly class-struggle role Marxists had expected of it. Labor's radical left wing dramatically deteriorated in many capitalist countries in the decades following 1950, with a significant radicalizing reversal in the late 1960s giving way to even more dramatic decline in the century's final decades. This took place even as capitalist reality had increasingly negative impact on various social groups. Commenting that such shifting realities mean that "new identities arise, [and] old ones pass away (at least temporarily)," social theorist Stanley Aronowitz observed that "new social and cultural formations—of nationality, race, gender, and sexuality, among others—have provided new bases of group and individual identities." In the late twentieth century, a specialized concept of *identity* was developed—particularly by theorists influenced by the philosophical current known as post-structuralism—which focused on the way in which specific groups in society have been culturally identified and/or have self-identified, a means for defining relationships with those around them. (Similarities can be found between this concept and, once again, Weber's notion of *status*.)

One can develop an understanding of this conception by realizing that each of us has many different identities that are important to defining who we are. Among such identities—some of which seem more vibrant to us than others—are (in no particular order): our place within a particular family; our gender; our race and/or ethnicity; our nationality; our age; our religious orientation; our attitude toward specific political ideas; our sexual orientation and preferences; the foods we like; our musical preferences, the clothes we choose to wear, and other cultural inclinations; our favorite hobbies and pastimes; organizations that we happen to belong to; whether we live in a city, a small town, or a rural area; our income level; our particular economic occupation and skill level within that occupation; and *the socioeconomic class that we happen to belong to (and our attitude, if any, to what that means)*.

It can be argued that for most people, there is not a natural inclination to "privilege" that final, italicized identity. The question can be raised as to why—

if the critical points made by C. Wright Mills and others are valid—one's class identity, particularly working-class identity, should be privileged. Many have argued that if one is concerned with revolutionary protest and change, a very different identity focus is far more relevant.

In the 1960s, for example, some African American radicals, critically respectful of the Marxist tradition yet intimately aware of harsh and complex realities, argued, in the words of James Boggs, that "white workers are by the very nature of U.S. development and history a class above all blacks," that "the blacks are an underclass that has developed despite the fact that they have been systematically damned by the system," and that "blacks, and particularly young blacks, are the revolutionary force inside this country, the only social force in irreversible motion." Some insisted with Harold Cruse that "white capitalist nations, including all the different classes within these nations, from upper bourgeoisie to lower proletariat, have become, in fact, bourgeois and relatively middle-class strata vis-à-vis the nonwhite peoples who have become, in fact, the 'world proletarians.'" Not long after, certain feminist theorists advanced somewhat similar arguments. (The most dramatic instances are Shulamith Firestone in *The Dialectic of Sex*, seeking "to take class analysis one step further to its roots in the biological division of the sexes," and Zillah Eisenstein in *Capitalist Patriarchy and the Case for Socialist Feminism*, advancing a conceptualization of women as a class.) However, in this case the theorists "privileged" the female identity, with a primary focus on women's liberation.

Yet some have questioned the value of elevating any identity to the position of being *the* primary one in the struggle for social change. In the 1980s, Ernesto Laclau and Chantal Mouffe generalized and elaborated the theoretical challenge to Marxism's emphasis on class, drawing on perspectives of French post-structuralists Michel Foucault and Jacques Derrida, and on a specialized reading of Italian revolutionary Marxist Antonio Gramsci. Dismissing "the ontological centrality of the working class" and "the illusory prospects of a perfectly unitary and homogenous collective that will render pointless the moment of politics," Laclau and Mouffe instead looked to a set of social movements representing various oppressed groups in society that would involve "a plurality of antagonisms and points of rupture." Alliances among such forces, cohering around a variety of issues, would establish a diverse but hegemonic "collective will" that could bring advances in struggles for gender and racial equality, human rights, economic justice, peace, defense of the environment, and other issues. The consequent enrichment of democracy would be far more real and meaningful than "the role of Revolution with a capital 'r,' as the founding moment in the transition from the one type of society to another."

Some Marxists have reacted with hostility to such challenges, arguing that "independent" social struggles around Black rights and women's rights—and/or "identity politics" as such—are actually either "bourgeois" or "petty-bourgeois" diversions from the class struggle and divisive of working-class unity. There have been other responses, however, from such diverse figures as Oliver Cox, C. L. R. James, George Breitman, Manning Marable, Lise Vogel, Sheila Rowbotham, and Nancy Holmstrom—all of whom have argued that the liberation struggles of oppressed groups (such as Blacks and women) are absolutely essential for social progress and for human liberation, and that independent social movements (controlled by Blacks and women respectively) are indeed needed to advance such struggles. They have also argued, however, that the majority of the people in such mass movements (regardless of how they consciously identify themselves) happen to be part of the working class, that such struggles are objectively in the interests of the working class as a whole, and that such movements and struggles can play a vanguard role in helping to radicalize the working class and lead it forward in the struggle against the capitalist status quo. Yet as historians such as David Roediger have demonstrated with such conceptualizations as "whiteness," the US working class has in fact been deeply fractured—in its consciousness, culturally and organizationally, by racism, and also by the distorted "maleness" of gender oppression.

Nonetheless, the decisive capacities attributed to the social movements by such theorists as Laclau and Mouffe have been sharply questioned by some analysts. Noting that "new social movements have made significant advances in recent decades and [that] they may reasonably hope to make more in the years to come," Ralph Miliband emphasized in 1989 that "what they cannot reasonably expect is that societies whose main dynamic is the pursuit of private profit and whose whole mode of being is suffused by deep inequalities of every kind can be made to do away with exploitation, discrimination, violence against vulnerable sections of the population, ecological vandalism, international strife, and all the other evils which have brought new social movements into being." Adding that "organized labor does have a greater potential strength, cohesion, and capacity to act as a transformative force than any other force in society," Miliband concluded: "So long as organized labor and its political agencies refuse to fulfill their transformative potential, so long will the existing social order remain safe from revolutionary challenge, whatever feminists, or black people, or gays and lesbians, or environmentalists, or peace activists, or any other group may choose to do, and even though their actions may well produce advances and reforms."

Uneven and Combined Development

The shifting and multifaceted realities of class and other identities in the dynamic global system of the past three centuries can be seen as a complex manifestation of "uneven and combined development," to use a phrase popularized by Leon Trotsky. There have certainly been confusions and complexities in determining the class position of some sectors. As C. Wright Mills and others have noted, although some occupations involve people who are paid for their labor-power (making them working class according to Engels's 1888 footnote to the *Manifesto*), they play managerial roles enhancing the exploitation of labor, sometimes receive a very high level of financial compensation, and are animated by a kind of consciousness, all of which seem to place them much closer to the capitalist class—causing analysts such as Erik Olin Wright to develop conceptualizations of "mixed-class locations."

In many so-called third world countries in Asia, Africa, and Latin America, there are sometimes even greater complexities: often within the same family, even in the same individuals, we find those who may shift back and forth between being a peasant, an agricultural laborer, an urban petty entrepreneur, a beggar, and a proletarian (causing some analysts, such as Carlos Vilas, to reach for more ambiguous formulations, such as "the working masses"). As Ronaldo Munck explains, the increasing prevalence of explosive urbanization in "peripheral" or "developing" societies has created what is often referred to as an "informal economy." He notes: "The urban informal sector (the petty-bourgeois self-employed and the informal proletariat) is seen as a subsidy to capitalist accumulation given its high levels of self-exploitation."

Harry Braverman's comments have relevance for such varied examples: "These difficulties arise, in the last analysis, from the fact that classes, the class structure, the social structure as a whole, are not fixed entities but rather ongoing processes, rich in change, transition, variation, and incapable of being encapsulated in formulas, no matter how analytically proper such formulas may be." This can be said to lend some credence to Thompson's assertion that "class is a relationship, not a thing." It also corresponds to Ira Katznelson's warning against seeing *class formation* (corresponding to the class-for-itself notion) simply as the logical outcome of *class structure* (class-in-itself) by maintaining a focus on theoretical formulas while "avoiding a direct engagement with the actual lives of working people." He summarizes the insights of a number of labor historians:

> Working-class formation as a process is not identical from country to country (or from place to place within countries). The histories of national working classes are composed not only of workplace relationships, trade unions, or the visible leadership of workers' movements and organizations. Inherited, preindustrial, precapitalist traditions count. Nonclass patterns of social division also affect class formation. Class, society, and politics cannot be conflated; their relationships are contingent. Class dispositions and behaviors are not fixed by interests but shaped by relationships.

Combining insights from the disciplines of political science, sociology, economics, and history, Manning Marable, Immanuel Ness, and Joseph Wilson (in light of the fact that in the United States "people of color" had shifted from minority to near-majority status within the working class) commented in 2006 that "the relationship between race and labor in America is a perpetually evolving condition that is changed, challenged, modernized, and ultimately revolutionized in light of leadership, historical struggles, social analysis, and not least importantly, mass consciousness and direct action." Each generation in the United States, they emphasized, had faced "epochal labor and civil rights battles," but complex combinations of racial and class differences have created various "rigidly segmented and antagonistic groupings," with a likelihood of "a continuum of progress and reaction in race relations framed around antagonistic labor and race relations." They extrapolated: "This combative tension between race and labor is imbedded in the ever-changing division of labor in the United States and extends across the entire world as race and labor issues have been internationalized, borders having been eviscerated, and global race-dependent economic relations emerge." Factoring in additional identities of gender, ethnicity, and religion—all of obvious and central importance to world realities at the beginning of the twenty-first century—would naturally bring additional "combative tensions" into relief.

Some scholars, such as Karen Brodkin-Sacks, have reached for what might be called a conceptual blending of identities relevant to protest and revolution, boldly working toward the unified conceptualization of race, class, and gender, although David Roediger suggests that "discussing the triad of race, class and gender would be difficult enough, but that is just the tip of the iceberg." He explains: "Once we acknowledge that the class identity of, say, an African American woman worker is influenced . . . by social relationships with, say, Chinese males (and vice versa), we see the practical difficulties associated with treating race, class and gender in what Tera Hunter brilliantly terms their 'simultaneity.'"

Yet in an insightful study of the Nicaraguan revolution that gives sustained attention to the identities of generation, gender, race, and class, anthropologist Roger Lancaster argues:

> The class dimension is privileged, if only circumstantially and politically (not analytically), and by this index: class exploitation necessarily produces an exploiting minority and an exploited majority. The same cannot be said for any other dimensions of oppression. Whether one is seeking to reform or overthrow *any* system of exploitation, the dynamics of class and class resistance remain, in Marx's sense, strategic and paramount.

Even the most penetrating observation, however, can hardly be expected to resolve such matters, given the complexities of social protest and revolutionary change.

Conclusions

"Capitalism is probably the most resilient and hegemonic system of production and distribution ever devised," radical economist Michael Yates has commented, "and its supersession by an egalitarian mode of production is going to take a long time and will involve a variety of tactics." Many will certainly ask if capitalism can in fact be replaced by another social system, although if it is not, this will be the first social system in history that proved to be permanent. Until such revolutionary change is brought about, however, it is likely that questions and debates will continue to arise regarding what social force or forces can bring about that change.

Inherent in capitalism is the fundamental class divide highlighted by Marx and others, but in this most dynamic of economic systems, additional divisions are brought into being, sometimes intensified and sometimes diminished, with the shifting balances and combinations of reality. Such "current realities" unavoidably generate ongoing debates and questions that will, undoubtedly, offer both stimulation and insights for those who wish to study revolutionary and protest movements of the past. It may also be the case that more profound explorations of the past will offer insights into future possibilities.

References and Suggested Readings

Anderson, Margaret L., and Patricia Hill Collins, eds. *Race, Age, and Gender: An Anthology*. Belmont, CA: Wadsworth Publishing, 1995.

Aronowitz, Stanley. *Dead Artists, Live Theories, and Other Cultural Problems*. New York: Routledge, 1994.

Bottomore, Tom, and Patrick Goode, eds. *Readings in Marxist Sociology*. Oxford: Clarendon Press, 1983.

Braverman, Harvey. *Labor and Monopoly Capital: The Degradation of Work in the Twentieth Century*. New York: Monthly Review Press, 1974.

Breitman, George, and Harold Cruse. "Marxism and the Negro Struggle," in *Malcolm X and the Third American Revolution: The Writings of George Breitman*. Edited by Anthony Marcus. Amherst, NY: Humanity Books, 2005.

Cohen, G. A. *Karl Marx's Theory of History: A Defence*. Princeton, NJ: Princeton University Press, 1978.

Cohen, Sheila. *Ramparts of Resistance: Why Workers Lost Their Power, and How to Get It Back*. London: Pluto Press, 2006.

Coser, Lewis A. *Masters of Sociological Thought: Ideas in Historical and Social Context*, 2nd ed. Long Grove, IL: Waveland Press, 2003.

Draper, Hal. *Karl Marx's Theory of Revolution*, vol. 2, *The Politics of Social Classes*. New York: Monthly Review Press, 1978.

Eisenstein, Zillah R., ed. *Capitalist Patriarchy and the Case for Socialist Feminism*. New York: Monthly Review Press, 1978.

Eley, Geoff. *Forging Democracy: The History of the Left in Europe, 1850–2000*. Oxford: Oxford University Press, 2002.

Firestone, Shulamith. *The Dialectic of Sex: The Case for Feminist Revolution*. New York: William Morrow, 1970.

Fischer, Ernst, and Franz Marek. *The Essential Marx*. New York: Herder and Herder, 1970.

Gerth, H. H., and C. Wright Mills, eds. *From Max Weber: Essays in Sociology*. New York: Oxford University Press, 1958.

Gorz, André. *Farewell to the Working Class: An Essay on Post-industrial Socialism*. London: Pluto Press, 1982.

Holmstrom, Nancy, ed. *The Socialist Feminist Project: A Contemporary Reader in Theory and Politics*. New York: Monthly Review Press, 2002.

Hunter, Herbert M., and Sameer Y. Abraham, eds. *Race, Class, and the World System: The Sociology of Oliver C. Cox*. New York: Monthly Review Press, 1987.

James, C. L. R. *C. L. R. James on the "Negro Question."* Edited by Scott McLemee. Jackson: University of Mississippi Press, 1996.

Katznelson, Ira, and Aristide R. Zolberg, eds. *Working-Class Formation: Nineteenth-Century Patterns in Western Europe and the United States*. Princeton, NJ: Princeton University Press, 1986.

Laclau, Ernesto, and Chantal Mouffe. *Hegemony and Socialist Strategy: Towards a Radical Democratic Politics*. London: Verso, 1985.

Lancaster, Roger N. *Life Is Hard: Machismo, Danger, and the Intimacy of Power in Nic-*

aragua. Berkeley: University of California Press, 1992.

Le Blanc, Paul. *From Marx to Gramsci: A Reader in Revolutionary Marxist Politics*. Amherst, NY: Humanity Books, 1996.

Lukács, Georg. *History and Class Consciousness: Studies in Marxist Dialectics*. Cambridge, MA: MIT Press, 1971.

Marable, Manning. *The Crisis of Color and Democracy: Essays on Race, Class, and Power*. Monroe, ME: Common Courage Press, 1992.

Marable, Manning, Immanuel Ness, and Joseph Wilson, eds. *Race and Labor Matters in the New U.S. Economy*. Lanham, MD: Rowman and Littlefield, 2006.

McLellan, David. *The Thought of Karl Marx: An Introduction*. New York: Harper and Row, 1971.

Miliband, Ralph. *Divided Societies: Class Struggle in Contemporary Capitalism*. Oxford: Oxford University Press, 1991.

Mills, C. Wright. *The Marxists*. New York: Dell Publishers, 1962.

Moody, Kim. *Workers in a Lean World: Unions in the International Economy*. London: Verso, 1997.

Munck, Ronaldo. *Globalisation and Labour: The New "Great Transformation."* London: Zed Books, 2002.

Panitch, Leo, and Colin Leys, eds. *Fighting Identities: Race, Religion and Ethno-Nationalism, Socialist Register 2003*. London: Merlin Press, 2002.

Reiss, Edward. *Marx: A Clear Guide*. London: Pluto Press, 1997.

Robinson, Cedric J. *Black Marxism: The Making of the Black Radical Tradition*. London: Zed Press, 1983.

Roediger, David. *Towards the Abolition of Whiteness: Essays on Race, Politics, and Working Class History*. London: Verso, 1994.

Rowbotham, Sheila. *Threads through Time, Writings on History and Autobiography*. London: Penguin Books, 1999.

Shanin, Teodor, ed. *Peasants and Peasant Societies*. Harmondsworth, UK: Penguin Books, 1971.

Thompson, E. P. *The Making of the English Working Class*. New York: Vintage Books, 1966.

Townsend, Jules. *The Politics of Marxism: The Critical Debates*. London: Leicester University Press, 1996.

Vilas, Carlos María. *The Sandinista Revolution: National Liberation and Social Transformation in Central America*. New York: Monthly Review Press, 1986.

Vogel, Lise. *Marxism and the Oppression of Women: Toward a Unitary Theory*. New Brunswick, NJ: Rutgers University Press, 1983.

Williams, Raymond. *Keywords: A Vocabulary of Culture and Society*. Rev. ed. New York: Oxford University Press, 1983.

Wolf, Eric R. *Europe and the People without History*. Berkeley: University of California Press, 1982.

Wright, Erik Olin. *Class, Crisis, and the State*. London: Verso, 1978.

Yates, M. *Naming the System: Inequality and Work in the Global Economy*. New York: Monthly Review Press, 2003.

5.

Democracy

"**D**emocracy does not come from the top, it comes from the bottom," Howard Zinn tells us at the beginning of his wonderful documentary *The People Speak*. "The mutinous soldiers, the angry women, the rebellious Native Americans, the working people, the agitators, the anti-war protestors, the socialists and anarchists and dissenters of all kinds—the troublemakers, yes, the people who have given us what liberty and democracy we have."[1] This insight from Zinn provides a key to our topic—the relation of democracy and socialism, especially the socialism associated with the outlook of Karl Marx.

The great democratic ideal of our country, historically, has been a land in which there is government of the people, by the people, and for the people, with liberty and justice for all. It is worth raising a question about how much democracy—how much "rule by the people"—actually exists in this American republic of ours. The definition of *republic* is "rule (or government) by elected representatives"—not quite the same thing as government by the people. We'll need to come back to that shortly. But certainly even an imperfect democracy is better than rule over the people by a government that decides it knows what is best for them. Many right-wingers today claim this is the goal of socialism.

That is a lie. Yet one of the tragedies of the twentieth century is that so many self-proclaimed partisans of socialism plugged themselves into that lie, leaving "rule by the people" out of the socialist equation. They defined socialism as government ownership and control of the economy, and government planning for the benefit of the people, who someday (but not yet!) would be permitted to have a decisive say in the decisions affecting their lives. This "socialism from above" was central to the ideology of certain elitist reformers associated with the so-called moderate wing of the socialist movement, and it was also central to the Stalin dictatorship in Russia. Even down to the present day, some well-meaning folks use this logic to describe despotic regimes (such as that in North Korea) as "socialist." Such thinking has disoriented millions of people over the years. But as the Afro-Caribbean revolutionary internationalist C. L. R. James insisted (using the word *proletarian* where many of us would say "working class"),

> The struggle for socialism is the struggle for proletarian democracy. Proletarian democracy is not the crown of socialism. Socialism is the result of proletarian democracy. To the degree that the proletariat mobilizes itself and the great masses of the people, the socialist revolution is advanced. The proletariat mobilizes itself as a self-acting force through its own committees, unions, parties, and other organizations.

Similar things were said in earlier years by the Italian Communist leader Antonio Gramsci, the Chinese dissident Communist Chen Duxiu, and the Peruvian Marxist José Carlos Mariátegui, to name three of many.[2]

"Socialists should not argue with the American worker when he says he wants democracy and doesn't want to be ruled by a dictatorship," said James P. Cannon—a founder of both the US Communist Party and US Trotskyism—in the wake of the 1956 Hungarian workers' and students' uprising against Stalinist bureaucratic tyranny. "Rather, we should recognize [the worker's] demand for human rights and democratic guarantees, now and in the future, is in itself progressive. The socialist task is not to deny democracy, but to expand it and make it more complete." Cannon stood in the revolutionary Marxist tradition of not only opposing capitalism but also opposing oppressive bureaucracies in the labor movement throughout the world, asserting that "in the United States, the struggle for workers' democracy is preeminently a struggle of the rank and file to gain democratic control of their own organizations." He added that—both in Communist countries and capitalist countries—"the fight for workers' democracy is inseparable from the fight for socialism, and is the condition for its victory." We can find the same kinds of points being made by Eugene Victor Debs and others during an earlier heyday of American socialism in the first two decades of the twentieth century and by revolutionaries in Europe—Rosa Luxemburg, Leon Trotsky, Vladimir Ilyich Lenin, and many others.[3]

The failure to recognize that genuine democracy and genuine socialism are absolutely inseparable is only one source of confusion. Another source of confusion has to do with the relationship of *capitalism* and democracy. Most of what I have to share here will actually focus on that question. A useful case study for us will be the American Revolution and its aftermath. Then we will need to touch on what some have called "the democratic breakthrough," for which Karl Marx and the labor movement with which he was associated are largely responsible. We should then consider descriptions of so-called democracy in the United States over the years by people in a position to know. We will conclude with some key insights from Lenin and Trotsky on combining the struggles for democracy and socialism.

First we should acknowledge an element of confusion that flows from a particular understanding—or misunderstanding—of Marxism. Marxist theory outlines different stages in human history based on different economic systems, first a primitive tribal communism that lasted for thousands of years, then a succession of class societies—in Europe, these included ancient slave civilizations, feudalism—and then capitalism, with its immense productivity and economic surpluses that have paved the way for the possibility of a socialist society.

The misunderstanding flows from the fact that according to Marxists, the transition from feudalism to capitalism is facilitated and largely completed by something that has been termed *bourgeois-democratic revolution*. *Bourgeois*, of course, refers to the capitalist class, and *bourgeois-democratic revolution* refers to those revolutionary upheavals, involving masses of people in the so-called lower classes, that sweep aside rule by kings and domination of the economy by hereditary nobles or aristocrats, creating the basis for both the full development of capitalist economies and more or less democratic republics.[4] Some Marxists, and many capitalist ideologists, have projected an intimate interrelationship between the rise of capitalism and the rise of democracy: just as "love and marriage go together like a horse and carriage" in the old song, so do capitalism and democracy naturally go together. But, as a number of sharp-minded historians and social scientists have argued, this notion is quite misleading. For clarification, we should take a look at an aspect of our own bourgeois-democratic revolution, the American Revolution of 1775 to 1783.

The big businessmen, the capitalists, the ruling elites of the thirteen North American colonies were the great merchants of the North and the great plantation owners of the South, and they did not want to be bossed around and constrained by the far-off government of an incredibly arrogant monarchy and aristocracy, working in conjunction with privileged merchants in England, who dominated the British Empire. To be able to pose an effective challenge, however, they needed to persuade a much larger percentage of their fellow colonists—small farmers, shopkeepers, artisans and craftsmen, laborers, and more—to make common cause with them. It became clear that these plebian masses were particularly responsive to the kinds of revolutionary-democratic conceptions that radicals like Tom Paine put forward in incendiary bestsellers like *Common Sense*. Such notions were consequently incorporated into magnificent rhetoric that Thomas Jefferson wrote into the Declaration of Independence in 1776. It was used to rally enough support throughout the colonies—now transforming themselves into independent, united states of America—to stand up to the greatest economic and military power in the world. "We hold these truths to be self-evident," it declared, "that all men are created equal, and endowed by their creator with certain unalienable rights, and among these are life, liberty, and the pursuit of happiness." The document went on, asserting that governments are not legitimate if they do not enjoy the consent of the governed, and that the people who are governed have a right to challenge, overturn, and replace governments not to their liking.[5]

Yet certain revolutionary leaders who wished to conserve the power of the wealthy minority of merchants and plantation owners were uncomfortable with the implications of such potent stuff. Early on, one such conservative, Gouverneur Morris, commented:

> The mob began to think and to reason. Poor reptiles! It is with them a vernal morning; they are struggling to cast off their winter's slough, they bask in the sunshine, and ere noon they will bite, depend upon it. The gentry begin to fear this.... I see, and I see it with fear and trembling, that if the disputes with Great Britain continue, we shall be under the worst of all possible dominions; we shall be under the domination of a riotous mob.

John Adams wrote, "I cannot but laugh. We have been told that our struggle has loosened the bands of government everywhere. That children and apprentices were disobedient—that schools and colleges were grown turbulent—that Indians slighted their guardians and Negroes grew insolent to their masters." Adams was dismayed by pressures to give propertyless men the right to vote (and by pressure from his own wife even to extend this right to women). He brooded: "It tends to confound and destroy all distinctions and prostrate all ranks to one common level." He warned: "Men in general in every society, who are wholly destitute of property, are also too little acquainted with public affairs to form a right judgment, and too dependent upon other men to have a will of their own."

Alexander Hamilton, a visionary enthusiast of an industrial capitalist future, was perhaps clearest of all. "All communities divide themselves into the few and the many. The first are the rich and well-born, the other the mass of the people." He goes on to say that since the "turbulent and changing" masses "seldom judge or determine right," the wealthy elite must be given "a distinct permanent share in the government." Or as he put it earlier, "that power which holds the purse-strings absolutely must rule."[6]

Three years after the Revolution was officially won, and reacting to the Massachusetts revolt of small farmers and poor laborers known as Shays's Rebellion, General Henry Knox wrote to George Washington: "Their creed is that the property of the United States has been protected from the confiscation of Britain by the joint exertions of all, and therefore ought to be the common property of all." Knox's exaggeration expressed the anxiety of the well-to-do in the early republic. "This dreadful situation has alarmed every man of principle and property in New England," Knox continued. "Our Government must be braced, changed, or altered to secure our lives and property." By the late 1780s, a majority of the states had given the right to vote to a minority—white male property owners. Of course, some of the property owners might be small farmers, artisans, and some shopkeepers with ties to what Hamilton called "the mass of the people." Most of the state governments had a more representative lower house for such folk—but it was held in check by a more powerful upper house that was controlled by the rich. In addition, many powerful state and local offices were appointed from above rather than elected.[7]

It is likely that a great majority of the founding fathers who gathered to discuss and compose a new constitution of the United States in the late 1780s saw things in the way Aristotle explained it many centuries earlier: "The real difference between democracy and oligarchy is poverty and wealth. Wherever men rule by reason of their wealth . . . , that is an oligarchy, and where the poor rule, that is democracy." The fact remained, as Ellen Meiksins Wood has commented, that "the colonial and revolutionary experience had already made it impossible to reject democracy outright, as ruling and propertied classes had been doing unashamedly for centuries and as they would continue to do for some time elsewhere." We will look at what happened "elsewhere"—at least in Europe—in a few moments. But what happened in the early American republic at the Constitutional Convention of 1787 was an attempt to fuse democracy (government by the many) with oligarchy (government by the few) in a way that would conserve the power of the wealthy. The key was the notion of *representative democracy*, in which the laboring multitude is represented by figures from the wealthy elite. Alexander Hamilton offers his own explanation in No. 35 of the *Federalist Papers*: "An actual representation of all classes of the people by persons of each class is altogether visionary;" instead, workers in the skilled and manufacturing trades, thanks to "the influence and weight and superior acquirements" of the wealthy merchants, should generally "consider merchants as the natural representatives of all these classes of the community." Meiksins Wood's paraphrase is nicely put: "Here shoemakers and blacksmiths are represented by their social superiors." She adds that "these assumptions must be placed in the context of the Federalist view that representation is not a way of implementing but of *avoiding* or at least partially circumventing democracy."[8]

Even the more liberal-minded founding father and close associate of Thomas Jefferson, James Madison, observes in No. 10 of the *Federalist Papers* that "the most common and durable source of factions [in society] has been the various and unequal division of property." He continues, emphasizing: "Those who hold and those who are without property have ever formed distinct interests in society." Here again we see the laboring *majority* and the wealthy *minority*. Insisting that "a pure democracy" will enable "a majority . . . to sacrifice to its ruling passion or interest both the public good and the rights of other citizens," Madison hailed the Constitution's conceptualization of a republic because it "opens a different prospect and promises the cure for what we are seeking." Madison returned to this concern in No. 51 of the *Federalist Papers*, praising the Constitution for creating structures and dynamics that will fragment the majority. Among other things, the checks and balances the Constitution established are able (as he puts it) "to divide the legislature into separate branches, and to render them by different modes of election and different principles of action, as little connected with each other as the nature of their common dependence on society will admit."

There is another element in Madison's calculations. He reminds us: "If the majority be united by a common interest, the rights of the minority will be insecure." The solution is to ensure that "whilst all authority [in the government] will be derived and dependent on the society, the society itself will be broken into so many parts, interests and classes of citizens, that the rights of individuals, or of the minority, will be in little danger from interested combinations of the majority." A geographically extensive republic, fragmented into states, with a "great variety of interests, parties and sects which it embraces," will block a majority coalition that could endanger the wealthy minority.[9]

Even setting aside its original embrace of slavery, the design of the US Constitution became a bulwark of privilege even as more and more men, and finally women as well, were able to win the right to vote. Three modern-day social scientists—Dietrich Rueschemeyer, Evelyne Huber Stephens, and John D. Stephens—flesh out this feature of the Constitution in their important 1992 study *Capitalist Development and Democracy*. They suggest that what was set up in the 1780s was a "constitutional or liberal oligarchy" (we could also call it an "undemocratic republic"). They go on to trace important gains that were made in the 1820s and 1830s, in the 1860s, in 1920, and in the 1960s, to expand the right to vote and to make the government more *responsive* to the desires and needs of the majority.[10]

The expansion of voting rights was not a gift from on high, but was achieved through tenacious, protracted, and sometimes violent social struggles, spearheaded by the kinds of "troublemakers" that Howard Zinn has so lovingly described. And yet even with all of this, we cannot say that genuine rule by the people has been established in our country—a reality we will explore shortly. But first we should turn our attention to what Rueschemeyer and his colleagues document as the democratic breakthrough in Europe in the nineteenth and early twentieth centuries.

Following, revising, and elaborating on studies of earlier social scientists such as Göran Therborn, they comment that "the bourgeoisie, which appears as the natural carrier of democracy in the accounts of orthodox Marxists, liberal social scientists and [others], hardly lived up to this role." Throughout Europe, the men of wealth and property were generally as reluctant as their US capitalist cousins to go in the direction of rule by the people, preferring some form of liberal or constitutional oligarchy, or sometimes even to cut deals with kings, aristocrats, and generals. They tell us:

> It was the growth of the working class and its capacity for self-organization that was most critical for the breakthrough of democracy. The rapid industrialization experienced by western Europe in the five decades before World War I increased the size and, with varying time lags, the degree of organization [of the working class] and thus changed the balance of class power in civil society to the advantage of democratic forces.

Their studies confirm "that the working class, represented by socialist parties and trade unions, was the single most important force in the majority of countries in the final push for universal male suffrage and responsible government." (It took additional feminist ferment, generally supported by socialists, to include women into the equation).[11]

Here too, genuine *rule by the people* cannot be said to have been established in these countries. But it is undeniable that these gains, the right to vote and to organize politically, made it easier for the laboring masses to pressure the wealthy minority. This definitely brought about meaningful improvements for millions of people.

There is one additional, very key point for us here. Another social scientist, August Nimtz, embracing the work of Rueschemeyer and his colleagues, finished connecting the dots, in his very fine study *Marx and Engels: Their Contribution to the Democratic Breakthrough*. Essential elements in the thrust of working-class democracy, Nimtz documents, were the intellectual and practical political labors of Karl Marx and Frederick Engels in the Communist League—in the 1848 revolutionary upsurge, during the quiescent interlude that followed, and then in the years of the International Workingmen's Association, the First International, and the Paris Commune. Nimtz is especially good at conveying a sense of the crucial importance of the First International in the larger political developments of the 1860s and 1870s, and particularly in the development of the labor movements of Europe and North America. He supplies extensive documentation for what he calls his "most sweeping claim"—that "Karl Marx and Frederick Engels were the *leading* protagonists in the democratic movement in the nineteenth century, the decisive breakthrough period in humanity's age-old struggle for democracy."[12]

And yet Marx and Engels themselves were highly critical of the so-called democracies that were emerging in various capitalist countries, not least of all in the United States. The two men were so critical *not* because they were antidemocratic, but precisely because they were fierce advocates of *genuine* democracy. For Marx, communism (or socialism, which for him meant the same thing) was what he once called "true democracy," which he passionately favored. He and Engels explained in *The Communist Manifesto* that under capitalism "the bourgeoisie has at last, since the establishment of modern industry and of the world market, conquered for itself, in the modern representative state, exclusive political sway," and that "the executive of the modern state is but a committee for managing the common affairs of the whole bourgeoisie." Against this, they argued that workers must increasingly unite in the struggle for a better life, waged in their workplaces and communities, which needed to amount, finally, to what they called "the organization of the proletarians into a class, and consequently into a political party" that would be capable of bringing about "the forcible overthrow of the bourgeoisie," laying "the foundation for the political sway of the proletariat." This meant that communists and all the other working-class parties needed to seek "the formation of the proletariat into a class, overthrow of bourgeois supremacy, conquest of political power by the proletariat." The "first step in the revolution by the working class is to raise the proletariat to the position of ruling class, to win the battle of democracy," and then to take increasing control of the economy in order to bring about the socialist reconstruction of society.[13]

Without this, genuine democracy would be impossible. In describing the first workers' government in history—the short-lived Paris Commune of 1871, which pro-capitalist military forces soon drowned in blood—Marx commented that "instead of deciding once in three or six years which member of the ruling class was to misrepresent the people in parliament, universal suffrage was to serve the people, constituted in communes." Twenty-two years later, Engels commented to a comrade living in the United States, "The Americans for a long time have been providing the European world with the proof that the bourgeois republic is the republic of capitalist businessmen in which politics is a business like any other."[14]

A brilliant description of this approach to politics has been offered by one of the outstanding working-class revolutionaries of the United States, Albert Parsons. One of the Haymarket Martyrs and a tireless activist and organizer, he described himself as a socialist, a communist, and an anarchist. He was also editor of the *Alarm*, the English-language paper of the International Working People's Association—which was a powerful force in Chicago during the 1880s.

Shedding light on what he sneeringly called "practical politics," Parsons put the following comments on page one of the *Alarm* during the election season of 1884:

> There is not one sound spot in our whole social system, industrial, political or religious. It is rotten to the core. The whole scheme as we now have was originated by pirates, founded upon fraud and perpetrated by force. The United States of America possesses in all its glory that sum total of all humbugs—the ballot. This country is now in the midst of its periodical craze—a presidential election. The voters are enthused by the politicians, parading with torches, bands of music and shouting for this or that nominee or party. A man can no more run for office without money than he can engage in business without capital.

The article argued that even if a poor man is nominated because of his popularity, his campaign is financed by wealthy friends in the party who expect him to "vote the right way" on particular issues; if he doesn't do this, he is replaced by someone who will.

> He takes his seat and votes to kill all legislation which would invade the 'sacred rights' of the propertied class, and guards like a watch-dog the 'vested rights' of those who enjoy special privileges. This is 'practical politics.' The poor vote as they work, as their necessities dictate. If the workingmen organize their own party, they are counted out; besides, those who own the workshop control, as a general thing, the votes in it. It is all a question of poverty; the man without property has practically no vote. 'Practical politics' means the control of the propertied class.[15]

Related to one of the points that Parsons makes here—regarding the workplaces where a majority of us spend our working lives (and so much of our waking lives)—it is worth taking time to reflect on the fact that, even if we don't let our employers intimidate us into voting one way or another, as soon as we walk through the doors of the workplace, we have entered a realm of economic dictatorship—sometimes a relatively benevolent dictatorship, sometimes a totalitarian nightmare, often something somewhere in between. But there is no democracy—no majority rule, limited freedom of expression, often (especially if there's no union) no bill of rights. A wealthy minority rules over us in the workplaces and in the entire economy on which all of us are dependent.

There are additional realities that flow from this, and you don't have to be a genius like Albert Einstein to figure out what they are. The fact remains, however, that Einstein *did* discuss the question in 1949 and expressed himself rather well. So let's see what he had to say:

> Private capital tends to become concentrated in few hands, partly because of competition among the capitalists, and partly because technological development and the increasing division of labor encourage the formation of larger units of production at the expense of smaller ones. The result of these developments is an oligarchy of private capital the enormous power of which cannot be effectively checked even by a democratically organized political society. This is true since the members of legislative bodies are selected by political parties, largely financed or otherwise influenced by private capitalists who, for all practical purposes, separate the electorate from the legislature. The consequence is that the representatives of the people do not in fact sufficiently protect the interests of the underprivileged sections of the population. Moreover, under existing conditions, private capitalists inevitably control, directly or indirectly, the main sources of information (press, radio, education). It is thus extremely difficult, and indeed in most cases quite impossible, for the individual citizen to come to objective conclusions and to make intelligent use of his political rights.[16]

Recently, Sheldon Wolin, professor emeritus of political theory at Princeton University, updated some of Einstein's points. To understand his argument, you need to understand Greek—so I will give you a short lesson. We got the word *democracy* from the ancient Greeks—*dēmokratia*, derived from *demos* (the people) and *kratia* (rule). Sheldon Wolin writes: "It is obvious that today—in the age of communication conglomerates, media pundits, television, public opinion surveys, and political consultants—the exercise of popular will, the expression of its voice, and the framing of its needs have been emptied of all promise of autonomy." No kidding! Noting that "American politicians and publicists claim that theirs is the world's greatest democracy," Wolin tells us that, instead (and remember, *demos* means "the people"), "the reality is a democracy *without the demos as actor*. The voice is that of a ventriloquist democracy."[17] That is, "we the people" *seem* to be expressing ourselves politically, but really what is being expressed comes from the wealthy elites and their minions who control the economy, the larger culture, the sources of information, the shaping of opinion, and the political process as a whole.

Many anarchists, quite understandably, reject all of this, denouncing the very concept of democracy as a swindle that should be rejected by all honest revolutionaries. Marxists argue, however, that while the swindle must be rejected, democracy should still be fought for. It does seem, however, that given the many ways in which the electoral process in the United States is stacked in favor of capitalism and capitalists, a case can be made, at least in the present time, for our efforts to be concentrated outside of the electoral arena. Just as politics involves much, much more than elections and electoral parties, so the struggle for democracy—as the comments of Howard Zinn suggest—can often be pursued far more effectively in workplaces, in communities, in schools, in the streets, in the larger culture through non-electoral struggles and creative work of various kinds. The key for us is to draw more and more people into pathways of thinking and pathways of action that go in the direction of questioning established authority and giving people a meaningful say about the realities and decisions affecting their lives. That is the opposite of how "democracy"—focused on elections—actually works in our country. This comes through brilliantly in the description of the wonderful anarchist educator Paul Goodman regarding the US political system in the early 1960s. This is how he describes it:

> Concretely, our system of government at present comprises the military-industrial complex, the secret para-military agencies, the scientific war corporations, the blimps, the horses' asses, the police, the administrative bureaucracy, the career diplomats, the lobbies, the corporations that contribute Party funds, the underwriters and real-estate promoters that batten on urban renewal, the official press and the official opposition press, the sounding-off and jockeying for the next election, the National Unity, etc., etc. All this machine is grinding along by the momentum of the power and profit motives and style long since built into it; it cannot make decisions of a kind radically different than it does. Even if an excellent man happens to be elected to office, he will find that it is no longer a possible instrument for social change on any major issues of war and peace and the way of life of the Americans.[18]

Elections can sometimes be used effectively by revolutionaries to reach out to masses of people with ideas, information, analyses, and proposals that challenge the established order. If elected, they may also find that—aside from proposing and voting for positive, if relatively modest, social reforms—they will also be able to use elected office to help inform, mobilize, and support their constituents in *non-electoral mass struggles*. But the insertion of revolutionaries into the existing capitalist state will not be sufficient to bring about the "true democracy" that Marx spoke of, because they would find themselves within political structures designed to maintain the existing power relations. They would not have the power to end capitalist oppression or to transform the capitalist state into a structure permitting actual "rule by the people." Marx and Engels themselves came to the conclusion that it would not be possible for the working class simply to use the existing state—designed by our exploiters and oppressors—to create a new society. The workers would need to smash the oppressive apparatus in order to allow for a genuinely democratic rule, through their own movements and organizations, and through new and more democratic governmental structures.

It is possible that some revolutionaries could be elected *before* such revolutionary change restructures the state. But they can be effective in what they actually want to do only by working in tandem with broader social movements and with non-electoral struggles. These movements and struggles must be working to empower masses of people in our economy and society, and to put increasing pressure on all politicians and government figures, as well as capitalist owners and managers, to respond to the needs and the will of the workers, of the oppressed, and of the majority of the people. Remember C. L. R. James's comment: "To the degree that the [working class] mobilizes itself and the great masses of the people, the socialist revolution is advanced. The [working class] mobilizes itself as a self-acting force through its own committees, unions, parties, and other organizations." These are, potentially, the seeds of the workers' democracy—germinating in the present—that will take root and grow, challenging and displacing the undemocratic and corrupted structures associated with the so-called bourgeois democracies.

Before we conclude, we need to look more closely, even if briefly, at a contradiction that seems to have arisen between the notion of democracy and the realities of what came to be known as communism. Within the tradition of twentieth-century communism, many (in sharp contrast to Marx) came to counterpose revolution and communism to democracy as such. This can't be justified, but it needs to be explained. Lenin, Trotsky, and the Bolsheviks led a super-democratic upsurge of the laboring masses, resulting in the initial triumph of the Russian Revolution of 1917. Immediately afterward, Russia was overwhelmed by foreign military invasions, economic blockades, and a very bloody civil war nurtured by hostile foreign capitalist powers. In that horrific situation, a brutal one-party dictatorship was established to hold things together. The Bolsheviks (even comrades Lenin and Trotsky) came up with highly dubious theoretical justifications for the dictatorship, which caused Rosa Luxemburg—correctly—to sharply criticize them, even as she supported the Russian Revolution. The justifications they put forward were soon used as an ideological cover for the crystallization of a vicious, bureaucratic tyranny propagated in the name of communism by Joseph Stalin and others, ultimately miseducating millions of people throughout the world.[19]

Both Lenin and Trotsky, and also many others who were true to the revolutionary-democratic essence of the Bolshevik tradition, sought to push back and bring an end to this horrendous corruption of the communist cause. But it was too late, and after the late 1920s such words as *communism*, *Marxism*, and *socialism* became wrongly identified throughout the world with that horrendous, totalitarian, murderous corruption represented by the Stalin regime. The ideology and practices of Stalinism are close to being the opposite of classical Marxism.

And it was the classical Marxist outlook that animated Lenin for most of his life—an outlook insisting that genuine socialism and genuine democracy are inseparable. In fact, this was at the heart of the strategic orientation that led to the victory of the 1917 revolution. It is an orientation that still makes sense for us today. Let's see how Lenin maps that out in a 1915 polemic:

> The proletariat cannot be victorious except through democracy, i.e., by giving full effect to democracy and by linking with each step of its struggle democratic demands formulated in the most resolute terms. . . . We must *combine* the revolutionary struggle against capitalism with a revolutionary program and tactics on all democratic demands: a republic, a militia, the popular election of officials, equal rights for women, the self-determination of nations, etc. While capitalism exists, these demands—all of them—can only be accomplished as an exception, and even then in an incomplete and distorted form. Basing ourselves on the democracy already achieved, and exposing its incompleteness under capitalism, we demand the overthrow of capitalism, the expropriation of the bourgeoisie, as a necessary basis both for the abolition of the poverty of the masses and for the *complete* and *all-round* institution of *all* democratic reforms. Some of these reforms will be started before the overthrow of the bourgeoisie, others *in the course* of that overthrow, and still others after it. The social revolution is not a single battle, but a period covering a series of battles over all sorts of problems of economic and democratic reform, which are consummated only by the expropriation of the bourgeoisie. It is for the sake of this final aim that we must formulate *every one* of our democratic demands in a consistently revolutionary way. It is quite conceivable that the workers of some particular country will

overthrow the bourgeoisie *before* even a single fundamental democratic reform has been fully achieved. It is, however, quite inconceivable that the proletariat, as a historical class, will be able to defeat the bourgeoisie, unless it is prepared for that by being educated in the spirit of the most consistent and resolutely revolutionary democracy.[20]

This uncompromising struggle for the most thoroughgoing and genuine democracy is one of the glories of the genuine Leninist tradition. It is something that can resonate with the needs, the aspirations, and the present-day consciousness of millions of people—and, at the same time, it leads in a revolutionary socialist direction.

In a similar manner, Leon Trotsky pushed hard against ultra-left sectarianism in the early 1930s when he insisted on the struggle to both defend "bourgeois democracy" and push beyond it to workers' democracy in the face of the rising tide of Hitler's Nazism. In this he stressed the need to defend the revolutionary-democratic subculture of the workers' movement. "Within the framework of bourgeois democracy and parallel to the incessant struggle against it," Trotsky recounted, "the elements of proletarian democracy have formed themselves in the course of many decades: political parties, labor press, trade unions, factory committees, clubs, cooperatives, sports societies, etc. The mission of fascism is not so much to complete the destruction of bourgeois democracy as to crush the first outlines of proletarian democracy." In opposing the fascist onslaught on democracy, the goal of revolutionaries is to defend "those elements of proletarian democracy, already created," which will eventually be "at the foundation of the soviet system of the workers' state." Eventually, it will be necessary—Trotsky says—"to break the husk of bourgeois democracy and free from it the kernel of workers' democracy." In the face of the immediate fascist threat, "so long as we do not yet have the strength to establish the soviet system, we place ourselves on the terrain of bourgeois democracy. But at the same time we do not entertain any illusions."[21]

The situation we face today is as different from that which Lenin faced in 1915 and Trotsky faced in 1933, as *their* situations were from what Marx and Engels faced in 1848 and 1871. But they are not *totally* different. Their insights and approaches may be helpful to us in our own situation as we struggle for rule by the people, genuine democracy, as the basis for a future society of the free and the equal.

6.

Making Sense
of Postrevolutionary Russia

This essay reviews two works: Kunal Chattopadhyay, The Marxism of Leon Trotsky (Progress Publishers, 2006), and Marcel van der Linden, Western Marxism and the Soviet Union (Haymarket Books, 2009).—P.L.

One of the many differences between the present global capitalist downturn and that of the 1930s is that back then there were millions of people throughout the world who believed the 1917 revolution that the Bolshevik/Communist vanguard led in Russia had actually opened the pathway to the socialist-communist future despite the dictatorial emergency measures brought on by foreign invasion and civil war. It seemed rule by democratic councils (soviets) of the workers and peasants had been established and a global Communist movement had taken shape for the purpose of carrying out similar revolutions throughout the world.

After the revolution's universally acknowledged leader, Vladimir Ilyich Lenin, died in 1924, a sharp struggle over future perspectives erupted between the intransigent revolutionary Leon Trotsky and the seemingly more patient and easygoing Joseph Stalin. Victory within the Russian Communist Party went to Stalin, who then guided the Union of Soviet Socialist Republics (USSR) into what was called a "revolution from above," involving the forced collectivization of land and a fiercely rapid industrialization. By the 1930s, the Stalin regime claimed that it had finally achieved "socialism," a claim accepted with hope and rejoicing by many workers, peasants, students, intellectuals, and others throughout the world.

As time went on, increasing numbers of people came to the conclusion that what existed in the USSR had little to do with the socialism forecast by Marx—a "free association of the producers" in which the laboring masses had won the battle for democracy to create an abundant society of the free and the equal. Instead, it was a society that continued to be marked by a considerable degree of inequality, drudgery, scarcity, and extreme restrictions on freedom.

If this was not the socialism that the Stalinists said it was, then what was it? How could its emergence be explained? The answers to such questions have obvious implications for other questions: Is a socialist alternative to capitalism actually possible? What are the preconditions, the barriers, and the possibilities for such a transition? Such questions as these have a greater edge than ever in the present period of capitalist crisis. Each in its own way, the books under review here have relevance for those facing this dilemma.

Trotsky's Marxism

The life and thought of Leon Trotsky have guided many seeking to understand the grandeur of the Russian Revolution and the tragedy of its betrayal. Kunal Chattopadhyay's *The Marxism of Leon Trotsky* is not the first book to deal with the topic indicated in the title.[1] The more serious biographies—by Isaac Deutscher and Pierre Broué (the latter still calls out for English translation)—naturally deal at length with Trotsky's revolutionary perspectives, as does Tony Cliff's more activist-oriented four-volume study.[2]

Important discussions of Trotsky's political orientation have been offered by such activist scholars as Ernest Mandel, Michael Löwy, Duncan Hallas, and John Molyneux—the first two inclined to embrace Trotsky without reservation, the latter two (along with Cliff) taking issue with him particularly for not seeing the USSR as "state capitalist" and for founding the fragile revolutionary socialist network known as the Fourth International.[3]

But before Chattopadhyay's volume, the only study reaching for a thorough and in-depth exposition was Baruch Knei-Paz's 1978 work *The Social and Political Thought of Leon Trotsky*.[4] When all is said and done, however, Knei-Paz is unsympathetic, even dismissive, of Trotsky's revolutionary Marxism, despite devoting 598 pages to it. Chattopadhyay's book (thirty pages longer) provides a more sympathetic, insightful, reliable account.

A professor at Calcutta's prestigious Jadavpur University, Chattopadhyay brings to this study a sensibility developed through his own family's longtime involvement in the substantial Indian Communist movement. In his youth, he himself was swept up in Maoist currents before experience and reflection brought him into the Fourth International. Such background may contribute to his ability to see and explain the coherence in the complexity and sweep of Trotsky's thought.

It is unfortunate that this splendid book is not easily available to US readers. Its length and polemical edge raise questions as to whether a US publisher will be inclined to rectify the situation. Yet the occasional reference Chattopadhyay makes to recent debates within the Fourth International, or between the Fourth International and other left-wing currents, cannot obscure the fact that we are presented here with a clear, rigorous, richly textured examination of an amazing political theorist and revolutionary leader. Those seriously concerned with Trotsky, Marxism, revolutionary history, and activism must take this massive contribution into account.

The book's chapters are grouped into four parts. Part One, "The Foundations," makes a distinction between classical Marxism (associated with Marx and Engels, Luxemburg, Lenin, and Trotsky) and the more rigid, mechanistic, dogmatic "Orthodox" Marxism supposedly predominant in the mainstream of the socialist movement in the late nineteenth and early twentieth centuries. Part Two, "The Strategy of Revolution," offers two chapters, one exploring the development of Trotsky's theory of permanent revolution in Russia, and the next exploring his generalization of it on a global scale.

Part Three, "The Revolutionary Process," consists of three chapters dealing with the interrelationship of the working class and the revolutionary party, the relation between democratic workers' councils and working-class political rule (or "dictatorship of the proletariat"), and the transition to socialism. The three chapters of Part Four, "Proletarian Internationalism," deal respectively with imperialism, the Communist International that Lenin and Trotsky helped to found and lead (and which Stalin helped to corrupt and dissolve), and the Fourth International.

Chattopadhyay helps us see in Trotsky's thought the dynamic interplay of democracy and class struggle, the self-activity of the masses of laboring and oppressed people reaching for their own liberation within—while at the same time straining beyond—the context of global capitalism.

Three elements of his theory of permanent revolution—(1) the possibility and necessity, under the right circumstances, of democratic and immediate struggles spilling over into the struggle for working-class political power, culminating in (2) a transitional period going in the direction of socialism, which

(3) can be realized only through the advance of similar struggles around the world—permeate Trotsky's orientation from his youth to his death.

His vision of workers' democracy and his appreciation of the radical subculture created by the embattled working class comes through in his failed effort to mobilize a Communist Party–Social Democrat united front against Hitler in the early 1930s:

> In the course of many decades, the workers have built up within the bourgeois democracy, by utilizing it, by fighting against it, their own strongholds and bases of proletarian democracy: the trade unions, the political parties, the educational and sports clubs, the cooperatives, etc. The proletariat cannot attain power within the formal limits of bourgeois democracy but can do so only by taking the road to revolution. . . . And these bulwarks of workers' democracy [which Hitler's Nazis were preparing to destroy] within the bourgeois state are absolutely essential for taking the revolutionary road.[5]

The commitment to workers' democracy also comes through in Trotsky's effort to mobilize Communists in the Soviet Republic of the mid-1920s against the bureaucratic onslaught represented by Stalin:

> We must not build socialism by the bureaucratic road, we must not create a socialist society by administrative orders; only by way of the greatest initiative, individual activity, persistence and resilience of the opinion of the many-millioned masses, who sense and know that the matter is their own concern. . . . Socialist construction is possible only with the growth of genuine revolutionary democracy.[6]

Chattopadhyay notes that in Trotsky's 1936 classic analysis of the USSR, *The Revolution Betrayed*, he rejected any "attempt to prettify the totalitarian regime." Insisting that "statization was not identical to the socialization of the means of production," he "denied the claim that the USSR was in any sense a socialist society."[7]

According to Chattopadhyay, "Stalinism (political counterrevolution within the workers' state) and fascism (political counterrevolution in the bourgeois state) heralded a long black night. It was necessary to raise a new, 'stainless banner,' around which the revolutionary workers of a new generation could unite."[8]

At the same time, running through Trotsky's orientation is a thoroughgoing revolutionary internationalism that is rooted in a conception of "world economy and the class struggle as a totality subject to uneven and combined development," as he put it, and an understanding that "today the entire globe—its dry land and water, its surface and interior—has become the arena of a worldwide economy; the dependence of each part on the other has become indissoluble."[9]

The relevance of his perspectives for the modern-day global justice movement seems striking:

> Imperialism represents the predatory capitalist expression of a progressive tendency in economic development—to construct a human economy on a world scale. . . Only socialism . . . which liberates the world economy . . . and thereby liberates national culture itself . . . offers a way out from the contradictions which have revealed themselves to us as a terrible threat to all of human culture.[10]

And in sharp contrast to the ethnocentrism of many European socialists, he commented in 1919: "We have up to now devoted too little attention to capitalism in Asia. However, the international situation is evidently shaping up in such a way that the [revolutionary] road to Paris and London lies via the towns of Afghanistan, the Punjab and Bengal."[11]

Critical Appreciation

While those inclined to take issue with key aspects of Trotsky's thought will be dissatisfied with the Chattopadhyay's almost invariable defense, this is always accompanied by an informative and well-reasoned discussion that even the most severe critic would do well to consider. Nor is the author himself completely uncritical of Trotsky's perspectives, and his contributions on this score deserve much more attention and debate than will be possible here.

One of the sharpest criticisms seems to focus on what he views as Trotsky's becoming, in a sense, too "Leninist." While hardly rejecting Lenin's fundamental orientation, Chattopadhyay approves of the young Trotsky's conflict with what he portrayed in 1904 (wrongly, I think) as Lenin's hyper-centralist deviations in *What Is to Be Done?* and *One Step Forward, Two Steps Back.*

Chattopadhyay is hardly an anti-Leninist, but he seems to view the pre-1905 Lenin as being insufficiently democratic, and that such an undemocratic residue could be found in Bolshevism even later. As a consequence, he is also critical of Trotsky for initially giving too much ground to Bolshevism when he joined Lenin's party in 1917.[12]

Chattopadhyay's argument is intriguing. He writes that Trotsky, in his anti-Lenin polemic *Our Political Tasks* (1904), "made a point to which we will find him returning all his life: 'The problems of the new [revolutionary] regime are so intricate that they can be solved only through the rivalry of the various methods of economic and political reconstruction, by long 'debates,' by systematic struggle—not only between the socialist and capitalist worlds, but also between the various tendencies within socialism, tendencies that must inevitably develop as soon as the dictatorship of proletariat creates tens and hundreds of new unresolved problems."[13]

This clear recognition of the necessity of political pluralism as an integral part of creating socialism is not present in Lenin's otherwise magnificent *The State and Revolution* (1917). The calamities of civil war, foreign intervention, economic blockade, and social chaos following the 1917 revolution caused Lenin, Trotsky, and the other Bolsheviks to establish a one-party dictatorship, curtail and ban various manifestations of political pluralism, and adopt other authoritarian measures on an "emergency" basis.

Some of Chattopadhyay's sharpest criticisms of Trotsky center on this period of 1919–22. In fact, the temporary expedients were never rescinded, contributing to the replacement of the power of workers' councils by the power of the state and party bureaucratic apparatus—and the crystallization of Stalinism. By 1923–24, Trotsky recognized the danger and began leading the ill-fated Left Opposition.

In his final years, now living in exile before being murdered by a Stalinist agent in 1940, he had—Chattopadhyay shows us—explicitly reintegrated into his Bolshevik-Leninist orientation the pluralist insights of 1904, calling for a revolution that would overthrow the bureaucratic dictatorship and pave the way for a multiparty soviet democracy. Trotsky viewed this as a political revolution, which he believed could and must rescue the social and economic gains of the 1917 revolution.

Making Sense of Stalin's "Socialism"

The political revolution never happened, however. Trotsky himself spent more than sixteen years seeking to make sense of Stalin's "socialism," a matter Chattopadhyay deals with capably, but not in great depth. He never expected the bureaucratic dictatorship to last as long as it did.

In fact, several generations of Marxists labored to make sense of what the USSR represented and how it might be squared with Marxist perspectives. Marcel van der Linden, research director of Amsterdam's prestigious International Institute of Social History, points out that "the 'Russian Question' was an absolutely central problem for Marxism in the twentieth century."[14]

In *Western Marxism and the Soviet Union*, van der Linden offers a survey of Marxist-influenced theorizations and debates. The discussion is not exhaustive but presents the thinking of more than a hundred people from 1917 to the dawn of the twenty-first century, whose works are listed here in forty-four pages. The eyes and mind of even veteran Marxists may begin to blur after spending excessive stretches of time with this volume—but the author's account is quite clear, coherent, fair-minded, and genuinely interesting.

The periodic crescendos of theory and debate (seven in all, van der Linden tells us, from 1917 to the end of the 1990s) have implications for the nature of socialism, and even its very possibility. The nature of capitalism is also at issue, as are the capacities of the working class to improve its own situation and the world, as well as the adequacy of Marxism as a tool for understanding the world.

Marx's materialist conception of history had posited a European historical development leading from a generalized primitive tribal communism, eventually giving way to the rise and fall of a succession of slave-based civilizations, then an extensive feudalism slowly evolving through the crystallization and expansion within it of a market economy, explosively giving way to a full-blown and dynamic capitalism, which would generate the possibility of immense productivity and abundance that would pave the way (after a working-class revolution) for a socialist future.

"It is necessary to reconsider the whole traditional structure of historical materialism," writes dissident-Marxists György Bence and János Kis (under the pseudonym Marc Rakovskii) in *Les Temps Modernes* as they sought to comprehend Soviet-style societies (247).

Indeed, how could such a society fit within the traditional Marxist schema? In 1980, Romanian dissident Pavel Campeanu suggested a variety of contradictory elements that added up to "some kind of pre-capitalist socio-economic formation" (284). Back in 1944, Czechoslovakian ex-Communist Josef Guttman, writing under the name Peter Meyer in the US radical journal *Politics*, suggested what many others had concluded before him: "Perhaps there is neither capitalism nor socialism in Russia, but a third thing, something that is quite new in history" (127).

As late as 1980, British economist Simon Mohun argued a point made by some other analysts, summarized by van der Linden in this way: "Just as the transition to capitalism could be understood only after capitalism was consolidated, the transition from capitalism to communism could only be fathomed once communism had become established" (197–98). But others refused to assume that the USSR represented any such transition to socialism or communism.

In his *samizdat* essays, written in the 1970s, Alexander Zimin, an old Bolshevik oppositionist who had somehow survived years in Stalin's labor camps, suggested that the USSR represented "a mongrel and freakish social

---

Samizdat refers to unpublished dissident writings, banned by the Communist dictatorship but illegally circulated, particularly in the less repressive post-Stalin years.

formation," a stagnant evolutionary byway, a dead-end detour going away from both capitalism and socialism (222). In the 1940s, German left-wing economist Fritz Sternberg had argued that the USSR was a hybrid form with progressive and reactionary tendencies (he increasingly saw the latter as predominant) and that one should resist giving it a label: "It is useless to attempt to cover with a name; it is misleading to mistake one side of the Russian development for the other" (131).

This has not stopped many from seeking and applying one or another label. Van der Linden notes: "Numerous attempts were made to understand Soviet society, some with solid empirical foundations, but most lacking them; some consistent and carefully thought-out, others illogical and superficial" (305).

The three "classical" theoretical labels for the USSR predominating in critical-minded circles (each with some connection to the Trotskyist tradition) have been (1) degenerated workers' state, (2) bureaucratic collectivism, and (3) state capitalism. Van der Linden argues that none of these matches up with what he calls "orthodox Marxism," but we will see that some theorists have insisted that major aspects of Marxism itself have been thrown into question by the evolving realities.

Challenge to Marxist Theory

Among the early critics, some insisted that the existence of the authoritarianism and bureaucratic aspects of reality in the early Soviet Republic and then the substantial concessions to market forces during the period of New Economic Policy (NEP), in the years 1921–29, were far from the socialist goal. This meant, from the standpoint of the stages that have been associated with the Marxist schema (primitive communal society, slave civilization, feudalism, capitalism, socialism, and communism), that what existed in Soviet Russia had to be some variety of capitalism, which the critics were inclined to call "state capitalism."

The Bolshevik leaders—Lenin and Trotsky most of all—never asserted that socialism had been established. Only Stalin and his followers would claim this, beginning in the 1930s. Lenin argued in 1921 that the 1917 working-class revolution had established a workers' state (political rule by the workers' councils, or soviets), but that under pressures of scarcity and war it was "a workers' state with bureaucratic deformations."[15] The transition to socialism could only be completed on the basis of further economic development, the deepening of workers' experience and power, and the triumph of the revolution in other parts of the world.

Bolsheviks could also point to Marx's comments that the future communist (or socialist) society must be seen "not as it has developed on its own foundations, but, on the contrary, just as it emerges from capitalist society, which is thus in every respect, economically, morally and intellectually, still stamped with the birth-marks of the old society from whose womb it emerges" (264).

Some socialists who had opposed the Bolshevik regime, such as the Menshevik Olga Domanevskaya, insisted that central dynamics of capitalism, such as economic competition and the insatiable quest for profit, were absent from the economy of Soviet Russia. Similarly, the famous Austrian Social Democratic economist Rudolf Hilferding argued that "wages and prices still exist, but their function is no longer the same" and that "while maintaining the form, a complete transformation of the function has occurred" in this emerging totalitarian order (92).

This partly dovetails with the analysis of another Austrian Social Democrat, Friedrich Adler, who (according to van der Linden's summary) claims, "Stalin's 'experiment' should be judged as an attempt to realize, through the sacrifice of a whole generation of workers, the primitive accumulation process which in developed capitalism had occurred earlier and in this way lay the foundation for a socialist Soviet Union" (53). Hilferding, on the other hand, stressed that the bureaucratic-authoritarian state in Soviet Russia had fractured the classical Marxist dictum that the economic system determines the class nature of the state. Under Stalin it had converted itself into "an independent power" ruling over the Soviet people (90).

Other challenges to traditional Marxist perspectives would crop up. For example, in 1933 Simone Weil developed an analysis arguing that under modern capitalist production the growing division of labor and specialization increasingly resulted in the mass of individuals losing their ability to "see society in its totality," which meant that they were "imprisoned in a social constellation" that prevented them from grasping the logic and history of socioeconomic reality. On the other hand, growing managerial and bureaucratic apparatuses were becoming essential for coordinating the "numerous fragmented activities." If a revolution removed the capitalists, a more likely outcome than working-class rule would be the conversion of rising administrative forces into a new bureaucratic caste ruling over the economy, as in Stalin's Russia (74–75).

In fact, many theorists had emphasized the division between intellectual and manual labor, identifying it as a source of bureaucratization within the workers' movement before World War I and—by logical extension—in the first effort to create a workers' state. This logic dovetailed with the perception of what actually manifested itself in the USSR, lucidly described in 1970 by US Marxist economist and *Monthly Review* editor Paul Sweezy:

> The Party established a dictatorship which accomplished epic feats of industrialization and preparation for the inevitable onslaught of the imperialist powers [which took place during World War II], but the price was the proliferation of political and economic bureaucracies which repressed rather than represented the new Soviet working class; and gradually entrenched themselves in power as a new ruling class (209).

Some would come to ascribe this inability to sustain workers' power to a fatal shortcoming in the working class itself. As another left-wing economist, the Greek/French political theorist Cornelius Castoriadis, put it in the late 1940s:

> Having overthrown the bourgeois government, having expropriated the capitalists (often against the wishes of the Bolsheviks), having occupied the factories, the workers thought that all that was necessary was to hand over management to the government, to the Bolshevik party and to the trade union leaders. By doing so, the proletariat was abdicating its own essential role in the society it was striving to create (118).

Such perceptions contributed to some theorists—such as East German Communist dissident Rudolf Bahro—concluding that since "the immediate needs of the subaltern strata and classes are always conservative and never positively anticipate a new form of life," the hope in bureaucratized "workers' states" was with the more intellectual middle strata of specialists and administrators pushing aside the privileged bureaucratic elites in order to guide society to genuine socialism (234–35).

For others, such as James Burnham—the most prominent Trotskyist intellectual in the United States before his rapid swing rightward to the Central Intelligence Agency and the editorial board of the conservative journal *National Review*—a different conclusion became obvious: socialism is impossible.

Dismantling his previous Marxist convictions in the 1941 classic *The Managerial Revolution*, Burnham asserted that the inevitable wave of the future, already well under way and destined to be completed within half a century, was a global transition to variations of "managerial society" (already evident in the USSR, Nazi Germany, and the extensive social liberalism of the New Deal in the United States). These different entities would enter into "direct competition in the days to come" for global empire (83).

Varieties of Socialist Affirmation

While van der Linden feels "it is perfectly clear that the Soviet society can hardly be explained in orthodox Marxist terms at all," his own sympathies bend toward those who refuse to abandon the Marxist method and the socialist goal. He gives greatest attention to those operating within the general revolutionary socialist framework personified by Leon Trotsky.

Trotsky himself followed the logic of Lenin (workers' state with bureaucratic deformations) by describing the USSR as a degenerated workers' state requiring a political revolution by the working class to replace the tyranny of the Stalinist bureaucracy with genuine workers' rule. The October 1917 revolution—the fruit of a mass insurgency of Russia's working class—had transferred "all power to the soviets," the democratic councils of the laborers, and this had resulted in the institutionalization of many gains beneficial to the working class. Thus, even with its bureaucratic deformations, the Soviet Republic continued to represent (in the view of Lenin and Trotsky) a variant of the original *workers' state*. To overcome the bureaucratic degeneration, it was essential to reestablish genuine rule by the working class, in alliance with the peasantry—*workers' democracy*.

"Democracy," he insisted, "is the one and only conceivable mechanism for preparing the socialist system of economy and realizing it in life." He forecast in 1938:

> That which was "bureaucratic deformation" is at the present moment preparing to devour the workers' state, without leaving any remains. . . . If the proletariat drives out the Soviet bureaucracy in time, then it will still find the nationalized means of production and the basic elements of the planned economy after its victory (66–67).

Led by Max Shachtman (and Burnham, fleetingly), some of Trotsky's US followers agreed with Trotsky's revolutionary-democratic thrust, concluding that by 1939 the bloated bureaucracy had indeed left "no remains" of the workers' state. They held that a qualitatively new form of class society had crystallized—what they termed *bureaucratic collectivism*. Its effective overthrow would require a much deeper break with the USSR than Trotsky was prepared to accept.

Van der Linden notes that for Trotsky, "planned economy and bureaucratic dictatorship were fundamentally incompatible" and that—as his French comrade Pierre Frank put it—"Stalinism was an accident, not a durable creation of history" (67). He envisioned that either the working class would once again take control of its own workers' state, clearing away the bureaucratic deformations and (within the context of working-class revolutions spreading to other lands) moving forward to socialism, or a period of continued bureaucratic decay would ultimately result in a collapse that would pave the way for capitalist restoration—which is, of course, what took place fifty years after his death.

The weak point in Trotsky's conceptualization was pinpointed by his one-time follower in Britain, Tony Cliff: "If the emancipation of the working class is the act of the working class, then you cannot have a workers' state without the workers having power to dictate what happens in society" (119).

This was exactly the point made by Shachtman and other proponents of the bureaucratic-collectivist analysis—although the existence of this purportedly "new stage of class society" for a mere half-century (in historical terms the blink of an eye) does suggest the possibility that it was an optical illusion.

State Capitalism

What Cliff and his co-thinkers came up with seems to avoid that problem. They asserted that the USSR under Stalin had evolved into a new variety of capitalism: state capitalism. Cliff and his followers have been among the most influential proponents of the "state capitalism" analysis (though van der Linden also discusses the version of this analysis advanced by other proponents such as the council communists as well as C. L. R. James and Raya Dunayevskaya).

As noted earlier, criticisms of the "state capitalist" theory have argued that that central dynamics that define capitalism and the capital accumulation process—that of economic competition and profit maximization—were absent in Soviet Russia. The state capitalist theorists have defended their conception by claiming (as van der Linden summarizes Cliff's thesis) "that the USSR should be defined as one big capital [or capitalist firm], which operated within the world market and in so doing competed with the West, above all through the arms race" (160).

One might question the analytical value of expanding the meaning of capitalism in this way. But, as was also the case with the bureaucratic-collectivism concept, it served the function of drawing the sharpest line of demarcation between revolutionary socialism and the bogus "socialism" of Stalin and his successors. It also helped prevent, among its adherents, the demoralization and disorientation brought on by the collapse of communism that afflicted so much of the left in the 1990s.

On the other hand, van der Linden points out that Cliff and his supporters "had originally assumed that state capitalism represented a higher stage of development than Western capitalism" (258) and, being ill-prepared for the crisis and impending collapse that became evident in the 1980s, were compelled to make dramatic if unacknowledged analytical shifts in their later theorizations. For that matter, even more mainstream Trotskyists—including such capable and brilliant figures as Ernest Mandel—were inclined to credit the USSR's "nationalized, planned economy" with much greater efficiency than later proved justified.

It was maverick theorist Hillel Ticktin who in the 1970s broke important new ground by noting that bureaucratic "planning"—by denying democracy—was increasingly inefficient and wasteful, a point that Trotsky himself had made more than once. This alleged planned economy was "really no more than a bargaining process at best and a police process at worst." Ticktin added that "the more intensive and more complex is the economy, the longer the chain of command and the less intelligible is industry to the administrators and so the greater the distortions and their proportionate importance" (242, 243).

Ticktin's view was that this represented neither a variety of capitalism nor a transitional phase leading to socialism nor a durable new form of society. His insights, in fact, influenced competing views, as van der Linden observes:

> Increasingly dominant in all currents of thought became the idea that the Soviet Union embodied a model of economic growth which, although it had initially been successful using extensive methods of industrialization and extra economic coercion, could not maintain its economic and military position in the competition with globalizing world capitalism, because of growing ineffi ciencies and the absence of a transition to intensive growth (303).

Open Questions

In his conclusions to this rich volume, van der Linden emphasizes that while he does "not mean to imply that the old theories are of no use whatever in further theoretical developments," his conviction is that a fully adequate analysis of the USSR has yet to be developed (318).

It may be that if we are able to build mass movements and struggles—in various parts of the world, as the twenty-first century unfolds—that add to our experience of bringing about transitions from capitalism to socialism, a more fully adequate analysis will come more within our grasp.

Marxist theory and history have often been dismissed with shrugs and giggles and eye-rolling, even on the left, with a few superficial comments deemed sufficient to sweep away such "ideological cobwebs." For those embracing that approach, the two volumes reviewed will seem explorations in irrelevancy. For serious activists, however, these books offer not only historical knowledge but insights on our struggle for a survivable future.

7.

The Darker the Night
the Brighter the Star

Trotsky's Struggle against Stalinism

This presentation was given at the Socialism 2016 conference on July 4, in Chicago.—P.L.

The title of this session—"The Darker the Night the Brighter the Star"—is the title of the fourth and final volume of Tony Cliff's biography of Leon Trotsky, who was a central leader of the 1917 Russian Revolution of workers and peasants, which turned the Russian tsarist empire into the Union of Soviet Socialist Republics. One of the founders of modern communism and the Soviet state, Trotsky is also the best known of those who fought against the degeneration of that revolution and movement brought on by a vicious bureaucratic dictatorship led by Joseph Stalin.[1]

I went online to find out where that book title came from, and I learned that it is often attributed to Fyodor Dostoevsky's great novel *Crime and Punishment*. But I also learned that this is contested, and I personally couldn't find it in Dostoevsky's novel. When I wrote to Tony Cliff's biographer, Ian Birchall, he checked with Cliff's son—Donny Gluckstein—who responded: "I think he might have taken the phrase from the Friedrich Schlotterbeck Left Book Club book—*The Darker the Night, the Brighter the Stars.*" Schlotterbeck was a young working-class Communist in Germany when Adolf Hitler's dictatorship was established in 1933, and his 1947 book is an inspiring and devastating account of left-wing workers' resistance to Nazi tyranny, in which we learn of the heroism and horrific destruction of his many comrades, friends, and family members who remained committed to socialist and communist ideals.[2]

But Trotsky has told us:

> No one, not excluding Hitler, has dealt socialism such deadly blows as Stalin. This is hardly astonishing since Hitler has attacked the working class organizations from without, while Stalin does it from within. Hitler assaults Marxism. Stalin not only assaults but prostitutes it. Not a single principle has remained unpolluted, not a single idea unsullied. The very names of socialism and communism have been cruelly compromised. . . . Socialism signifies a pure and limpid social system which is accommodated to the self-government of the toilers. Stalin's regime is based on a conspiracy of the rulers against the ruled. Socialism implies an uninterrupted growth of universal equality. Stalin has erected a system of revolting privileges. Socialism has as its goal the all-sided flowering of individual personality. When and where has man's personality been so degraded as in the U.S.S.R.? Socialism would have no value apart from the unselfish, honest and humane relations between human beings. The Stalin regime has permeated social and personal relationships with lies, careerism and treachery.[3]

So wrote Trotsky in 1937. And those in Soviet Russia who believed such things were repressed no less ruthlessly than the German Communists had been.[4]

The Left Oppositionists that Trotsky led persisted after his expulsion from the Soviet Union, and they were rounded up and sent to Siberian prison camps called "isolators." "When you can no longer serve the cause to which you have dedicated your life—you should give it your death." These were the words of Adolf Joffe, one of Trotsky's close friends and co-thinkers who had committed suicide as a protest against Stalinism in 1927. His young wife Maria ended up in internal exile in 1929. As the situation of the condemned Oppositionists worsened by degrees, she held out, and when it became the horrific "one long night" that she describes in her memoir of the late 1930s, she was one of the few who somehow survived to tell what happened. She was sustained by a core belief: "It is possible to sacrifice your life, but the honor of a person, of a revolutionary—never."[5]

Pressures to give in were intense because capitulation could mean freedom, while remaining in the Opposition meant never-ending jail and exile. By 1934, after seven years, Trotsky's close comrade Christian Rakovsky himself was ready to capitulate, his views later recounted by Maria's stepdaughter, Nadezhda Joffe, in whom he confided and whom he won over: "His basic thoughts were that we had to return to the party in any way possible. He felt that there was undoubtedly a layer in the party which shared our views at heart, but had not decided to voice their agreement. And we could become a kind of common sense core and be able to accomplish something. Left in isolation, he said, they would strangle us like chickens."[6]

Trotsky rejected this logic, as did many co-thinkers exiled in the small village isolators. One survivor recalled the toasts they made in the early 1930s on New Year's Day: "The first toast was to our courageous and long-suffering wives and women comrades, who were sharing our fate. We drank our second toast to the world proletarian revolution. Our third was to our people's freedom and our own liberation from prison."[7]

Instead, they would soon be transferred to the deadly Siberian labor camps into which hundreds of thousands of victims of the 1935–39 purges (including most of the capitulators plus many other Communist Party members) were sent as Stalinist repression tightened throughout the country. Arrested while in Moscow in 1936, Secretary of the Palestinian Communist Party Joseph Berger later remembered the Left Oppositionists he met during his own ordeal:

> While the great majority had "capitulated," there remained a hard core of uncompromising Trotskyists, most of them in prisons and camps. They and their families had all been rounded up in the preceding months and concentrated in three large camps—Kolyma, Vorkuta, and Norilsk. . . . The majority were experienced revolutionaries who had fought in the Civil War but had joined the Opposition in the early twenties. . . . Purists, they feared contamination of their doctrine above all else in the world. . . . When I accused the Trotskyists of sectarianism, they said what mattered was "to keep the banner unsullied."[8]

Another survivor's account, published in the émigré publication of Russian Mensheviks, the *Socialist Messenger*, recalls "the Orthodox Trotskyists" of the Vorkuta labor camp who "were determined to remain faithful to their platform and their leaders," and, "even though they were in prison, they continued to consider themselves Communists; as for Stalin and his supporters, 'the apparatus men,' they were characterized as renegades from communism." Along with their supporters and sympathizers (some of whom had never even been members of the Communist Party), they numbered in the thousands at this site, according to the witness. As word spread of Stalin's show trials designed to frame and execute the Old Bolshevik leaders, and as conditions at the camp deteriorated, "the entire group of 'Orthodox' Trotskyists" came together. The eyewitness remembers the speech of Socrates Gevorkian:

> It is now evident that the group of Stalinist adventurers have completed their counter-revolutionary *coup d'etat* in our country. All the progressive conquests

of our revolution are in mortal danger. Not twilight shadows but those of the deep black night envelop our country. . . . No compromise is possible with the Stalinist traitors and hangmen of the revolution. But before destroying us, Stalin will try to humiliate us as much as he can. . . . We are left with only one means of struggle in this unequal battle: the hunger strike. . . ."

The great majority of prisoners, regardless of political orientation, followed this lead.[9]

Lasting from October 1936 to March 1937, the 132-day hunger strike was powerfully effective and forced the camp officials and their superiors to give in to the strikers' demands. "We had a verbal newspaper, *Truth Behind Bars*," Maria Joffe was told by an Oppositionist who had survived, "we had little groups—circles, there were a lot of clever, knowledgeable people. Sometimes we issued a satirical leaflet, *The Underdog*. Vilka, our barrack representative, was editor and the illustrations were formed by people against a wall background. Quite a lot of laughing, too, mostly young ones there." And then "everything suddenly came to an end."[10]

In 1938 the Trotskyists of Vorkuta were marched out in batches—men, women, children over the age of twelve—into the surrounding arctic wasteland. "Their names were checked against a list and then, group by group, they were called out and machine-gunned," writes Joseph Berger. "Some struggled, shouted slogans and fought the guards to the last." According to the witness writing in the *Socialist Messenger*, as one larger group of about a hundred was led out of the camp to be shot, "the condemned sang the 'Internationale' joined by the voices of hundreds of prisoners remaining in camp."[11]

In her memoir, Maria Joffe tells us the "tortures, murders, mass shootings of many thousands of Trotskyists in Vorkuta and Kolyma" actually impacted many more, constituting "the complete destruction of the October and Civil War generation, 'infected by Trotskyist heresy.'" It has been estimated that more than two million people were condemned from 1934 through 1938—with more than seven hundred thousand executions and over a million sent to increasingly brutalized labor camps, where many more perished.[12]

In the rest of these remarks I want to touch on aspects of the so-called Trotskyist heresy that analyze how a profoundly democratic workers' and peasants' revolution, inspired by the deepest socialist idealism, could turn into one of the worst tyrannies in human history. This is something that Trotsky wrestled with as it was happening—and there is much we can learn from that, as my friend Tom Twiss brilliantly demonstrates in his important book, *Trotsky and the Problem of Soviet Bureaucracy*.[13]

The bottom line, however, is that Trotsky's analysis clearly emerges from the fundamental analysis of Karl Marx eighty years earlier. It is also inseparable from the basics of his own theory of permanent revolution. In my remaining time I will offer in very broad strokes two analyses—one dealing with permanent revolution and the other with the bureaucratic degeneration of the Soviet Union.

The rise and industrial development of capitalism has done three things, according to both Marx and Trotsky. First there was a process sometimes known as "primitive accumulation," which involved a horrific and murderous displacement and oppression and brutal exploitation of masses of peasants and indigenous peoples on a global scale. Second, there has been a massive process of proletarianization—making a majority of the labor force and population into a modern working class (those whose livelihood is dependent on selling their ability to work, their labor-power, for wages). This working-class majority is the force that has the potential power, and the objective self-interest, to replace the economic dictatorship of capitalism with the economic democracy of socialism—and the awareness of all this is what Marxists mean when they speak of workers' *class consciousness*. Third, the spectacular technological development generated by capitalism—the ever self-renewing Industrial Revolution—creates the material basis for a new socialist society. As Marx put it in 1845, the creation of this high level of productivity and wealth "is an absolutely necessary practical premise [for communism] because without it want is merely made general, and with destitution [there is a resumption of] the struggle for necessities," generating a competition for who gets what, and then (according to one translation) "the same old shit starts all over again."[14]

Drawing from Marx, Trotsky and a growing number of his Russian comrades came to see the coming revolution in backward Russia in this way. The democratic struggle against the semi-feudal tsarist autocracy would only be led consistently and through to the end by the small but growing Russian working class in alliance with the peasant majority—and the success of such a revolution would place the organizations of the working class into political power. There would be a natural push to keep moving in a socialist direction (with expanding social improvements for the masses of people)—although the socialism that Marx had outlined and that the Russian workers were fighting for could not be created in a single backward country. But a successful Russian Revolution would help push forward revolutionary struggles in other countries, and as these revolutions were successful—especially in industrially more advanced countries such as Germany, France, Italy, and Britain—the Russian workers and peasants could join with comrades in a growing number of countries in the development of a global socialist economy that would replace capitalism and create a better life and better future for the world's laboring majority. This is why Lenin, Trotsky, and their comrades labored to draw revolutionaries and insurgent workers from all around the world into the Communist International, to help advance this necessary world revolutionary process for international socialism. Because socialism cannot triumph if it is not global.[15]

But the anticipated revolutions in other countries were not successful, and seven years of relative isolation—with military invasions, foreign trade boycotts, civil war, economic collapse, and other hardships—had three results. First, the projected government by democratic councils (soviets) of workers and peasants was delayed as the overwhelming social-political-economic emergency brought about what was originally seen as a temporary dictatorship by the Communist Party. Second, a massive bureaucratic apparatus crystallized in order to run the country and administer the economy. As Trotsky would later explain in *The Revolution Betrayed*, when there aren't enough necessities to go around, there is rationing and people "are compelled to stand in line. When the lines are very long, it is necessary to appoint a policeman to keep order. Such is the starting point of the power of the Soviet bureaucracy. It 'knows' who is to get something and who has to wait."[16]

While some of the Communists remained absolutely dedicated to the original ideals and perspectives that had been the basis for the 1917 revolution, there were many who became corrupted or compromised or disoriented. Stalin was a central figure in the increasingly authoritarian bureaucratic apparatus, and along with the brilliant but disoriented Nikolai Bukharin, he disconnected the idea of socialism not only from democracy, but also from the revolutionary internationalism that is at the heart of Marxism, advancing the notion of building socialism in a single country—the Soviet Union. Trotsky and his co-thinkers denounced this notion as "a skinflint reactionary utopia of self-sufficient socialism, built on a low technology," incapable of bringing about genuine socialism. Instead, the same old shit would start all over again. But it was Stalin who won this battle, fiercely repressing Trotsky and the Left Opposition.[17]

Stalin didn't stop there. While Bukharin and others had envisioned building their "socialism in one country" slowly and more or less humanely, Stalin and the powerful figures around him decided to initiate a "revolution from above"—a forced collectivization of the land and a rapid, authoritarian industrialization process (all at the expense of the peasant and worker majority) to modernize Russia in the name of "socialism in one country."[18]

Bukharin and his co-thinkers were smashed politically, but unlike Trotsky and the intransigent Left Oppositionists, they quickly capitulated to Stalin—

although this didn't save them in the end. Peasant resistance was dealt with brutally, and famine resulted. Worker resistance was also savagely repressed. All critical discussion in the Communist Party was banned. All independent and creative thought and expression—in education, art, literature, culture—throughout the country was compelled to give way to authoritarian norms that celebrated the policies and personalities of Stalin and those around him—but especially, more and more, of Stalin himself.[19]

Although they claimed that the modernization policies they oversaw added up to socialism, and that they were the loyal and rightful heirs of Lenin and the 1917 revolution, the functionaries in the increasingly massive bureaucratic apparatus enjoyed an accumulation of material privileges, with authority and a lifestyle that placed them above a majority of the people. As Trotsky put it in *The Revolution Betrayed*, "It is useless to boast and ornament reality. Limousines for the 'activists' [that is, the bureaucrats], fine perfumes for 'our women' [that is, wives of the bureaucrats], margarine for the workers, stores 'deluxe' for the gentry, a look at delicacies through the store windows for the plebs—such socialism cannot but seem to the masses a new re-facing of capitalism, and they are not far wrong. On a basis of 'generalized want,' the struggle for the means of subsistence threatens to resurrect 'all the old crap,' and is partially resurrecting it at every step."[20]

Several years later, the knowledgeable analyst David Dallin noted that government employees (the bureaucracy from top elite to lowliest functionaries), constituting at least 14 percent of the labor force, consumed as much as 35 percent of the wealth; that the working class, constituting about 20 percent of the labor force, received no more than 33 percent of the wealth; that peasants, 53 percent of the labor force, received 29 percent of the wealth; and the forced laborers (the millions whose labor was exploited in the Stalinist gulag), estimated at a minimum of 8 percent of the labor force, received 3 percent of the wealth. By all accounts, the lifestyle of the elite rivaled that of capitalists in other lands. While this inequality is somewhat different from ours (where the top 1 percent has at least 40 percent of the wealth and the bottom 80 percent has no more than 20 percent of the wealth), what existed under Stalin was still a mockery of the socialist goal of 1917.[21]

In the 1930s, many in the USSR remembered the democratic and egalitarian ideals of the revolutionary cause, and some remained committed to these. Among those dissident Communists defeated and repressed by the regime (including those who capitulated) were experienced revolutionaries who had helped to overthrow the tsar. They couldn't be trusted, especially because all was not well in the Union of Soviet Socialist Republics. Despite the unending pseudo-revolutionary propaganda and positive improvements in economic and social opportunities for some workers, there was widespread suffering and dissatisfaction within the population. The dynamics of "socialism in one country," accelerated by the "revolution from above," were bound to explode into the murderous authoritarianism we looked at earlier. The program of the heroic Left Oppositionists who gave their lives was a definite threat to the Stalinist system, and it was outlined eloquently in Trotsky's *The Revolution Betrayed*:

> It is not a question of substituting one ruling clique for another, but of changing the very methods of administering the economy and guiding the culture of the country. Bureaucratic autocracy must give place to Soviet democracy. A restoration of the right of criticism, and a genuine freedom of elections, are necessary conditions for the further development of the country. This assumes a revival of freedom of Soviet parties, beginning with the party of Bolsheviks, and a resurrection of the trade unions. The bringing of democracy into industry means a radical revision of plans in the interests of the toilers. Free discussion of economic problems will decrease the overhead expense of bureaucratic mistakes and zigzags. Expensive playthings—palaces of the Soviets, new theaters, show-off subways—will be crowded out in favor of workers' dwellings. 'Bourgeois norms of distribution' will be confined within the limits of strict necessity, and, in step with the growth of social wealth, will give way to socialist equality. Ranks will be immediately abolished. The tinsel of decorations will go into the melting pot. The youth will receive the opportunity to breathe freely, criticize, make mistakes, and grow up. Science and art will be freed of their chains. And, finally, foreign policy will return to the traditions of revolutionary internationalism.[22]

This continues to be relevant to our situation today.

Which brings us back to this session's title. When we look up at night, the blackness of the universe is vividly punctuated by the stars, whose glow has traveled light-years for us to see. Even though some of those stars no longer exist, we see them shining from where we are. And their wondrous illumination may help us find our way in the dark terrain of our own times.

8.

Origins and Trajectory of the Cuban Revolution

This essay reviews Samuel Farber, The Origins of the Cuban Revolution Reconsidered *(University of North Carolina Press, 2006).*—P.L.

O ne of the most useful works on the Cuban Revolution has appeared with Samuel Farber's *The Origins of the Cuban Revolution Reconsidered*. Its succinct, clearly written, straightforward account draws widely on a range of primary and secondary sources, and also on the author's personal experience as someone who grew up in pre-revolutionary Cuba and retains a connection with revolutionary socialist perspectives.[1]

Of interest is the author's intelligent utilization of Leon Trotsky's formulations of the theory of uneven and combined development and the theory of permanent revolution to develop thoughtful analyses of Cuban history. No less important is the fact that this volume was designed as a serious intervention against current scholarly and political discussions and debates of today, particularly against liberals and conservatives in the United States and within the Cuban exile community (and more covertly within Cuba) who—in contrast to Farber himself—want to advance the notion that capitalism in Cuba was in the interests of the Cuban people before 1959 and could yet remain in their interests in the future.

The fact that Farber is a sharp critic of the Cuban Revolution, and even more so of the Castro regime, in a sense adds to the value of his contribution.

The Revolutionary Leader

Full disclosure: I have always been a supporter of the Cuban Revolution, and I do not share Farber's particular characterization of the Cuban government. I will indicate some of my differences at the conclusion of this review. But Farber's passion for objectivity enables him to reconstruct the events of the late 1950s and early 1960s in a manner that both partisans and critics will find useful.

Now more than ever, such a contribution is vitally important as Cuba enters a new era, with the present incredibly fluid and future difficult to predict, and truly—as the old cliché goes—"with great stakes trembling in the balance."

As we try to understand where Cuba is going, it is essential not to lose sight of where it has been. Although I was young, I can recall how profoundly we were all affected by that crazy, heroic, joyous reality of the Cuban Revolution—scruffy, dedicated young guerrilla fighters with a buoyant sense of humor surging into their country's cities, their numbers swelled by exultant crowds, as the army and police and torturers and hangers-on of the vicious pro-US dictator Fulgencio Batista melted away.

The revolutionaries took power on January 1, 1959. In the wake of this victory, revolutionary Cuba soon challenged the economic and political domination of the United States that had afflicted the island since the 1890s. Among those who hated the Revolution, the rich and the gangsters led the way to Miami. In Havana, the suits of "respectable" politicians were briefly on the scene, but then were crowded out by the military fatigues of the guerrilla fighters who were not willing to compromise away the struggle for social and economic justice for the oppressed and exploited classes that they had initiated in the mountains.

Leading the revolution on to an increasingly radical course was a bearded and eloquent militant named Fidel Castro (coming out of the clean-shaven conformist 1950s of the United States, we considered his look amazing). Despite the inevitable collision with US imperialism, he refused to back down. Enthusiastic masses of the Cuban people followed him into a successful confrontation with US power, and both Fidel and Cuba became powerful symbols of anti-imperialism and successful liberation struggle.

US and Latin American radicals continued to watch and debate events in Cuba over the years. I recall a discussion back in the late 1970s with a comrade less inclined to be critical than I was of Castro's top-down leadership style and the absence of institutions of workers' democracy at all levels of Cuba's government. "Okay," I said, "let's say that Fidel's decisions are always in the best interests of defending the interests of the masses of the Cuban people and advancing the Cuban Revolution—but what happens when Fidel isn't there anymore?"

My friend responded: "Well, Fidel is still pretty young and healthy—I think he'll be around for a while."

As this review is being written, in mid-September of 2006, a National Public Radio report on Cuba by Tom Gjelten stresses what all of the US media keeps harping on: "Castro is now an old man, still recovering from abdominal surgery and unable to make an appearance at a summit of non-aligned nations in his own capital of Havana."[2]

The NPR report sports a couple of sound bites from Mexican journalist Jorge Castañeda (author of the "revolution is passé" bestseller of the early 1990s, *Utopia Unarmed: The Latin American Left after the Cold War*).[3] Castañeda tells us what he thinks is the view of Castro among radicalized young people in Latin America: "They know he's not a revolutionary, they know the Cuban experience is a failure"—and yet "they still say, 'Well, yes, but he stands up to the Americans.'"

Castañeda's generalizations are thrown into question by some of what Farber tells us. The fact that this "failed" revolutionary experience greatly enhanced the quality of life for a majority of Cubans comes through in these pages. And Farber shows us that, regardless of what criticisms one may advance, there is no question that Fidel Castro, for all of his adult life, has been a revolutionary.

He emerged, as Farber indicates, from a radical-populist subculture that "repudiated a long history of betrayal and corrupt political behavior in Cuba, particularly after the mid-1940s, and rejected the deeply entrenched view that public office was, more than anything else, a source of unlimited personal enrichment and social mobility." Given the nature of Cuban politics and society at this time, this orientation could only be realized through "revolutionary social change."[4]

Radical-Populist Roots

The radical-populist subculture in Cuba was rooted in the early Auténtico Party that arose in the 1930s, a current influenced by democratic, anti-imperialist, and socialist ideas, but which became utterly compromised and corrupt when it came to power in 1944. Castro was part of a radical split-off, the Ortodoxo Party, led by the volatile and uncompromising Eduardo Chibás, who died by his own hand in 1951.

As Farber comments, from his student days, Castro, while graced with a remarkable "political radar and rapport with people," also "seems to have been somewhat more educated and cultured than the typical populist activist," in fact "transcending the traditional populist tradition" as he familiarized himself with Marxist thought, which he tended to blend with the radical-nationalist ideas of a left-wing Cuban revolutionary of the nineteenth century, José Martí.[5]

As Farber explains, "The nature of populist politics, with its ambiguous class commitments, allowed Fidel Castro, at least for a while, to be different things to different people.... Fidel Castro had political designs that he shared with no one. They were pragmatic in the sense that although Castro wanted to make a radical revolution, he left it to historical circumstances, the existing relations of forces and tactical possibilities, to determine specifically what kind of revolution it would be, all along making sure that he would be in control."

The phenomenon of the benevolent leader who maintains tight control is part of a widespread political-cultural phenomenon in Latin America known as *caudillismo*, but as Farber notes, Castro was "a caudillo with political ideas" whose approach "did not involve a long-term strategic plan but rather a series of tactical adjustments and innovations by an intelligent revolutionary politician."[6]

The Revolutionary Struggle

Genuine revolutions such as this one are dependent not simply on dynamic individual leaders but also on cadres, vanguards, organizations, political and social movements, masses of people, classes, and social forces, as well as complex and contradictory political institutions and economic formations.

All these are part of Farber's account—although for those seeking the story in all of its fullness, there is more that must be sought in the works of Carlos Franqui, Robert Taber, Marta Harnecker, K. S. Karol, and others. One could also do worse than to utilize, along with such works, the 2003 anthology *The Cuba Reader*, splendidly edited by Aviva Chomsky and others.[7]

In the introductory remarks in his *Diary of the Cuban Revolution*, Franqui— one of the most radical of the revolutionaries (who later joined the ranks of anti-Castro dissidents)—writes: "And if we prevailed then over tyranny and domination, it was because the people joined in the struggle and became its real protagonist."[8]

Farber concurs—although with an interesting and perhaps problematical twist: "Although the social revolution and class struggle were *always controlled from above*, they were accompanied by mass radicalization and participation."[9]

This insistence on an invariable, one-way, top-down dynamic strikes me as questionable and certainly worthy of deeper investigation, but the mass nature of the revolutionary phenomenon cannot be questioned.

The important element of truth in Farber's "twist" is the fact that the mass revolutionary upsurge was not spontaneous but was dependent in large measure on intermediary formations, of which three were particularly important. An uncharacteristic gap in Farber's account is that there is only a fleeting mention of one major component of the revolutionary anti-Batista struggle, the student-based Revolutionary Directorate—although, in his defense, this formation turned out not to have the central importance of the other currents on which he focuses: the July 26th Movement (M-26) and the Popular Socialist Party (PSP, the "old-line" Communists).

Farber provides an informative and insightful analysis of the PSP—the serious limitations that made it incapable of providing serious revolutionary leadership, and the genuine strengths that made it almost indispensable when Castro and those around him came to power and decided on an uncompromisingly radical turn that guaranteed a collision course with the United States.

Although the ideology of PSP was, for many, synonymous with "Marxism," Farber correctly points out that this was a "crude Stalinist Marxism" promulgated by the one-party dictatorship of the Soviet Union from the time of the consolidation of Joseph Stalin's bureaucratic tyranny back in the 1930s.

In addition to representing schematic and dogmatic theoretical constructs and a strong tendency toward political opportunism, "Stalinism meant a contempt for principled and consistent democratic practices whether inside the party . . . or in society at large (dismissing the need for civil liberties and democracy under socialism as a bourgeois notion)."[10]

As Farber shows, the freewheeling nature of Castro's diverse M-26 proved far more capable of inspiring masses of Cubans and leading them into revolutionary struggle. He goes on to make an important point, however. "The Soviet Union and the Cuban Communists shared a bureaucratic approach to revolution that differed from both the classical Marxist approach and that of Fidel Castro." While authentic Marxism "posited a rising autonomous workers' movement struggling for its self-emancipation and that of its class allies," a traditional Stalinist Communist Party "defined itself as the representative of the working class regardless of the actually expressed views and wishes of that class and . . . felt free to substitute its own interests for those of the working class."[11]

In contrast, "Fidel Castro . . . was a tactical master at detecting the readiness of public opinion for whatever political steps he was contemplating," so that "the Castro-led forces came to power with a great deal of popular support, prestige, and credibility." Far from classical Marxism's "autonomous workers' movement" engaged in "self-emancipation," however, Castro's radical policies "moved from the leaders to the masses rather than the other way around. The various forms of the leaders' radicalism filtered in various ways down to the masses, who continued to support the various measures Castro periodically and unexpectedly produced after long sessions with close associates."[12]

Also on the political scene leading up to 1959, of course, were the more well-to-do anti-Batista moderates, with liberal-to-conservative ideological perspectives, who constituted the traditional political elite that had been sidelined by Batista's "Bonapartist" dictatorship. But with no mass base and an inclination toward safe respectability, such "leaders" could only be a significant factor because of their relationship with US economic and political interests and in partnership with popular struggles organized by others—in this case, M-26.

As Farber puts it, in seeking to be different things to different people, Castro's "behavior and pronouncements involved a great deal of secrecy and deception"—which meant "manipulating people and hiding his political agenda, with the purpose of dividing and conquering his actual and potential opponents," particularly those who would seek to block the radical trajectory of the revolutionary change to which he was committed. For example, "Castro's political dissimulation of his anti-imperialist politics significantly helped to delay U.S. hostility toward his movement while it was in opposition and, to a degree, after it came to power."[13]

"History Will Absolve Me"

To their extreme chagrin, the respectable moderates among the Cuban political elite and the anti-Batista business interests discovered all too soon (yet too late) that Castro had far more radical designs than they had bargained for.

Evidence of his social-radical intentions, though, was there from the beginning. Farber cites Castro's eloquent courtroom speech of 1953, when he was on trial for leading the failed assault of July 26th on the Moncada barracks, which had been meant to spark a national insurrection. That speech was turned into a pamphlet—*History Will Absolve Me*—meant to recruit people to the new revolutionary organization, M-26.

While addressed to "the people in general," it was also "more narrowly directed at the militant anti-Batista students and young workers who had not yet joined his group. Castro sensed that several thousand of these young people were ready to be brought into his nascent movement."[14]

The content of the speech, according to Farber, is not "class-based" and represents a "radical, non-socialist platform" typical of much of Latin American populism. But this strikes me as somewhat misleading. He offers a brief quote from the speech to give a sense of its tone: "When we speak of the people, we do not mean the comfortable and conservative sectors of the nation that welcome any regime of oppression, any dictatorship, and any despotism. . . . We mean the unredeemed masses to whom everything is offered but nothing is given except deceit and betrayal."[15] But it is worth looking at more of this revolutionary classic:

> In terms of struggle, when we talk about people we're talking about the six hundred thousand Cubans without work, who want to earn their daily bread honestly without having to emigrate from their homeland in search of a livelihood; the five hundred thousand farm laborers who live in miserable shacks, who work four months of the year and starve the rest, sharing their misery with their children, who don't have an inch of land to till and whose existence would move any heart made of stone; the four hundred thousand industrial workers and laborers whose retirement funds have been embezzled, whose benefits are being taken away, whose homes are wretched quarters, whose salaries pass from the hands of the boss to those of the moneylender, whose future is pay reduction and dismissal, whose life is endless work and whose only rest is the tomb; the one hundred thousand small farmers who live and die working land that is not theirs, looking at it with the sadness of Moses gazing at the promised land, to die without ever owning it, who like feudal serfs have to pay for the use of their parcel of land by giving up a portion of its produce, who cannot love it, improve it, beautify it, nor plant a cedar or an orange tree because they never know when a sheriff will come with the rural guard to evict them from it; the thirty thousand teachers and professors who are so devoted, dedicated, and so necessary to the better destiny of future generations and who are so badly treated and paid.[16]

True, *History Will Absolve Me* goes on to talk of the plight of twenty thousand small businessmen and ten thousand young professionals, but the greater emphasis of this particular brand of radical populism, as we can see, is only a step away from a class-struggle and anticapitalist orientation, and this is consistent with the ideological balance and social composition within the M-26 membership.

Farber acknowledges that "many of them seem to have been workers by origin or occupation," but he emphasizes that "very few had been active or even involved in trade union or working-class political organizations" and that the two thousand or so peasant recruits (responding to the M-26–initiated guerrilla war that spread in the mountains and rural areas after 1956), with a few exceptions, similarly "had little or no history of previously organized peasant struggles." He argues that this allowed Castro "to mold these men into faithful followers of his caudillo leadership," that this particular vanguard formation, "an inner circle of 'classless' men unattached to the organizational life of any of the existing Cuban social classes became Fidel Castro's political core."[17] As we shall see, however, the reality was more complex.

A new stage of the anti-Batista struggle had opened after 1956, once M-26 established a guerrilla base in the Sierra Maestra, proving too formidable a force for Batista's military to defeat.

Castro successfully sought "the formation and consolidation of a politically militant but socially moderate coalition to overthrow Batista and avoid alarming the United States," even though "Castro wrote privately to his confidante, Celia Sánchez . . . that when the current [anti-Batista] war ended, a bigger and much longer [anti-imperialist] war would begin against the United States."[18] Marx and Lenin, no less than José Martí, informed this vision of the Cuban Revolution's trajectory.

The Revolution's Course

Farber effectively challenges the common notion advanced by some US liberals and even elements of the Left that Fidel was leading a potentially "friendly" revolution that veered toward revolutionary extremism only because of the blind hostility of a short-sighted US foreign policy.

"The revolutionary leaders [of Cuba] acted under serious external and internal constraints but were nevertheless autonomous agents pursuing independent ideological visions," he argues, although the course of the revolution can be viewed as a "predetermined response to objective economic, social, and political conditions as understood and acted upon by men whose guerrilla experience conditioned them to act as realistic revolutionaries to survive."[19]

Farber offers a sense of the diverse and divergent elements in M-26 and among its allies, although in some passages of Carlos Franqui's bitter, contradictory but illuminating memoir, *Family Portrait with Fidel*, we get a clearer picture. Within M-26 was a cluster of those who "were staunch fidelistas and contributed to Fidel's mystique," inclined to back Castro in whatever tactical permutations he felt the need to pursue.

Among the others, "the strongest, most powerful group was that of the pro-Soviet comandantes," which included Raúl Castro, Che Guevara, and Ramiro Valdés; there was also Camilo Cienfuegos, who was "loyal to Fidel, but . . . followed Che and other Marxists." (Franqui, coming from a different M-26 current, praises Che's "force of will, talent, and sheer audacity" as a revolutionary leader, and also tells us that Che was "a sort of free-lance Communist," but that "his brand of communism" was tempered by his "independence of character and his sense of morality.") This pro-PSP/pro-Soviet current saw such alliances as essential to enable the Cuban Revolution to move forward to socialism and survive the consequent US hostility; they were not confident, even as late as 1959 (when the revolutionaries came to power), that Castro's commitment to radical revolution would withstand US pressures, and at times considered openly challenging the M-26 leader. Franqui, an ex-Communist, was part of an independent radical current (which included David Salvador, Faustino Pérez, Marcelo Fernández, and Enrique Oltuski), with a base among intellectuals and in the trade unions. No less anti-imperialist and anticapitalist than the current of Che and Raúl, Franqui and his co-thinkers were critical of the Soviet Union and hostile to the PSP, favoring instead what Franqui called "a free socialism and a humanist revolution." Elements of this cluster of independent radicals broke with Castro soon after the 1959 triumph (trade union leader Salvador ending up in prison) while others remained—Franqui breaking only in the late 1960s, Pérez and Oltuski remaining for the duration. There was also a smaller, less influential group of "democratic liberals" in M-26 that included Raúl Chibás, Huber Matos, Manuel Ray, and others with a background in the Ortodoxo Party. They were eliminated as a force (most went into exile, though Matos went to prison) when they opposed the revolution's radical turn and accommodation with Cuban Communists and the Soviet Union.[20]

As Farber emphasizes, "although [Castro] did not necessarily foresee membership in the Soviet bloc, he also did not preclude it a priori"; but when he concluded that the only way to advance the Cuban Revolution along the radical path that he had indicated in his 1953 courtroom speech was to align himself with the Soviet Union, he threw his weight fully to the M-26 current led by his brother Raúl and Che Guevara, and to an intimate working relationship with the PSP. As Farber notes, "Castro always resisted subordinating himself to any organizational apparatus," and he engineered the merger of the M-26, the Revolutionary Directorate, and the PSP into "his own ruling Communist Party . . . only in 1965, when virtually all the major social and economic changes in Cuban society had already been carried out under his personal leadership and control."[21]

These revolutionary changes led to a qualitative improvement in the lives of the majority sectors of the Cuban population specified in Castro's *History Will Absolve Me*, and their support for Fidel's leadership and general policies consequently endured for decades.

"A strategic and tactical continuity existed in Fidel Castro's leadership both before and after Batista's overthrow," Farber writes. "He knew or could anticipate that he could more or less take mass support for granted, since his radical measures would find support among those deriving material benefit from them." The revolutionary regime's radical course "alienated some sections of the upper and upper-middle classes, [but] it cemented popular support and definitively established that the revolution was dedicated to the material improvement of the working class and the poor." US business interests and the US government naturally responded with horror and extreme hostility to this turn of events, but as Farber notes, "the multifaceted U.S. opposition to the Cuban government that developed after May 1959 raised popular anti-imperialism" to almost unprecedented levels throughout the island, and—in stark contrast to other "third world" regimes seeking to stay on good terms with US corporations and policy-makers—"instead of quieting down popular anti-imperialism, Cuban leaders typically raised the ante and encouraged its development, often at massive demonstrations.[22]

Larger Contexts, Past and Future

Among the most interesting aspects of Farber's study involve his discussion of US foreign policy in relation to Cuba and also his discussion of the Soviet Union's shifting Cuban policy. Both discussions are characterized by a high degree of sophistication, with information drawn in both cases from a variety of sources, including previously inaccessible US government archives.

Regarding the interplay of policies of the US government and Cuba's new revolutionary regime, Farber comments that "an institutional analysis requires some overall notion of what kind of revolution, broadly speaking, the United States would and could have accepted in the Latin America of the 1950s and 1960s." Certain key US policy decisions that culminated in the breakdown of relations "were not errors at all but inflexible policies institutionally determined by the system of U.S. imperial commitments and business needs."[23]

Historically US-Cuban relations "represented *de facto* if not fully *de jure* colonialism," he observes, concluding that US policy toward the Cuban Revolution was obviously conditioned, first, by the need for "defense and protection of the political and juridical conditions necessary for the functioning of private property and capitalism, particularly insofar as U.S. investments in Cuba were concerned," and, second, by "the related but not identical Cold War aim of opposition to Communism, domestic or foreign."[24]

We have already noted the desire of Cuban revolutionaries to connect with the Soviet Union, to secure both protection against the United States and material assistance for the radical course they wished to chart for their revolution.

"The Soviet Union was guided by tactical considerations influenced by a number of factors, including the existing state of relations with Washington, the Soviet Union's fears of economic and military overcommitment to Cuba, and the gradually emerging pressures from Communist China and its effect on the Soviet Union's standing in the international Communist movement," writes Farber. While the Soviet Union "did not seem to have a strategically coherent approach to dealing with developments in Cuba," its leader Nikita Khrushchev tended to favor a policy that "pushed the Soviet Union into a proactive presence in the Third World" in a manner that would tilt the international relation of forces in favor of the Soviet Union. "The Soviet Union of the Khrushchev period typically supported Third World governments that broke with the West and adopted independent foreign policies, preferably tilting somewhat toward anti-imperialist, pro-Soviet positions." The Cuban Revolution, and especially its Marxist-influenced trajectory, were completely unexpected. Initial confusion and caution quickly gave way, however, to Khrushchev's buoyant embrace. "You Americans must realize what Cuba means to us old Bolsheviks," his emissary Anastas Mikoyan later confided to the US secretary of state. "We have been waiting all our lives for a country to go communist without the Red Army. It has happened in Cuba, and it makes us feel like boys again."[25]

Something odd happens, however, at the very beginning of the chapter in which the Soviet Union is discussed. Farber puts forward a theoretical generalization that strikes this reviewer as highly dubious. "By 1959, the Soviet Union, a relatively new imperial state, was involved in a serious conflict with the United States, the most powerful of all imperial states," he asserts. "Beyond the geopolitical elements underlying the clash between the two major powers, a major conflict existed between two competing modes of production: the traditional capitalist system represented by the United States versus a new class system based on nationalized economy administered by a Communist Party–dominated bureaucracy."[26]

There are several questions that can be raised about this. One deals with the characterization of what existed in the Soviet Union as "a new class system," which implies a certain durability that history has not confirmed. Unlike the class systems associated with ancient slave civilizations, feudalism, and capitalism—what existed in the Soviet Union failed to survive for even a century.

To equate the Soviet Union and the United States as "imperial states" raises additional questions, if one is to interpret this as involving the kind of economic expansionism traditionally associated with the Marxist conception of imperialism. US business interests were driven by a capital accumulation process (involving the voracious, unstoppable need for more and more investments, leading to more and more profits, necessitating more and more profit-seeking investments). This was inseparable from and necessary for the health of the US capitalist economy (i.e., the national interest), and this reality has necessarily guided the foreign policy of the US government.

These facts are consistent with the information and analysis provided in Farber's book. But the informative analysis he offers on the workings of Soviet foreign policy—while demonstrating a dictatorial regime's power struggle with the United States, with ample indications of a manipulative and opportunistic orientation and an absence of any concern for socialist democracy—provides no corroboration of anything in the USSR equivalent to the primacy of the US capital accumulation process.

One more question is raised by Farber's dubious generalization. According to the author, the development of the Cuban Revolution under Castro's leadership had "an elective affinity with the Soviet model of socialism," that it represented "a left-wing authoritarian populism that under existing circumstances evolved into a variety of Communist nationalism."[27]

Does this mean that what was established in Cuba is "a new form of class system" that deserves to be overthrown by the oppressed and exploited laboring masses? In wrestling with this question, it is worth giving attention to the descriptive specifics that Farber presents: "Castro's politics are inextricably bound with his *caudillismo*, by which I mean, among other things, the politics of blindly following the leader. This constitutes a major obstacle to raising the Cuban people's political consciousness and increasing their organizational autonomy." Farber does not claim "that the revolution was not popular or that it did not involve a radical social and political change," but he insists that "although the great majority of the population was encouraged to participate, it was not allowed to control or direct the revolution."[28]

This is hardly a new criticism. Two critical-minded supporters of the revolution, Leo Huberman and Paul Sweezy, made the point in 1969:

> The revolutionary leadership might have seen in this situation an opportunity to attempt the difficult feat of bringing the people more directly into the governing process, forging institutions of popular participation and control and encouraging the masses to use them, to assume increasing responsibility, to

share in the making of the great decisions which shape their lives. In practice, however, the relationship between government and people continued to be a paternalistic one, with Fidel Castro increasingly playing the crucial role of interpreting the people's needs and wants, translating them into government policy, and continuously explaining what had to be done, and what obstacles remained to be overcome.[29]

More than twenty years later, such knowledgeable and sympathetic observers of revolutionary Cuba as Janette Habel and Frank Fitzgerald offered detailed studies in which the same observations were repeated with ample documentation, and with calls for radical reforms to establish democratic control by Cuba's laboring masses over Cuba's political economy.[30]

Should those favoring socialism now urge a struggle for radical-democratic reform in Cuba, or a struggle of class-against-class, culminating in new social revolution? Actually, Farber seems to think, in fact, that capitalist restoration is Cuba's most likely future.

Today, from within Cuba itself, there are some revolutionary-minded elements—even in the Cuban Communist Party—who speak of "the Stalinism which contaminated us . . . [as] a contagious virus, in spite of which, and not without battles, the ideal of socialism was able to survive, because it was the very essence of the revolutionary process."[31]

These are the words of Celia Hart (daughter of two historic leaders of the Cuban Revolution, Armando Hart and Haydée Santamaría) in one of her many articles popularizing the ideas of Trotsky in her homeland. More recently, in an interview with French Trotskyists, she commented: "The interpenetration of the bureaucracy and the market economy, that's where the danger lies. We have to demolish the foundations of the bureaucracy, because it is on these foundations that the bourgeois class can develop—we saw in the USSR, in Poland, and elsewhere how the bureaucrats, who were managers, men of power, became owners, became capitalists."[32]

Actually, there is some overlap between this and the conclusion of Farber's book, which asserts that with Fidel Castro's death "a capitalist transition is highly likely to be led, as in the Soviet Union and China, by Cuban Communists and would restore . . . much of the power that the United States lost in Cuba almost fifty years ago." This and the ideological confusion that accompanies it will, he predicts, "be challenged by those upholding the legacy of Fidel Castro as well as by those trying to create a new revolutionary and democratic Left in Cuba."[33]

The question remains whether positive elements in the legacy of the Cuban Revolution are stronger than Farber is inclined to acknowledge and—

perhaps intertwined with revolutionary developments and counter-influences elsewhere in Latin America—will push aside bureaucratic afflictions and capitalist restoration, resulting in the ideal of socialism (the free association of the producers) being made real "as the very essence of the revolutionary process."

9.

Nicaragua

Revolution Permanent or Impermanent?

T he incredibly rich and complex revolutionary experience of late twentieth-century Nicaragua, a small Central American country then inhabited by three million people (almost six million in 2015), merits careful study by students of popular protest and revolution. The Frente Sandinista de Liberación Nactonal (FSLN—Sandinista National Liberation Front) led the fierce insurgency of 1978–79 that brought down the Somoza dictatorship. This triumph initiated a decadelong revolutionary process. It was a process that brought many gains to the country but also hardships, and ultimately it failed to realize the far-reaching goals that its initiators and supporters had envisioned. In 2006, sixteen years after being dislodged, a new FSLN government took power through elections—generating controversy about its very nature. To understand both triumph and failure, as well as the later controversy, one must explore not only the FSLN but also much larger forces that have shaped and limited it.

I. The Sandinista Revolution

To comprehend the roots and historical context of the Nicaraguan Revolution, one must go back to the early nineteenth century and even before.

Historical Background

The earliest roots can be found in the impact of the mercantile capitalism of the Spanish empire that colonized most of Latin America, including what is now Nicaragua, at the expense of indigenous peoples—most of whom became blended with the Spanish to form a mestizo majority, which became the bulk of the large peasantry and the small working class. When Nicaragua became independent from Spain in the early nineteenth century, its social structure was that which had been forged by the colonial experience. At the top was a local ruling class of landowner capitalists and merchant capitalists, whose decades-long feud with each other would be reflected in the competition of their respective political groups, the Conservative Party and the Liberal Party. This divided elite rested on top of the laboring majority of Nicaraguans. Also, each upper-class faction at various times sought to gain assistance from the British and then the US capitalists and governments in order to enhance wealth and secure state power in Nicaragua, which introduced another key element in the coming of the Nicaraguan Revolution.[1]

By the end of the nineteenth century, the United States was unquestionably the dominant power in the Western Hemisphere, but the so-called Open Door foreign policy precluded US government and business leaders from seeking to make Nicaragua an outright colony. Rather, they sought to advance their interests by ensuring the existence in Nicaragua of friendly governments through "gunboat diplomacy" that involved frequent military interventions throughout much of Latin America and the Caribbean.[2]

It was in reaction to such US military intervention that the plebian radical nationalist Augusto César Sandino led an immensely popular and very successful guerrilla war in the 1920s and early 1930s. His troops were made up of peasants and workers. Influenced by diverse ideological currents, Sandino explained to mine workers in 1926 "the sad fact that we were exploited and we ought to have a government really concerned for the people to stop the vile exploitation by the capitalists and big foreign enterprises." Sandino was able to outfight and confound US military forces, becoming a hero throughout Latin America and an international symbol of anti-imperialism.[3]

The most perceptive and influential foreign policy-makers in the US government concluded, by the 1930s, that such direct intervention into the political life of countries such as Nicaragua was becoming counterproductive. The so-called Good Neighbor Policy of President Franklin D. Roosevelt was a reflection of this change, but it had been initiated earlier under the Republican administration of Herbert Hoover, whose State Department personnel fashioned a new policy mandating an independent and constitutional Nicaraguan government, in which a stable two-party system (with the Liberal and Conservative parties) would be established, US military forces withdrawn (as Sandino demanded), the US interventionist pattern terminated, and a US-trained Nicaraguan National Guard established to maintain law and order and political stability. Then a durable "Good Neighbor" relationship could more effectively maintain US economic interests in the region.[4]

What happened was that (1) Sandino agreed to accept the new Nicaraguan government, (2) the US-trained head of the National Guard, Anastasio Somoza, had Sandino and many of his followers murdered, and then (3) Somoza kicked out the traditional Liberal and Conservative politicians and established his own family's forty-five-year rule of the country—thanks to its control of the National Guard—while always maintaining the facade of the US-arranged constitutional government. Although he was careful to adapt to and support all major aspects of US foreign policy, Somoza was not simply a US puppet. The US government was never happy with the way he had shunted aside the traditional bourgeois politicians in favor of his own dictatorship. But policy-makers in Washington, having abandoned the norm of direct military interventionism and understanding that Somoza had established political stability and on all major questions would be pro-U.S., concluded that Somoza was acceptable. As Roosevelt is said to have put it: "He's a son of a bitch, but he's our son of a bitch."[5]

By the 1940s, the United States secured 95 percent of Nicaraguan exports (chiefly bananas, tropical produce, mahogany, gold) and furnished 85 percent of its imports. The US-created Export-Import Bank loaned money for projects in Nicaragua, under imposed conditions of US control of them, and the Somoza regime encouraged agricultural and small industrial enterprises that fit into, and would not compete with, North American enterprises.

Just as Somoza was not a US puppet, neither was he a puppet of Nicaragua's capitalist class. Enjoying considerable autonomy and assuming a posture of being above the divisions in society, the dictator nonetheless ensured the stability of capitalist property relations and facilitated the rapid development of the capitalist economy. The Somoza family's strength always rested on their absolute control of the powerful and vicious National Guard. But they were accepted by the upper classes in part because they kept down the living standards of the masses. As old "Tacho" Somoza warned those among the Nicaraguan bourgeoisie who were not happy with him: "My opponents should remember that we, the better people, are only 6 percent; if trouble arises, the

94 percent may crush us all."[6] The upper classes in general, and leaders of the traditional opposition, were therefore generally prepared either to support, to compromise with, or at least to soften their opposition to the Somoza regime. This upper-class fear of generating popular unrest remained even in the face of the utter corruption and gangster-style business tactics represented by the regime of the final Somoza, known as Anastasio II, or "Tachito," which caused the relative autonomy of the regime to be replaced by resentful isolation even among the country's upper 6 percent.

Crystallization of Revolutionary Conditions

Yet the post–World War II economic development of Nicaragua generated a process of proletarianization that, in turn, created a social force capable of challenging the Somoza dictatorship. A basic economic infrastructure was created: electrification, highways, communications, port works, financial structures. This laid the basis for the intensive cultivation of cotton, a cash crop geared for the world market, which transformed Nicaraguan agriculture in the 1950s. Cotton quickly surpassed coffee, livestock, and sugar as the country's main export. There was also a significant expansion of light industry, especially chemicals, textiles, metal processing, and food processing.

Not only was there a growth in both the industrial and service sectors of the working class, but peasants were increasingly pushed into supplementing their income through wage labor. There was a dramatic increase in urbanization, with a growing informal sector that combined unemployment with occasional wage work plus petty commerce (selling chewing gum, lottery tickets, flowers, even plastic bags of water, etc., on the streets), sometimes traveling back and forth from city to countryside. The repressiveness of the Somoza regime—systematically violating civil liberties, holding down unions, failing to provide for the impoverished majority badly needed social services (health and sanitation, education, electricity, and so on)—increasingly alienated and radicalized growing sectors of the population.

By the end of the 1970s, 46 percent of the labor force was agricultural, of which about 70 percent was semi-proletarian (needing to supplement small landholdings with part-time wage work) proletarian (full-time, rural wage workers), or sub-proletarian (landless workers without stable employment). Among the economically active population in nonagricultural sectors, 9.6 percent were property owners (large, middle, and petty bourgeoisie) while 90.4 percent were non–property owners (18 percent constituting a relatively well-off, white-collar, and professional sector, and 73 percent consisting of more or less proletarian layers).

Analyst Carlos Vilas once termed these layers as Nicaragua's "working masses," stressing that those who made up this entity were far from being a traditional factory proletariat. Consider such different occupational categories as small landowner, agricultural worker, urban artisan, urban wage worker, unemployed worker, domestic servant, street vendor. Not only would one family contain all of these, but at different times one individual might be each of these things. The class realities in Nicaragua were fluid and complex. On the one hand, this could facilitate a certain cohesion among the so-called working masses of Nicaragua. On the other hand, it could contribute to a fluidity, a diversity, a greater range of contradictory qualities in their consciousness.[7]

The fact remained that for every layer of the working masses, living conditions were very difficult. According to studies by the United Nations, the standard daily caloric requirement for a human being is 2,600. In the 1970s the poorest 50 percent of Nicaragua's population (which enjoyed only 15 percent of the nation's income) averaged 1,767 calories a day—more than 800 below the requirement; the next 30 percent of the labor force (with 25 percent of the income) averaged 2,703 daily calories, a bare 100 above the minimum requirement. Taken together, roughly, this 80 percent constituted the working masses. The richest 5 percent of the population, with 28 percent of the total income, averaged a whopping 3,931 calories per day, with the "middle sectors"—15 percent of the population—getting about 32 percent of the wealth with an average of 3,255 calories per day. Only 1.1 percent of the Nicaragua population had completed all the years of primary education, and half the population lacked any formal any education at all. Of every ten deaths, six were caused by infectious diseases—that is, curable diseases. Forty percent of health care expenditures served less than 10 percent of the population. Workers who tried to form unions, peasants who tried to defend their interests, those in the barrios (poor neighborhoods) seeking better services, students organizing for educational reform—all could find themselves targeted for brutally repressive action by Somoza's National Guard.[8]

Revolutionary Leadership, Revolutionary Mobilization

It was the mobilization of these growing numbers and increasingly discontented working masses that brought down the Somoza dictatorship in 1979. This did not happen spontaneously. In the 1960s, and with increasing effectiveness through the 1970s, the Sandinista National Liberation Front posed an alternative to the Somoza dictatorship, to the reformist Conservative and Liberal oppositions, and to leftist groups, particularly Nicaragua's pro-Moscow

Communists of the PSN (Nicaraguan Socialist Party), inclined to compromise with bourgeois parties. In fact, FSLN founders Carlos Fonseca and Tomás Borge broke from the PSN precisely because that organization resisted applying to modern Nicaragua either the revolutionary tradition of Sandino or the more recent example of the 1959 Cuban Revolution.[9]

Formed in 1961 and evolving in an increasingly dynamic manner over a period of fifteen years, the FSLN drew from diverse ideological sources. Essential were the perspectives of Marx and Lenin, blended with the inspiration of the Cuban Revolution led by Fidel Castro and Che Guevara, and especially the plebeian radicalism of Sandino. Other influences among the Sandinistas were the Chinese and Vietnamese revolutions, as well as—for many—the radical Christian perspectives associated with "liberation theology" and, for some, the views of such revolutionary Marxists as Leon Trotsky. The first decade and a half of the FSLN was by no means overwhelmingly promising, particularly as efforts to apply the strategy drawn from Che Guevara's *Guerrilla Warfare* and popularized in Régis Debray's *Revolution in the Revolution*—the creation of small groups of revolutionary warriors in the countryside—resulted in initial disastrous losses. This eventually led to a serious split in FSLN ranks. Fonseca, Borge, and Henry Ruiz represented the Prolonged People's War tendency, based on the notion that a patient strategy of rural guerrilla warfare concentrated in the mountains would be the key to bringing down the Somoza dictatorship. Jaime Wheelock, Carlos Nuñez, and Luis Carrón led an opposition, the Proletarian tendency, which argued—in more classical Marxist fashion—that patient organizing around social and economic issues among rural and urban workers made more sense than armed struggle in the countryside.

In the same period, there was emerging a substantial bourgeois-led opposition to Somoza, which formed a liberal reformist coalition (in which almost all anti-Somoza organizations including the Nicaraguan Stalinists of the PSN participated) from which the FSLN remained independent. The coalition's most effective leader, *La Prensa* publisher Pedro Joaquín Chamorro, was murdered in 1978 by Somoza's henchmen—bringing further discredit to the regime and pushing more people, including significant sectors of the business community, into the overtly revolutionary struggle. The new opportunity intersected with yet another split in the FSLN—an Insurrectional tendency headed by Humberto Ortega, Daniel Ortega, and Victor Tirado López. They argued that patience was no longer a virtue, that a broad alliance of social and political forces were ready to support an armed insurrection capable of bringing down the dictatorship in the very near future.

This three-way split initially had a devastating impact on FSLN cadres. "The split and the process of reuniting were difficult times for us," Dora Maria Tellez remembered later. "An organization which many of us thought indestructible fell apart right before our eyes." She added: "Perhaps the division wasn't necessary, but the process that gave rise to it was—the internal discussion of our problems, our line, our strategy and its application to our people's struggle."[10] The fact that such internal discussion could not take place without splits relates to the top-down organizational structure and lack of democratic process in the FSLN, later criticized by some of the group's militants as "verticalism," which would also create problems between 1979 and 1990. The fact that there were three factions of the FSLN pursuing different orientations, however, turned out to have positive consequences. As Humberto Ortega commented: "Actually the efforts made by the three separate structures were furthering a single strategy for victory."[11] This fact led to an FSLN reunification in the months before the final victory, with a central leadership—the nine-person National Directorate—consisting of the three leading personalities from the three different tendencies.

The specifics of the FSLN's winning strategy had not been blueprinted beforehand but rather evolved from practical experiences in the course of the struggle, which actually involved a diverse number of struggles. In urban areas there were struggles of poor neighborhoods for utilities and social services as well as a proliferation of protests by students and youth, organized women, nurses, journalists, teachers, public employees, and construction and factory workers. Of special importance were peasant conflicts over the problem of access to land. All of this was increasingly interwoven with the work of the FSLN, involving the guerrillas in the countryside as well as armed fighters and clandestine organizations in the cities. Also essential in the forward surge of the struggle were a number of mass organizations, in many cases organized by FSLN militants and sympathizers—neighborhood councils, women's organizations, organizations of students and youth, trade unions, and peasant groups—all pushing for meaningful reforms while interlinked with forces pressing for revolutionary change. "With the development of the mass organizations, social hegemony began to change and Sandinismo replaced Somocismo as the legitimate force in the eyes of the Nicaraguan people," FSLN theorist Orlando Nuñez later commented. "The questioning of Somocismo waged by the mass movements had an important voice in the organized journalists of all the national media. This questioning began with a democratic character and progressively became revolutionary."[12]

The coherence of these diverse struggles in 1978–79 was ensured by the leading Sandinista militants, who were determined to maintain FSLN hegemony during and after the revolutionary process in order to move the revolutionary in a socialist direction. This was not evident to many observers and even some participants, who assumed that the influence of the Insurrectional tendency, with its commitment to broad-based alliances, meant a move away from revolutionary radicalism and toward a more moderate pragmatism. The Insurrectionals' founding document of 1977, asserted that "Nicaraguan capitalism, unlike that of Europe and other highly developed and industrialized nations, does not facilitate the immediate establishment of socialism," but it went on to say: "The fact that we do not immediately establish socialism does not mean that we support a bourgeois-democratic revolution." The document explained:

> The present struggle against tyranny should lead us to a true democracy of the people (not a bourgeois democracy) that will form an integral part of the struggle for socialism. Our struggle should never be left midway, even if conciliatory, bourgeois forces should strive for such a goal. The popular democratic phase should be, for the Sandinista cause, a means used for consolidating its revolutionary position and organizing the masses, so that the process moves unequivocally toward socialism. The necessary popular-democratic revolutionary phase, to be fulfilled once the tyranny is toppled, should not lead us to capitalism, reformism, nationalism, or any other development.[13]

This orientation guided the Sandinistas as they mobilized for the final victory. This was a victory won at a very high cost, however. The Somoza regime—fighting for its life against what seemed increasingly like an insurgent population—unleashed an incredible amount of military violence on the country's people and resources. Before the fighting had ended, there were as many as fifty thousand dead and several hundred thousand maimed or wounded. Before Somoza and a few others fled to Miami, they had left one-fourth of the people homeless and a good part of Managua's industrial district bombed out. On July 19, 1979, however, the FSLN and its masses of exultant supporters took possession of Nicaragua with high hopes for a better future.

Evolution of the Revolutionary Regime
When the Somoza dictatorship was finally demolished, the Sandinistas formed a revolutionary regime that at first included an alliance with the bourgeois liberal opposition. Violeta Chamorro, widow of martyred *La Prensa* publisher Pedro Joaquín Chamorro, and millionaire businessman Alfonso Robelo joined with top Sandinista leaders to head the government. It quickly became clear,

however, that the Sandinistas—basing themselves on the new revolutionary army and the popular mass organizations—were intent upon maintaining real political control. It also became clear to the would-be bourgeois allies that their own liberal-modernization orientation was incompatible with an FSLN ideology that blended the revolutionary nationalism of Sandino with the revolutionary socialist perspectives of Marx and Lenin (and a substantial dose of Castro and Guevara). The Sandinistas also saw their effort as part of an international revolutionary process that would soon triumph throughout Central America and beyond. As this process advanced, their long-range goal of bringing socialism to Nicaragua would be realized.

Chamorro and Robelo left the government to become leaders, respectively, of the peaceful, legal wing and the armed struggle wing of the anti-Sandinista opposition, which came to include a broad array of forces: veterans of the old Somoza National Guard; major sectors of the Catholic Church (although many Catholics, partly inspired by "liberation theology," were solidly pro-Sandinista); conservative businessmen and landowners; a narrow but vocal minority in the trade union movement aligned with the traditionally anti-Communist leadership of the AFL-CIO in the United States; oppositional politicians indignant at being pushed aside by the new regime; liberal reformers who believed that the Sandinistas' leftist goals and opposition to US foreign policy would place Nicaragua in a no-win situation in the "real world." Some of these oppositionists established close ties with the Central Intelligence Agency and received enormous quantities of money, while US politicians debated whether such aid should go primarily to the legal opposition or to the murderous contras seeking to overthrow the Sandinistas through violent civil war.

Jaime Wheelock asserted in December 1979, five months after the revolutionary victory, that "the state now is not the same state, it is a state of the workers, a state of the producers, who organize production and place it at the disposal of the people, and above all of the working class." Similarly, in 1983 Tomás Borge commented that "here political power is not in the hands of the businessmen," that "they will not resign themselves to losing political power," but that "this is a revolution of the working people. It is not a revolution of the bourgeoisie."[14]

We have seen that the FSLN fostered the growth of a number of mass organizations during the period of revolutionary struggle. In the period after the victory of 1979, these mass organizations became consolidated and initially enjoyed substantial popular participation. They became dominant in what was originally the central organ of the new government, the Council of State. Together with the FSLN, these pro-Sandinista forces controlled between 60 and

75 percent of the seats in that central governmental body. In the early period, the Sandinistas functioned in a National Patriotic Front, which included the Popular Social Christian Party, the Independent Liberal Party, and the Nicaraguan Socialist Party (the name of the country's old-line Communist Party). The rival Democratic Coordinating Committee rallied anti-FSLN forces— concentrated in the Nicaraguan Social Christian Party, the Social Democratic Party, and elements aligned with the Superior Council on Private Enterprise (COSEP)—ensuring that sharp debate, and some subsequent compromises, marked the deliberations of the Council of State.

Yet political debate became increasingly polarized, and critics of the FSLN regime predicted that it would seek to establish a one-party state similar to what had come into being in the wake of the 1959 Cuban Revolution. While there were some violations of civil liberties in this period—often due to the difficult conditions created by the US-sponsored contra war—there was more freedom of expression, greater political openness, more opportunity for popular involvement in the political process, and even greater opportunity to maintain critical and oppositional activity than ever before. The first honest elections in decades were organized in 1984 under the Sandinistas, with sharp critics of the FSLN, in six opposition parties on the left as well as the right, competing with it for the popular vote. Voter turnout was massive—all citizens sixteen years or older were eligible to vote, over 94 percent of whom actually registered, and 75 percent of these voted—with 67 percent of valid ballots cast (and 63 percent of all ballots) going to the FSLN.[15] This support was given, it can be argued, because the Sandinistas, through their statements and policies, represented the hope for a better life to large sectors of the working people and the poor of Nicaragua.

Serious campaigns were launched to provide health, education, and other much-needed social services to all sectors of the population, especially to those who had been excluded in the past. The concept of a "social wage" was advanced— the notion that all who were part of the country's "laboring masses," in whose interests the revolution had been made and whose labor was essential to the country's future, must with their families be assured the necessities of life: food, clothing, shelter, health care, cultural opportunities. There was a commitment to land reform and to the creation of public sectors of the economy—both policies having problematical aspects, but representing to many very positive moves in the right direction. Unlike previous regimes, the Sandinista government seemed committed to drawing the masses of people into discussions and debates about the future of the country and to giving them greater control over their communities. The army and the police, previously alien bodies that inspired fear throughout the population, assumed a popular character. Just as important, as we have seen, the government encouraged the endeavors of mass organizations: trade unions in the various urban workplaces and among agricultural workers, unions of peasants and small farmers, neighborhood committees, organizations of women and youth, and so forth, which possessed, and in some cases realized, the potential to give what had been oppressed sectors of the population a voice and an opportunity to take action for advancing their own interests.

The Sandinistas' economic orientation involved creating a "mixed economy" in their tiny country. This consisted of three ownership categories: state or collective property (accounting for 25 percent of agriculture, 40 percent of industry, 38 percent of internal trade, 100 percent of public services); a purely capitalist sector (accounting for 17 percent of agriculture, 30 percent of industry, and 12 percent of internal trade); and a sector of small and medium producers, in many cases organized into cooperatives (accounting for 58 percent of agriculture, 30 percent of industry, and 50 percent of internal trade). Of Nicaragua's gross domestic product, the state and collective property sector accounted for 45 percent, the capitalist sector accounted for 25 percent, and the small and medium producers accounted for 35 percent.[16] While much of the economy was in private hands, the government controlled all the banks, all access to foreign currency, and all jurisdiction over imports, and it set production quotas and designated priorities, leaving businessmen with far less power over their enterprises than had been the case in prerevolutionary times.

Capitalism was by no means overturned. The FSLN leadership believed that the Nicaraguan economy would unavoidably remain tied to, and dependent upon, the world capitalist economy for some time to come—and that, with the refusal of the Brezhnev regime and of the Gorbachev regime in the USSR to provide massive aid, it would not be feasible to take the Cuban road of rapid and generalized nationalization of the economy. Given this reality, the functioning of the Nicaraguan economy would in large measure continue to be dependent on the willingness of at least some Nicaraguan capitalists (and also foreign companies) to be involved in maintaining their enterprises. This need to maintain a mixed economy introduced sharp contradictions in the policies of the Sandinista regime and in the life of the Nicaraguan people.

Ultimately, the leaders of the Nicaraguan Revolution believed its success depended on the spread of revolutions beyond the borders of Nicaragua. Sandinista spokesman Omar Cabezas explained in 1986 that his government was in fact trying "to buy time and give time to our brothers and sisters in Central America [and undoubtedly elsewhere] to deepen and advance their revolutionary movements. . . . The most important thing," he stressed, "is to preserve power so that those [capitalist] socio-economic structures can be overturned at an appropriate time in the future; at a time [when] the objective and subjective conditions in Nicaragua and Central America are gathered."[17]

The Contra War

Another feature of Nicaraguan economic life under the Sandinistas was the US government's sustained assault on it. This included organizing and funding a massively destructive contra war, plus a nonmilitary legal opposition, in order to dislodge the Sandinistas. The US government also orchestrated a fairly effective effort to damage the economy through a blockade and the cessation of trade and assistance from many other countries and institutions that are part of the world capitalist economy. This, combined with the problems inherent in maintaining a mixed economy, increasingly eroded the quality of life of the masses of the people, as well as undermining the ability of the Sandinistas to maintain, let alone extend, the sweeping social reforms that had characterized the first years of the triumphant revolution.

Surveying the damage after Somoza's overthrow, the World Bank had observed: "Per capita income levels of 1977 will not be attained, in the best of circumstances, until the late 1980s." The World Bank initially recommended that "it would be highly desirable for the country to receive external assistance," adding that "any untoward event could lead to a financial trauma." The Reagan administration soon persuaded the World Bank to reverse its recommendation, and the administration also labored diligently to pile one "untoward event" upon another in order to traumatize the Nicaraguan economy.[18]

There was also the ongoing threat of a US military invasion, enhanced by official US statements as well as troop and fleet deployments in the region, and also by the successful US invasion of what had been the revolutionary island of Grenada. The Central Intelligence Agency oversaw the organization of a Nicaraguan counterrevolutionary army (the contras)—a project that by 1984 had absorbed hundreds of millions of dollars.

The contras, numbering more than ten thousand, had demonstrated (according to human rights organization Americas Watch) that they "were capable of controlling neither population nor territory for any significant period of time; they did not enjoy popular support, nor did they represent any serious threat to the stability of the Nicaraguan government." Economic losses from the contra war totaled around $3 billion. By 1985 more than half of the Nicaraguan government's budget was being diverted into defense spending. By

1984, more than 7,400 people had been killed. By 1990 the casualties had risen to almost forty thousand—including twenty thousand killed. The terror of contra operations was enhanced—in the words of the London-based Catholic Institute for International Relations—by "the torture and killing of civilians and the disgusting mutilations of the bodies of the victims." The contras especially targeted social services—health, education, rural cooperatives—through which the FSLN had generated popular support.[19]

In addition to devastating economic losses and the terrible loss of life, there were widespread and profound physical and psychological injuries. The Nicaraguan government argued before the World Court that "the impact of such a policy on a small, impoverished nation is simply incalculable." In fact, the World Court itself sharply criticized US policy: "The right to sovereignty and to political independence possessed by the Republic of Nicaragua, like any other state of the region or of the world, should be respected and should not in any way be jeopardized by any military and paramilitary activities which are prohibited by the principles of international law."[20] This resulted in the United States simply withdrawing from the World Court's proceedings in righteous indignation.

There was considerable truth, however, to the World Court's accusations. "We were a proxy army, directed, funded, receiving all intelligence and suggestions, from the CIA," one contra leader, Edgar Chamorro, later commented. "We had no plan for Nicaragua, we were working for American goals." Some US officials closest to contra operations complained, on the other hand, that contra leaders were "liars and greed and power motivated. . . . They are not the people to build a new Nicaragua."[21] But the point was not actually to build "a new Nicaragua." The primary goal was simply to engineer the erosion of popular reforms, the decline of living standards, the implementation of unpopular military conscription, and possible restrictions on civil liberties, which in turn would increase popular discontent and dissent inside the country. A US diplomat summarized the purpose of the contra war this way:

> The theory was that we couldn't lose. If they took Managua, wonderful. If not, the idea was that the Sandinistas would react one of two ways. Either they'd liberalize and stop exporting revolution, which is fine and dandy, or they'd tighten up, alienate their own people, their international support and their backers in the United States, in the long run making themselves vulnerable. In a way, that one was even better—or so the idea went.[22]

From this standpoint, the US-perpetrated contra war—much of it carried on secretly, illegally, and in violation of decisions made by the US Congress—was quite effective.

Decline and Fall

The high-water mark of Sandinista strength and popularity was reached in 1984, as indicated by several realities: the proliferation of mass organizations, combined with their institutionalization and integration into a radical-democratic Council of State; the campaigns and policies to advance the health, educational, economic, and cultural benefits of the "social wage"; and the embrace of the democratic elections of 1984, which seemed to provide the FSLN with a decisive victory and mandate.

Yet amid the electoral enthusiasm there was a deepening political polarization leading to the erosion of FSLN alliances with growing sectors of the country's sociopolitical culture. By the early 1980s, as already noted, there was a break with the Roman Catholic Church hierarchy that had, initially, been remarkably sympathetic to the Sandinista Revolution. The 1984 elections saw new breaks with political parties initially aligned with the FSLN—the Independent Liberal Party, the Progressive Social Christian Party, and the Nicaraguan Socialist Party. Even though the FSLN won a decisive electoral victory, a process had advanced that was destined to accelerate dramatically in coming years.

Also, as we have noted, this moment saw a dramatic escalation of US government hostility and a consequent intensification of the contra war, which would take an incredible toll on the country and destroy the initial socioeconomic gains of the 1979 Revolution. As these gains deteriorated, so did an important aspect of popular support for the FSLN.

Furthermore, there was a freeze and reversal of revolutionary developments in Central America and the Caribbean, on which the future of the revolution had depended. When the FSLN had swept to victory, there was also a revolutionary victory led by Maurice Bishop and the New Jewel Movement on the small island of Grenada, and in El Salvador a revolutionary coalition, the Farabundo Martí National Liberation Front (FMLN), seemed similarly poised to replace an unpopular regime with radical and anticapitalist forms of "people's power." In 1983, however, there was a violent split in the New Jewel Movement leading to the shocking murder of Bishop and his closest comrades, creating sufficient confusion to allow a US military invasion of Grenada that established a pro-US regime. And throughout the 1980s, massive US military and economic aid were poured into El Salvador in sufficient measure to ensure a bloody stalemate in which the FMLN could not be defeated but also could not take power. On top of this, the late 1980s erosion and collapse of the Communist bloc in Eastern Europe, ultimately culminating in the fall of the USSR, closed off possibilities of assistance from a once-significant adversary of US power.

There were, in addition, profound socioeconomic developments within Nicaragua that had an impact on FSLN prospects. We have noted that a process of proletarianization had led up to the 1979 revolution. By the late 1980s, an antithetical de-proletarianization process had been greatly advanced. This process involved some agricultural workers and impoverished peasants receiving land and shifting increasingly to a small-farmer mode of life and consciousness as opposed to a proletarian one. Also, the economic deterioration in the cities led to many workers losing their jobs and becoming more dependent on petty commercial activity through the informal sector. Indeed, the gains for the masses of the laboring poor that had been won in the 1979–84 period—improved health care, consumption, and living standards—were destroyed by inflation (which fluctuated between 1,000 and 37,000 percent), shortages, and austerity measures designed to shift resources toward economic revitalization. Increasingly, the inspiring rhetoric of the revolution began to seem empty.

The close connection between the government and the masses of working people dramatically eroded, and it was not only because of disappointment over deteriorating living conditions. To a large extent, the Sandinista-led mass organizations no longer remained instruments of popular expression but instead were used by the government to mobilize support for the war effort against the contras as well as contain militant class-struggle sentiments that could jeopardize relationships between the capitalists and the regime that were necessary for maintaining the mixed economy. Therefore, poor peasants might find the regime and the peasants' union aligned in opposition to the peasants taking over the large estates of rich landowners. Workers might find their union repeating exhortations of the FSLN's top leaders to demonstrate their patriotism and their loyalty to the revolution by working longer and harder, by avoiding strikes, by forgetting about wage increases, and so on.

The Sandinista regime seemed to feel that it could nonetheless keep the revolution on course, making necessary decisions and providing popular justifications for them, safeguarding (when appropriate) the radical principles that would once again be used to rally the people, and maintaining formal democratic trappings that—although not really giving power to the people—would be good for public relations. Despite all of the revolutionary rhetoric and all the formalized electoral machinery, the working masses were increasingly removed from meaningful decision-making.

The problem of *verticalism*—a top-down approach to governing—was not simply a product of the contra war. It was related to the top-down and undemocratic internal structure of the FSLN itself. Not long after the 1979 revolutionary victory, this approach created serious complications on Nicaragua's Atlantic Coast regarding the new regime's relations with indigenous peoples (the Miskito, Rama, and Suma peoples) and with Creole communities, which thereby created a base for contra activity. It also gradually eroded FSLN support among sectors of the peasantry, with similar effect. Verticalism also reared its head more than once in regard to women's rights, with the all-male *comandantes* overruling the efforts of their feminist comrades in deference to conservative social and cultural pressures.

Verticalism inevitably played out in abuses of power, ranging from personal arrogance to bureaucratic mismanagement to outright corruption, with some leaders using their political authority to accumulate material privileges. Such practices were especially problematical in a political movement purporting to represent the notions of power to the people and social equality. To the growing extent that such developments manifested themselves, the morale, credibility, and popularity of the FSLN were bound to suffer.

As an apparent countervailing tendency, the FSLN leadership fostered a wide-ranging national discussion on the development of a new constitution designed to create a relatively traditional form of parliamentary democracy. In fact, this was at best a development with mixed intentions from the standpoint of actual "rule by the people." It had already been preceded, in 1985, by the replacement of the Council of State, which was based on the visions of radical-democratic mass organizations—by a National Assembly consisting of representatives elected on a geographical rather than a class basis. This earlier development actually stemmed from the mass organizations having withered and become transmission belts for government policy rather than vibrant entities existing "of the people, by the people, for the people."

Harry Vanden and Gary Prevost, summarizing the work of a number of analysts, have argued that such traditional democratic forms as the National Assembly outlined in the new constitution are "only meaningful if real popular power lies below the form of representative democracy."[23] The gradual decline and evaporation of radical-democratic mass organizations threatened to give to Nicaraguan political life the same quality that characterizes the politics of many other allegedly democratic countries—expensive campaign glitziness, hollow sound-bite rhetoric, and politicians' remoteness from genuine popular control.

The decline of the mass organizations of the initial revolutionary period also had the effect of tending to channel dissatisfaction with the status quo into those organizations that stood in opposition to the FSLN. In spite of this, the FSLN enjoyed greater popular support than any other party in the country. But by the 1990 presidential and parliamentary elections, fourteen other political parties—left, right, and center—had joined together in a broad coalition to vote the Sandinistas out: the United Nicaraguan Opposition (UNO), with its attractive symbolic leader, Violeta Chamorro, running for president against the FSLN's Daniel Ortega. It was no secret that the US government was intimately involved in supporting and advising UNO, and US leaders made it clear that if Chamorro won, US economic pressures and threats of military aggression would cease. An Ortega victory, it was made clear, would have the opposite effect.

The FSLN leadership was convinced that its legitimacy would be validated by holding elections in 1990, which—according to what turned out to be faulty opinion polls—the FSLN was widely expected to win. The cost of preparing and administering the elections exceeded $15 million, and the Sandinistas spent $7 million on a fancy campaign in an effort to compete with the UNO campaign that was financed not only by Nicaraguan business and oppositional sources but also by the US government, which spent $12.5 million. All of this stood in stark contrast to the impoverished conditions faced by a majority of Nicaraguans, contributing to growing popular alienation from the FSLN. A campaign poster showing FSLN leader Ortega holding a child and looking visionary proclaimed: "Everything Will Be Better." More credible for many were such UNO assertions as "there will be no peace under a Sandinista government," and "only UNO can end the economic crisis."[24]

The election of February 25, 1990, brought an end to the revolutionary process that had culminated almost twelve years before. Although the FSLN leadership had expected yet another decisive victory, it was the UNO coalition that was swept into power. Chamorro secured 55 percent of the votes for president, with UNO taking fifty-one out of ninety-two seats in the National Assembly, and 102 of the country's 131 municipal councils. The election returns found the Sandinistas reduced to 41 percent of the vote—a critical drop of 22 percent since 1984—with only thirty-nine National Assembly seats going to FSLN delegates.[25]

Aftermath of Revolutionary Defeat

The FSLN declared, in accepting the UNO victory, that it would "support the government's positive steps" but promised "a firm and unwavering opposition to any measure intended to destroy [revolutionary] achievements and all that affects popular interests." It also indicated an intention—through revitalized mass organizations—of "governing from below" and predicted that "the change of government in no way means the end of the revolution."[26] The UNO victory did bring an end to the contra war, as promised, but its market-oriented, neoliberal policies did not fulfill the deep desires of the Nicaraguan poor and laboring classes for economic improvement. This seemed to offer opportunities for a revitalized FSLN.

In 1991, the FSLN held the first democratic convention in its history, where a rhetorical consensus formed around a condemnation of verticalism, losing touch with the masses, undemocratic practices, arrogance, corruption, and so forth. At the same time, the Ortega brothers and others around them—who were targets of criticism for those universally condemned sins—success-fully maintained control of the organization, with the deflection of critical discussion and organizational reforms resulting in a number of militants leaving the organization, some charging that the principles of Sandinismo had been betrayed. Along with this development, what remained of the mass organizations embarked to a dramatic degree on a trajectory of radical independence from FSLN control (although, as it turned out, they found it difficult to sustain themselves into the twenty-first century as independent entities).

Within the FSLN's top echelon, leaders articulated divergent commitments to revolutionary socialism and to global capitalism (to be humanized by modest social reforms). When the diverse UNO coalition inevitably disintegrated, the FSLN moved to secure a practical political alliance with pro-capitalist technocrats around Violeta Chamorro. Despite its expressions of concern over the continued decline of social and economic conditions for the majority of the Nicaraguan people, the FSLN no longer represented a revolutionary alternative to the status quo (an alternative that seemed to be precluded by the new international situation of the 1990s). This continued to be so when the re-constituted Constitutional Liberal Party—headed by an extreme conservative and former Somocista, Arnoldo Alemán—won 50 percent of the vote and the presidency (compared with Daniel Ortega's 38 percent of the vote). Alemán's administration went further than Chamorro's in reversing social and economic policies beneficial to the working masses, and it was marred by incredible corruption, yet the approach of the FSLN tended toward pragmatic accommodation. In fact, the Constitutional Liberals and FSLN, the country's two largest parties, cooperated closely in marginalizing other political parties to their mutual benefit.

It cannot be argued, however, that the radical spirit of Sandinismo vanished from Nicaragua as the twentieth century was coming to an end. "Like social movements across the Americas, Nicaragua's (formerly) Sandinista popular/mass organizations were adjusting to a reality characterized by the multiplication of social demands on an increasingly unresponsive state," write scholarly observers Pierre La Ramée and Erica Polakoff. "Confronted by the neoliberal state and the inexorable rollback of the modest gains in social justice and development experienced during the 1980s . . . the leaders and activists of the popular organizations are . . . the true 'Sandinistas'—the living legacy of the revolution, regardless of their current party affiliation."[27]

In 1991, a surprisingly positive assessment of the Sandinista Revolution was offered by former *New York Times* correspondent Stephen Kinzer, who had been a sharp critic of the Sandinistas for being "by many standards undemocratic" (although he acknowledged that they had "never resorted to the kind of savagery common in nearby countries" by regimes backed by the US government). His comments merit consideration in any evaluation of the revolution:

> By destroying the repressive apparatus of the Somoza family, the Sandinistas at least provided a basis on which a genuine democracy could be built. They made it possible for Nicaraguans to go peacefully to the polls and choose the kind of government they wanted, something unthinkable in Guatemala, El Salvador, or Honduras. Had they done nothing more than that, they would deserve a place of historic importance.
>
> Sandinista leaders could claim other successes as well. They encouraged Nicaraguans to take pride in their nationality and their heritage. They destroyed the rigid class structure that had confined Nicaraguans since time immemorial. And their policies . . . were based on the premise that government's greatest responsibility was to the poor and dispossessed. No Nicaraguan regime to come, even the most avowedly anti-Sandinista, would be able to ignore those advances.[28]

It is likely, however, that there will be ambiguity about the legacy of the Sandinista Revolution as long as the fate of the poor and dispossessed remains unresolved.

II. Nicaragua in the Twenty-First Century (2015–17)

In the twenty-first century, the ambiguities about the legacy of the Sandinista Revolution have certainly increased, just as the fate of the poor and dispossessed have remained unresolved. Neither efforts by dissident Sandinistas to establish a substantial political presence nor the various mass organizations that some projected as "the living legacy of the revolution" have proved to be particularly durable. On the other hand, in a remarkable turnabout, after sixteen years of disappointment and suffering among the great majority of Nicaraguans, and after sixteen years of persistent organizing and shrewd maneuvering, Daniel Ortega's FSLN took power in 2006 after he won the presidential elections with a 38 percent plurality. In his inaugural address, Ortega proclaimed "the second stage of the Sandinista revolution." In the 2012 elections, the FSLN secured a 62 percent majority for the presidency, and a decisive majority of the seats in the National Assembly. "The Sandinista Revolution Continues!" read the headline of one news story. Another insisted: "Daniel Ortega Is a Sandinista in Name Only."[29]

To find one's way through the ambiguities, one must look at what happened to the revolutionary vanguard as well as at the underlying social and economic realities shaping Nicaragua's destiny.

The New FSLN

The FSLN suffered serious of splits in the 1990s, as Daniel Ortega labored to reimpose a verticalist internal regime and realize his vision of retaking power and this time holding it. His orientation blended a rhetorical leftism with a ruthless pragmatism that could not afford or tolerate the internal debate and questioning inseparable from a truly democratic FSLN. Combined with this was what many saw as a material corruption related to "*la piñata*" (a slangy reference to a distribution of "goodies" and what one militant later termed "the original sin" of the defeated Sandinistas). After the 1990 electoral defeat, but before the FSLN government stepped down, there was a debate inside the upper circles of the FSLN. Should they be prepared to defend the state and cooperative property, initially created through confiscations from wealthy contras (valued at $1.5 billion), from a now-inevitable privatization to be inaugurated by the incoming Chamorro government? Or should they transfer as much property as possible to leading FSLN personnel? The second course was followed, justified by a rationale that the property would be transferred to the FSLN itself for safekeeping until a revolutionary regime returned to power (a plan never realized, as it turned out). The enriched pragmatists around Ortega also "assumed that in order to survive the Sandinistas had to employ the same means and morality as their opponents," as one critical comrade later put it. In the face of all this, there were brushed-aside protests, flurries of angry resignations, and waves of expulsions, through which a new FSLN was forged.[30]

Some of the most prominent FSLN dissidents formed the MSR (Sandinista Renovation Movement) but, suffering from a lack of political clarity, they proved unable to build a coherent force—not able to "recruit the poor, the peasants, the workers, nor mount a significant electoral challenge." Such were the observations of Orlando Nuñez, who made his peace with Ortega and for whom he became a prominent ideologue. The bitterness among anti-Ortega Sandinistas was no substitute for a clear political program. After several ineffectual years attempting to orient to the FSLN from the outside, the MSR moved in the direction of forming alliances with forces that had been long-time Sandinista foes (including some fairly conservative groups, such as the Independent Liberal Party), which caused some militants to pull away. As it turned out, the Ortega-led FSLN would make compromising alliances no less dramatic, but they showed more impressive results than those shown by the dwindling MSR.[31]

As Nuñez noted, it was Ortega's organization, with its mass base and substantial resources, that proved capable of actually vying for power. But this was certainly not the force that had made the 1979 revolution. Veteran FSLN militant Mónica Baltodano, who broke both from and the FSLN and the MSR, explains: "The FSLN itself is just an electoral franchise. Nicaragua no longer has an organization of revolutionaries with critical thinking, a leftist organization. This particular mutation has been very profound: the autocrat has used money to subject the leaders of the past and present, making them submissive." The internationally renowned revolutionary writer Eduardo Galeano would refer to the Ortega's FSLN loyalists as those "who were once capable of risking their life [but] are now incapable of risking their positions." Baltodano concludes: "With that they liquidated the philosophy and ethics of Carlos Fonseca, who had proclaimed ethics as a heritage handed down by Sandino to the FSLN leaders."[32]

A Strategy for Taking and Keeping Power

Yet Ortega and those around him definitely had a multifaceted plan for retaking—and retaining—power. And in this he proved more astute and capable than critics from the left and the right. As Sergio Ramírez, FSLN vice president in the revolutionary "good old days," wistfully mused, "Ortega outsmarted us all."[33]

One facet of the plan involved an understanding of the nature and dynamics of the bourgeois opposition that would replace the FSLN government, and the negative achievements of which it would be capable once it took power, reversing FSLN policies that had been beneficial to substantial numbers of Nicaraguans. Maintaining the FSLN's organization and its mass organizations would be essential for taking advantage of the popular dissatisfaction resulting from such negative achievements. But it would also be necessary—and possible—to reach out to elements within this opposition, and to elements of the opposition's own base, to bring shifts in the constellation of power within the country. Such shifts would allow the return of an FSLN government. The policies of such a new

FSLN government must build greater popular support, either by including or neutralizing old enemies. Crucial for the regime's survival in a capitalist world would involve being adept at playing on contradictions and complexities within that world and adapting fully (in a manner incompatible with the old Marxism initially prevalent within the FSLN) to capitalism itself.

After the FSLN government was turned out in 1990, Ortega and his co-thinkers foresaw that the governments of the old bourgeois political parties would not fare well. There were three succeeding governments: the ineffectual UNO coalition of Violeta Chamorro, the fantastically corrupt regime of Arnoldo Alemán of the Constitutionalist Liberal Party (PLC), and finally the administration of Enrique José Bolaños. This third government, headed by the man who had served as Alemán's vice president, went after Alemán for being corrupt—which resulted in Bolaños being kicked out of the PLC. In 2004 he formed the Alianza por la República (APRE, Alliance for the Republic) a politically unsuccessful formation that aligned with the Nicaraguan Liberal Alliance (ALN) in the 2006 elections but went down to defeat as Ortega's FSLN once again swept into office.

Chuck Kaufman of the pro-FSLN Nicaragua Network can certainly be expected to give a hostile summary of the sixteen-year period of non-FSLN rule: "Free education and health were eliminated. Public employee jobs were cut to the bone. The backbone of Nicaragua's economy, peasant farming, was starved for lack of government credit. The result was displaced farmers and desperate families who served to provide cheap labor for foreign sweatshops." As another critic commented, for the rich there were "free trade zones, malls and motorways"; for the poor, "illiteracy, malnutrition and disease." The *Guardian*'s Rory Carroll, hardly an Ortega fan, offers a succinct description of these wretched years: "Corruption blossomed and the poor were forgotten. Jobs were scarce and most people scrabbled on less than $2 a day." A line from an Ortega campaign speech resonated widely: "We've had 16 years of these democratic governments, and what have they given us? They've turned us into beggars! They've plundered the people and robbed from our youth."[34]

Ortega's FSLN—with its old revolutionary rhetoric, its residual presence in sectors of the state apparatus, its continuing control of many of the old mass organizations, and its mass voting base—was able to pose as representing a credible alternative. But it was not interested in a repetition of the earlier scenario in which its enemies would join in a coalition to once more turn it out of power. "By forging alliances with his former enemies," Stephen Kinzer noted, "he has built a regime that appears likely to remain in power for a long time."

Especially important were increasingly effective efforts to win over the traditionalist hierarchy of the Catholic Church (embracing the infusion into the political discourse of a relatively conservative Christianity with a "pro-family" social agenda that strictly banned all abortions, opposed gay marriage, and so forth). Persistent bridge-building with former contras, from the poorest peasant to the wealthiest landowner, became another priority. The FSLN also prioritized making three deals with the PLC: (1) to adopt legislation marginalizing political forces aside from the FSLN and PLC; (2) to protect Alemán from paying the price for his immense corruption, while protecting Ortega from being prosecuted for the sexual abuse of his own stepdaughter; and (3) to carry out far-reaching constitutional reforms that would make it easier—eventually—for the FSLN to win elections and enhance its power when in government. And the message was conveyed to the business community (including in the United States) that not only would the FSLN regime have no intention of overthrowing capitalism, but it would also accept the strictures of the International Monetary Fund and World Bank and foster a business-friendly climate.[35]

Social Reform in a Capitalist World

The other key to maintaining power was shoring up the FSLN's mass base. When Ortega returned to the presidency in 2007, his government's policies evolved along several tracks that greatly enhanced its chances for survival. One involved continuing the orientation of either winning over enemies or marginalizing them, of course. But no less important was carrying through, in modest but meaningful ways, on the radical-populist promise that had been embedded in the Sandinista program from the beginning. Even sharp critics acknowledged that Ortega's government "has made some progress in addressing the needs of the poor. Examples in the areas of education and health include reducing the illiteracy and infant mortality rates, and providing free access to health care." A more supportive Katherine Hoyt emphasized "the provision of food, transport and energy subsidies for the poor. With free school meals, these have allowed Nicaragua to reduce malnutrition," assertions backed by more than one observer. Hoyt also reported that infrastructure projects "have included the construction and improvement of 6,000 kilometres of roads and new bridges connecting the Pacific and Caribbean coasts," and that "much work has also gone into improving water systems, providing clean water to hundreds of thousands of people."[36]

Maurice Lemoine reported "tens of thousands of poor Nicaraguans given 854,000 sheets of zinc by the government to mend their leaky roofs," adding

that hundreds of Managua residents benefitted as well from a dignified housing project that built affordable homes in place of the ruins left from the 1972
earthquake. He also told the story of Yaira Mayorga, who used to live in the
ruins of an old building. "She and 360 neighbors, nearly one-quarter of whom
say they are 'non-Sandinistas,' now have real homes: 'Look at my beautiful
house!' she said." He also cited the case of Rosalia Suárez, "one of the 80,000
female beneficiaries of the Zero Hunger plan who was given a cow, a pig and
six hens: 'My cow has already had two calves. I sell the milk we don't drink, my
children have eggs to eat ... Before that, we had nothing.'" Lemoine pointed to
"the many women, including single mothers, who have used zero-interest loans
to set up bakeries, small businesses selling *nacatamales* (stuffed corn cakes) or
tortillas, or establish cooperatives." Although there have been charges of voting irregularities that have contributed to the dramatic rise in FSLN election
totals, there was also an obvious feeling on the part of many working-class and
peasant voters that the government is on their side.[37]

"The strength of this regime lies in the country's poverty," one critical observer, Arturo Cruz, noted, adding that Ortega has become "a father figure for
the campesinos—he can resolve their needs." Often this adds up to "knowing
how to distribute the scarcities with more abundance than other politicians."
In chronically impoverished Nicaragua, expectations among the majority are·
modest. "It can be resolved for many people with a few pieces of roofing tin
and a handful.of nails. The voter thinks, 'Now I won't get wet.' And when it
rains he thinks of Ortega."[38]

At the same time, Ortega and his wife, Rosario Murillo (a political force
in her own right), openly and ostentatiously present themselves as devout
Catholics, interweaving Catholic social teachings (including prohibition of
all abortions) with other pronouncements and policies. "These days, Cardinal
Miguel Obando y Bravo, an old opponent from the Reagan years, appears ·
alongside Ortega and Murillo in public, blessing whatever they do," notes
journalist Jon Lee Anderson. One FSLN cadre in Managua, Lucy Vargas, observes: "In many countries, abortion is not restricted, but they don't look after
women and children's health, and many of them die. Here, we help women, if
only by providing free healthcare." A former FSLN official adds: "The conservative peasants who thirty years ago may well have shouted 'Long live Reagan'
may today shout 'Viva Ortega.'"[39]

The Reagan-Bush governments of the United States had previously undermined and blocked—"by any means necessary"—Sandinista financial ability to
implement such beneficial policies, a hostile goal decisively achieved with the

collapse of the USSR and Communist bloc. Despite continuing US hostility, however, a shifting international situation now opened up new financial lifelines that made possible the sweeping social reforms. While US global power is still quite strong, new developments have brought relative decline. The global economic downturn and crisis in the first decade of the twenty-first century, combined with increasing competitive dynamics among the most powerful capitalist countries, have certainly contributed to the decrease of US hegemony, as have disastrous and debilitating military interventions in Iraq and Afghanistan.

Within this new context, leftist insurgencies in Latin America caused a number of left-nationalist governments to take power and to form a new political-economic power bloc, initiated by Cuba and Venezuela—the Alianza Bolivariana para los Pueblos de Nuestra América (ALBA—Bolivarian Alliance for the Peoples of Our America). Russia under Vladimir Putin, as well as Iran and (before its overthrow) the regime of Muammar al-Gaddafi in Libya, provided additional potential allies in the global arena. Especially important was the People's Republic of China, which had now become a universally acknowledged world power of the first rank and a keystone of the global capitalist economy. Not only did this new international reality provide space within which Ortega's FSLN could reconquer and hold power in Nicaragua, but especially thanks to the oil-rich and radical Venezuelan government of Hugo Chavez, an annual $500 million of life-giving aid could now flow to the Ortega regime, making possible the economic projects and social programs generating such widespread popular support.[40]

This was supplemented by a proliferation of foreign investors whose interest in making profits in Nicaragua would generate further development that allowed for the uptick in the country's economy. This was possible because the Ortega regime—despite its oft-repeated slogan of "Cristiana, Socialista, y Solidaria" (Christianity, Socialism, and Solidarity)—had committed itself fully and intimately to a pathway of capitalist development. A central "pillar of the new regime is big business," writes Stephen Kinzer. "As an anticapitalist revolutionary, Ortega had confiscated hundreds of farms, factories and other assets. Many businessmen fled the country. Now Ortega counts them among his closest allies. He recently pushed a tax law through Congress giving a host of concessions to the wealthiest Nicaraguans and foreign investors. One provision allows the tax-free importation of yachts and executive helicopters. The flood of foreign investors now includes behemoths such as Cargill, the agro-industrial conglomerate that recently unveiled a 'master plan' aimed at making it one of Nicaragua's major food producers and distributors."[41]

Traveling on the Capitalist Road

Mónica Baltodano notes that "the economic pragmatism shown by the FSLN with respect to privatizations and neoliberal policies was fully displayed" from the beginning of Ortega's return to office, with a "rapprochement process with the other pillar of national power: the heads of big business grouped under the Superior Council of Private Enterprise (COSEP) umbrella," involving an acceptance of privatization and neoliberal policies. She insists that it is "a symbiosis rather than an alliance because what defines the nature of the current regime is that its main mission is to create or strengthen the market economy conditions, buttressing big capital, while handing out crumbs to the poor to keep them pacified."[42]

Daniel Ortega's speeches are sometimes peppered with anticapitalist and anti-imperialist rhetoric. Yet his brother Humberto (onetime guerrilla fighter and FSLN minister of defense) has cautioned that people shouldn't pay too much attention to this, because "one thing is discourse for the political clients, and another thing is what the reality shows you are doing." Policies of the new FSLN, according to critics from the left, have in fact involved far-reaching adaptations to neoliberalism, highlighted early in the party's reascension by two indicators: "First, the FSLN did not oppose a free trade agreement when it was negotiated by President Bolaños, and did not attempt to reject or renegotiate it once it took office in 2006. Second, while the Ortega government has received massive financial support from Venezuela, it has channeled it through the Sandinista business sector rather than through the state." Observers friendly to the FSLN have noted the same thing: "Foreign investors and organizations such as the International Monetary Fund and the World Bank cannot fault the way Nicaragua has been governed over the last five years. The private sector—which includes some very rich Sandinista entrepreneurs, among them Ortega—has been favored. It has even been able to take advantage of the government's strategic decisions: by joining ALBA and turning to South America, the government has opened up new markets." José Adán Aguerri, president of the big-business confederation Consejo Superior de la Empresa Privada (COSEP—Superior Council on Private Enterprise) noted approvingly that "there is not a single law that the Sandinista government has passed that has not been consulted on first with us in the private sector," adding that in terms of "non-intervention in the private sector," Ortega's government "is ranked No. 8 in the world." Tax policies, too, favor the wealthy: leftist critic Mónica Baltodano notes that fiscal policy is still regressive, based on indirect taxes, "which basically punish the poor and middle classes, while the wealthiest are privileged with exonerations and exemptions."[43]

As early as 2006, one conservative observer, Emilio Álvarez Montalván, commented with grudging admiration: "Ortega has turned his movement into a buffet lunch and everyone is invited: conservatives and radicals, Sandinistas and anti-Sandinistas, pro-Americans and anti-Americans," adding that "the essential question people are asking themselves is if Daniel Ortega has really changed." One man who decided that perhaps he had "really changed" was Jaime "the Godfather" Morales, a wealthy former contra leader whose luxurious home had been confiscated for Ortega's personal use and who became Ortega's vice president, serving from 2006 to 2012. This unlikely alliance was explained by FSLN leaders as part of a policy of "reconciliation," although another old adversary of Ortega's, Edén Pastora, observed that "reconciliation is just a synonym for opportunism." Pastora had been a prominent Sandinista up to 1982—then, in opposition to the revolution's radicalization, went into armed opposition, joining the contras. (He was the famous target of a failed FSLN assassination attempt in which a bomb killed and maimed a number of aides and journalists.) By 2010, however, he also reconciled with Ortega and took a position in the government, admiringly commenting (with special reference to a major business deal with the Chinese): "None of the previous Presidents had Daniel Ortega's *hormones*. Strength and political ability are needed to carry out the job."[44]

One critic of the regime has argued that "the FSLN has economic interests in various sectors of the economy: tourism, construction, financial sector, agricultural production, trade, services and petroleum products, among others. This has facilitated it [in] reaching agreements with Nicaragua's traditional big capital and leading families, which has undermined the transformative potential of the FSLN." But this hardly captures the full extent of what has happened. Baltodano, writing in 2014, noted that 8 percent of the Nicaraguan population control 46 percent of the country's wealth and that the number of multimillionaires has been growing—from 180 to 190 between 2012 and 2013 alone. These multimillionaires include prominent FSLN figures, although some argue that their business success is nothing to be ashamed of. "If there is a free market, there needs to be a system in which people are free to get rich, so the poor can stop being poor, so the poor can become middle class and the middle class can become business owners and be better off," insists Humberto Ortega. Having broken the economic stranglehold of a small ruling class, he adds, the Sandinistas can become vital "new actors" in today's modern free-market economy. Not all Sandinistas are millionaires,

of course, although salaries among the upper levels of the FSLN are significantly higher than the incomes of the common worker. "Roberto Rivas, the
head of the Supreme Electoral Council, earns more than 17 times what the
average Nicaraguan worker does," points out Alejandro Gutiérrez. "Paradoxi-
cally, Orlando Nuñez, chief architect of Ortega's anti-hunger and anti-poverty
programs, earns 12 times the salary of the average Nicaraguan."[45]

The implications of what is described here go far beyond a simple contradiction between the old Sandinista and socialist ideals and present-day realities of inequality. As Baltodano notes, "Ortega and his group are with big
capital because they themselves are now an important capitalist group and the
government represents its community of interests with the traditional oligarchy and transnational capital." But she goes on to point to the more essential
aspect of the new reality:

> The leaders of the big businesses affiliated with COSEP, who congratulate
> themselves for having gotten five years of salary agreements that benefit them,
> 68 laws by consensus and 39 models of public-private alliances in these seven
> years of the Ortega government . . . don't say a word about the interests of the
> workers, peasants, small and medium businesses or the middle classes among
> all these accomplishments. So we can see that the "bourgeois State" has been
> consolidated and the state institutions are obeying *the logic of capital*.

The phrase I have italicized here has profound importance. Baltodano ac-
idly notes that "the wealthiest are obtaining the greatest benefits of this 'Christian, socialist and solidary' model." But she also acknowledges that the sincere
defenders of the current FSLN (foreign supporters plus a strong residue of sincere and idealistic cadres in Nicaragua) are certainly describing reality when
they argue that "there are benefits for the poor." Yet these gains are built on sand,
given the logic of capital that guides the economy. "The private sector generates
96% of the GDP," she notes (which is "totally the opposite of the Sandinista revolution's project, in which the public sector was hegemonic"). The state's
institutions are controlled by a layer of bourgeoisified "Sandinistas" who are
interlinked with a national and transnational bourgeoisie. "A symbiosis between
them [is] based on the interests of the 'free' market, which prohibits, rejects or
fights any regulation." Which means that the new FSLN has established a government "incapable of promoting a socialized vision of the economy."[46]

After taking power in the twenty-first century, the Ortega regime was
able to rely on vital and generous support from the leftist government of Venezuela, allowing for modest but meaningful reforms that secured a mass base
sufficient for mobilizing the votes to keep the regime in power—at least for

a time. Not only were there no guarantees about the permanence of this arrangement, however, but the death of Hugo Chavez and the growth of problems and instabilities in Venezuela raised questions about the future.

Some feel this has given urgency to the remarkable push by the Ortega government to undertake an immense project of building a new Nicaraguan Canal. The waterway, running between the Atlantic and Pacific Oceans and rivaling the Panama Canal, is projected for completion in 2019. With support from the Nicaraguan and Chinese governments, an agreement was signed in 2013 by Daniel Ortega and Wang Jing, president of the Hong Kong Nicaragua Canal Development Investment Company (HKND). The terms of the agreement guarantee Nicaragua receipt of $1 million each year beginning immediately, and also receipt of 10 percent ownership in the company each decade for fifty years, at which time it would own 51 percent of the canal, with the original agreement up for renewal for another half-century. In a 2013 statement, an HKND spokesman explained the anticipated results of the canal in this way: "Nicaragua will become by far the richest country in Central America—and that will affect the entire region. Investment in this project is three to four times the GDP of Nicaragua, there will be an effect of full employment and prosperity." Multiple questions have been raised—regarding the canal's technical feasibility, actual profitability, and environmental impact, as well as (especially because of lack of transparency) what is or is not being given away to the Chinese investors. Defenders of the FSLN have responded: "Opposition parties, including those of former Sandinistas, are scared to death that the FSLN will continue to increase employment and decrease poverty. They are concerned that development spurred by the canal will increase the FSLN's popularity and further marginalize their own electoral ambitions."[47]

One relatively conservative opponent, Antonio Lacayo, once a senior official in the Chamorro regime, has offered a fairly negative analysis:

> Daniel can see the disaster that is coming in Venezuela. So he looks around. It's not a long list: there's Russia, China, Iran. With Iran, there was nothing to get. From Russia, he got some buses and some reconnaissance planes. So Daniel decides to attract China to Nicaragua—to "defend" it from the U.S., and to contribute economically. How does he do it? By offering the Chinese a hundred-year concession to do whatever they want.[48]

Edén Pastora, on the other hand, argues that the benefits will be transformative:

> The opposition calls it a surrendering of national sovereignty, but investors need security for their investment. And not a single foreign soldier is coming

to Nicaragua! What really bothers them is the prestige that this signifies for Daniel Ortega. Keep in mind: this will change the economy of the world. The natural resources won't have to go around Cape Horn anymore, but come straight through here to China, on megaships! There will be two-hundred-ton trucks doing earthmoving and specialized drivers earning a thousand dollars a day! . . . There are going to be railroads, refineries, satellites, hydroelectric plants, airports, and over thirty-seven social projects—all of it achieved in an atmosphere of freedom and democracy, without even so much as a tear-gas cannister fired, without persecuting anybody. In five years, Managua will be a canal city, the most beautiful of Central America.[49]

It remains to be seen whether the sort of Marxist analysis articulated by Mónica Baltodano can be made irrelevant by the projected wonders of the canal. Of course, she is still animated by the Sandinista vision of old:

> We Sandinistas struggled to give workers and peasants direct control of the wealth so they could manage it and grow, develop and be subjects of their own transformation. What we have now is a compassionate socialism, in which things are done for the poor through charity, with gifts or handouts that link grassroots religiosity to power, like the long lines of the poorest people before the Púrisima altars where the government gives them some food. The slight reduction of poverty that some indicators point to has been achieved with programs that allow the poor to receive something immediately: sheets of zinc roofing, farm animals, seeds . . . but that doesn't imply any in-depth transformation of the material conditions in which they live so they'll stop being poor.[50]

Yet in the present moment, there are no longer significant forces mobilized around the vision to which Baltodano gives voice. Journalist Jon Lee Anderson suggests that in the new Nicaragua, "past allegiances, even mortal rivalries, mean nothing; the only important things seem to be power and profit." He describes a discussion he had with Victor Tirado López, one of the old FSLN comandantes: "Of the Sandinista revolution, there is nothing left—just projects that were unfinished," Tirado said. "If it hadn't been for us, there wouldn't be this new epoch, this new country. But the ideology—the Marxism and all that—that's history; it's over." Baltodano agrees: "Critical thinking—Marxism, which was the 'intellectual sword' of Sandinismo, to evoke Rosa Luxemburg's phrase—has been replaced with the most corroded religious ideas."[51]

The Regime Today

The global performance of capitalism in the twenty-first century seems to militate against stability, certainty, and harmony. And there remain those inequalities and consequent tensions between the "haves" and the "have-nots" that have been intensifying in so many countries. Is it some sense of these inequalities—the potential source of challenges to his authority—that troubles Daniel Ortega? Or is it the old bad memories of losing power in 1990? Or is it a compulsive pragmatism preventing him from simply relying on the popularity that a plan for a new canal generates, with the promise of increasing employment and decreasing poverty? Whatever the motivation, he has consistently sought to firm up control. Mónica Baltodano has described the process this way:

> In recent years we've witnessed both the annihilation of organizations that don't subordinate themselves, and the proscription of the Left. At the same time the rightwing leaders have been reduced by their own errors and limitations or by the manipulation of the electoral and judicial apparatuses Ortega controls. Whatever the cause, they no longer exist. They've been unable to put together any alternative force in recent elections. What exists in Nicaragua today is a single party, the party of perks and divvying-up power, of "you scratch my back and I'll scratch yours," in which it no longer even matters who wins. Those willing to play can sit at the same table. What exists is the determination to proscribe the emergence of any leftist party or parties, any party that could promote an alternative project.[52]

Maneuvering to control the judiciary, to establish greater integration of the military into his regime, and to push through sweeping reforms that will enshrine the canal deal with China into the constitution, while also clearing the way for him to run for presidency as many times as he wants—all these moves have created considerable discontent among those who are not FSLN loyalists.[53]

Another former FSLN leader from the revolutionary days, Dora Maria Tellez, elaborates:

> Today all the institutions have collapsed because President Ortega wants to be re-elected perpetually. His ambition for eternal power has brought about the collapse of judicial power, which has collapsed not only institutionally but ethically as well. None of the magistrates who are there is credible as a judge, because they are all political arms of Ortega or Alemán. Who could believe a judge who endorses a caudillo's positions? This supreme court has collapsed institutionally and ethically. The comptroller as well. The human rights prosecutor also. With his lust for re-election, Ortega has forced the principles of the country into an abyss and now he is doing everything possible to buy votes so he can have a majority for changing the constitution for the purpose of permitting him to stay in power.[54]

Even Humberto Ortega (retired from politics, now concentrating on his memoirs and his businesses) has expressed uneasiness that his brother's government has become too "closed and authoritarian." It is time, in his opinion, for what he terms the "political class" to "sit down and sort this out." He warns: "If we lose all sense of law and order and respect for institutional authority, then none of the important macroeconomic advances we have made here will mean anything."[55]

The "important macroeconomic advances" that the old general (despite tactical and rhetorical differences) values fully as much as his brother—the integration of the regime's policies with the interests of big capital—are seen in a different light by an erstwhile comrade such as Mónica Baltodano, who yearns for the revolutionary democracy of genuine socialism.

Unlike the Ortegas, she has never moved away from the vision that motivated her when the FSLN was a revolutionary organization. While many FSLN members and supporters see Ortega's government as representing a variant of the left, this is not how she and others like her see it. "This is not a leftist government," argues her like-minded comrade, Dora Maria Tellez. "It is a rightist populist government. Their principal ally is large-scale capital. Their policies have favored Nicaraguan capital, the concentration of capital in a few hands, the creation of a cloak of corruption in the country. This is a rightist government. The poor are still poor, as in Nicaragua of 2006."[56]

Comparisons have been made by some critics between the old Somoza regime and that of Ortega. "Ortega grew up under the dictatorship of the Somoza family, which endured for 40 years through the rule of a father and two sons," writes Stephen Kinzer. "As a Sandinista leader, Ortega helped destroy this corrupt dynastic system. Now he is emulating it, turning into just the kind of pro-business autocrat he spent years of his life fighting." Other critics take issue with this. "The Nicaragua of today still is not a dictatorship like we had when we confronted Somoza, who had closed all democratic space and forced us to take up arms and employ violence against the regime," insists Humberto Ortega. "We need to know how to respond in an appropriate manner to authoritarian expressions, which all power has to one degree or another." Baltodano agrees: "I don't believe this is a regime that can be catalogued as a dictatorship as it is today. Much less should we catalog it as a dictatorship that's worse than the Somoza one. In my view, when we say things like that it weakens our discourse and our critique." She adds, importantly: "I do believe it's an authoritarian regime with a dictatorial ambition and dictatorial actions. And I believe it could become a dictatorship. All the steps Ortega and his followers are taking are leading toward a dictatorial regime."[57]

It is Baltodano who seems to have articulated the most incisive and balanced analysis of the Ortega regime, from which it is worth quoting at length. There are four features, in her view, that must be grasped:

First feature. We aren't in any second stage of the revolution, as FSLN spokespeople would have us believe. No transformations are being implemented to put us on the road to a system of social justice. To the contrary, a social-economic regime has been strengthened in which the poor are condemned, like never before, to eke out a living in informal, precarious self-employed jobs, work long hours for miserable wages or migrate to other countries in search of work. If they're at all lucky, they can look forward to pathetic retirement pensions, if they ever hold a formal job long enough to be eligible. We're talking about a regime of social inequity with an increasing concentration of wealth in the hands of small groups.

Second feature. The country's subordination to capital's global logic has been intensified. Almost without our realizing it, our country is being turned over to large transnational corporations and foreign capital in general, which come to exploit our natural wealth or take advantage of our cheap labor force, as is happening in the free trade zones. The most pathetic case of this logic of handing over the country and its resources is the concession for the construction of an interoceanic canal, but many other mining, forestry and energy generating concessions have been made to foreign companies all over the country.

Third feature. Such a social-economic system needs to do away with social resistance and the Ortega regime is accomplishing that by exercising severe social control. It controls the unions, producer and professional associations and grassroots organizations, facilitating the alienation of those sectors, which would otherwise be inclined to resist were they not under the impression we are being governed by a leftist revolutionary party.

Fourth feature. An unconscionable concentration of power has been taking place in the clique surrounding Ortega and his wife, Rosario ("Chayo") Murillo. It's a process of expansion and growth that in our judgment still hasn't topped out. It threatens to destroy every vestige of democratic institutionality, as there's no force even able to slow it much less halt it right now.[58]

Future Struggles?

It is impossible to know how Nicaraguan realities will unfold in the coming years and decades. It seems unlikely—given the complexities and contradictions of global capitalism, and how they are apt to combine with Nicaraguan realities—that the Ortega regime can secure the permanence for which it seems to be striving. Inevitably there will be crises and struggles. The nature of those struggles, and their outcome, cannot be predicted at this moment. Former Sandinista militant Silvia Torres, commenting on "internal fractures" within the FSLN, notes that her old organization "has displaced the old guerrilla militancy in favor of young people . . . with very little understanding of history and no class positions, along with the *alianza* with big capital." She adds: "In the case of the peasantry and the workers, the Sandinista Front abandoned its representation. The only alliance that stands firm is the one it maintains with the big businessmen organized in the COSEP, with whom the government consults all its economic policies." Struggle for change in the FSLN's "anti-poor policies, and its relationship with the financial oligarchy and transnational capital," according to Torres, "is being organized and led from the periphery." She adds that "civil society organizations and representatives of some political parties support this mobilization," but admits that such efforts "at the moment do not show a medium-term resolution." It will take time.[59]

This matches Baltodano's view that "there are no organized political forces with a social base capable of resisting this [Ortega] project in a holistic way." She adds that the "transformations the country needs aren't going to come from" elements among the Nicaraguan Liberal parties. "They'll come from the Sandinistas as a whole, from that mass forged in a quarter century of struggle against the Somocista dictatorship, ten years of revolution and all these years of resistance." This is a point she returns to again and again. "That's where the transforming potential is, even though many of these people are working with Ortega today, are employees of his government or have to go to his traffic-circle rallies to keep their job." Arguing with some of her fellow dissidents, she stresses: "There's potential there, but there are some messages that don't get through to that potential. We have to be able to find the right messages to get through to them and make them think. We have to be there, close to those people."[60]

The force capable of bringing the kind of solution Baltodano wants to see can be built and mobilized, she is convinced, by those who "unravel and unfold flags, values and ideals of those who gave everything for justice and freedom." Insisting that "there's no possibility of a progressive solution in Nicaragua without taking the Sandinista grass roots into account and without the banners of the Sandinista ideology and vision," she argues—here addressing the position of onetime comrades such as Humberto Ortega and Victor Tirado López—that "it is not true that the cause of revolutionary transformation is now a goal for which there is no point fighting," adding "whenever we see a greater concentration of wealth, greater injustice, violence against women, destruction of the environment, capital wants to destroy everything . . . you have to keep fighting."[61]

She calls for "an alternative project with a medium- and long-term strategy," and with "an identity and a clear progressive profile that's clear about its objectives, those that are vital for Nicaragua, its people and democracy." It is necessary to build "a force that rejects caudillo logic and insists on educating the people to turn popular conscience into a material force for change." Such a force (1) "can't be at the mercy of short-term electoral interests or subjected to utilitarian alliances" and (2) cannot have its focus restricted to "denouncing how the institutional foundations of a dictatorship are being constructed, how political rights and the law are being violated."[62]

On this second point, she notes, "There's a disassociation between struggle and the denunciation of these big political issues, which don't seem to interest people, don't mobilize them, because they feel remote from the major daily issues that do interest them and make them victims of this regime." The regime's "pragmatism and accommodation can only be confronted by taking up the struggles in response to social problems, linking the social problems to the big political issues such as the constitutional reforms, the canal concession." She points to the FSLN's revolutionary experience:

> The original links we worked on to get people convinced they had to strug-
> gle against the Somocista dictatorship began with social problems. We were
> among the people, with the people. We have to identify what government mea-
> sures are disappointing and frustrating people and accompany them until some
> victory is achieved. Because achieving something reaffirms the awareness and
> conviction that the way to progress is by being organized and united.[63]

Baltodano clearly sees differences between (a) Oretega's FSLN regime, (b) the actual FSLN organization, and (c) the FSLN base. "This regime, based on concentrating wealth in few hands and bestowing advantages on the trans-nationals, is generating a lot of contradictions." On the other hand, within the organization there are different elements. Some still adhere to and attempt to act upon the old ideals—they are "good people" who "firmly believe that they are making the revolution, and are doing very good things for their commu-nity." Others are firmly ensnared by the opportunism and authoritarianism of the regime and "are little party bosses, little caudillos." At the same time, "con-tradictions are emerging within the Sandinista base," with some beginning to "see the authoritarianism operating in their barrio, community and work-place." In her opinion, "the day will come when that guy who's now satisfied with the 10 sheets of zinc roofing they gave him is going to start asking why he's supposed to be grateful for them" while, at the same time, the "upper eche-lons are living like millionaires. That day will come, just as the moment always comes in humanity in which the oppressed ask themselves if the oppression they're suffering is fair."[64]

Those adhering to the revolutionary organization that Baltodano envisions serve the function of patiently building around a long-term political program, rather than around some pragmatic and electoral quick-fix. They must grapple with the underlying problems: "We need to work on them, revealing, thinking about, analyzing and explaining them." This can happen by "energizing people to express their frustrations through struggle in the social movements. Connections have to be built between the social problems that concern people and the political issues." At one point she emphasizes: "We have to foment indignation. We need to organize indignation. Because it will not happen here on its own. . . . We need to organize it in the neighborhoods and communities. . . . There are circumstances that cannot be predicted, but they trigger a social explosion," she says. "The idea is to be organized and ready for when it happens."[65]

Such generalizations have defined the approach of revolutionary Marxist groups in many countries for many years. It remains to be seen how effectively and successfully they can be applied in Nicaragua as the twenty-first century continues to unfold.

10.

South Africa

Race, Class, Vanguard

For decades the Republic of South Africa had a dual reputation as a republic for its privileged white minority (except for radical dissidents) and a super-racist, fascistic police state for its large Black majority. The ideology and policy of racial separation—or, more accurately, domination —was known as apartheid. The momentous and relatively peaceful overturn of South Africa's apartheid regime in the twilight of the twentieth century, in the same historical moment as the collapse, one after the other, of Communist dictatorships in Eastern Europe, utterly contradicted most knowledgeable observers' expectations of violence. Perhaps we can only comprehend what happened through an application of materialist dialectics—the analytical methodology of change through contradictory interpretations.

Apartheid posited a racial hierarchy in which European "whites" (making up 12.8 percent of the South African population) were seen as supreme, under whom Asians, including Indians, Malays, and Chinese (2.6 percent) and mixed-race "coloreds" (8.5 percent) were viewed as superior only to the Black majority of South Africa's people (76 percent). This majority group was fragmented into distinct tribal categories—which have included such disparate ethnic and cultural groupings as the Xhosa, Zulu, Swazi, Sotho, Bapedi, Tswanga, Shangan-Tsonga, Venda, and Lemba. According to apartheid partisans, each of these is a very distinct "people" whose nationality should be kept distinct (both excluded from and subordinated to the government of "racially superior" whites). The fact that perhaps as many as one-third of the whites may have had some percentage of colored/Black genetic material somewhere in their biological makeup was—of course—not even acknowledged.[1]

For many years it seemed as if this incredibly repressive system could never be brought down—and then suddenly, dramatically, it was. South Africa was rich in what could be called vanguard organizations (organizations involving activist cadres who were influential among a significant percentage of the politically alert layers of the population). We find a thick alphabet soup of interactive elements: the African National Congress (ANC), the South African Communist Party (SACP), the Congress of South African Trade Unions (COSATU), the Pan-Africanist Congress (PAC), the Black Consciousness Movement (BCM), South African Students Organization (SASO), the Azanian People's Organization (AZAPO), the United Democratic Front (UDF), the Workers Organization for Socialist Action (WOSA), the National Forum (NF), the Mass Democratic Movement (MDM), and more.

The fluctuating fortunes of these interrelated and often contentious vanguard elements can only be understood within the framework of broader interpenetrating binaries—capitalism/apartheid and race/class. We must also look at the mutual influence of internal, regional, and global factors. There are the complex relationships, as well, between violence and nonviolence, and between the patient work of organizing and the explosiveness of spontaneous upsurge. Not to mention the wobbling and shifting balance of idealism and pragmatism.

From European Invasion to Apartheid

South Africa's apartheid regime came to power in 1948, deeply rooted in almost three centuries of white racist colonization. This first involved Dutch settlers (calling themselves Afrikaners), then the English (who imported a significant number of Indian and other Asian laborers), then the English again, fighting and dominating the more numerous Afrikaners—both groups progressively taking land from, demanding labor from, and systematically subjugating and degrading the majority-Black populations. Apartheid's triumph was part of a post–World War II Afrikaans resurgence at the polls (from which non-whites had historically been barred) under the recently formed National Party. Although sectors of the English had a reputation (particularly in the Cape Town area) for greater racial tolerance, racist policy and ideology had been a central and consistent component of English colonialism from the very beginning, and it had permeated government personnel, businessmen, the intelligentsia, farmers, and workers of both British and Dutch origin, with few exceptions.[2]

The forging of modern South Africa was an outcome of a dynamically developing world capitalist system. Rosa Luxemburg gave one of the earliest Marxist accounts in her classic *The Accumulation of Capital* (1913), describing— especially after the discovery of diamonds and gold—the three-way conflict between the Dutch Boers (simple commodity production farmers), the "primitive communistic" Black African tribes, and modern capitalist British imperialists. By the early twentieth century, in the wake of the Anglo-Boer War (1899–1902), a Union of South Africa had been firmly secured within the British imperial project and fully opened to a modernizing industrial capitalism. "There is no doubt that segregation was the product of South Africa's industrial revolution," comments historian Nigel Worden, and he goes on to summarize recent scholarship tracing the growth of aggressive Afrikaner business interests that combined with populist concerns of white workers and farmers to create the basis for a new "Afrikaner nationalism." (Afrikaners constituted well over half of white South Africans, while the English speakers made up barely more than one-third.) This dynamic ideology rallied its constituents around a white racist vision designed to create a prosperous modern economy, soaring capitalist profits, and across-the-board rising white living standards, at the expense of Black labor.[3]

When Britain's Conservative prime minister Harold Macmillan—touring colonial areas that were being transformed into independent nations—warned against maintaining anti-Black racism as "winds of change" swept Africa in the late 1950s, the apartheid regime detached the Republic of South Africa from the British Commonwealth. This was accomplished without slowing in any way the forward surge of its industrializing economy. As Marxist analyst Harold Wolpe asserted, "The consequence of this is to integrate race relations with capitalist relations of production to such a degree that the challenge to the one becomes of necessity a challenge to the other." This came to be a common perception among the Left. "While the national oppression of Blacks has favored a rapid accumulation of capital in South Africa, the development and growth of the country's capitalist economy has in turn led to a strengthening of white supremacy," wrote Ernest Harsch in the mid-1980s. "The two elements—national oppression and capitalism—are inseparably intertwined and mutually reinforcing."[4]

Apartheid, no less than the earlier colonial racist policies from which it flowed, cannot be grasped if seen as an effort simply to keep the races separate. "The major components of South Africa's racial system—the Bantustans, pass laws, labor bureaus, residency rules—were instituted, not primarily to keep blacks and whites separate," analyst Kevin Danaher pointed out in the mid-1980s, "but to secure white control over black workers." Despite myths perpetuated by the ideologists of apartheid, historic economic development and migration patterns throughout the nineteenth and twentieth centuries were forging a more or less cohesive Black working class. Apartheid ideology and policy allowed for the exploitation of Black labor in urban and industrial areas while restricting as many Blacks as possible to artificial "homelands"—which consequently placed 80 percent of all South African land in white hands. The industrialization and urbanization processes that had crystallized modern Afrikaner nationalism had, as Allister Sparks has pointed out, "ripped apart the fabric of black tribal life, turning a landless peasantry into an urban proletariat, and awakening a political consciousness that eventually demanded its own national liberation from white mastery just as Afrikaners had demanded theirs from the British."[5]

This was the context in which we can understand the development and interrelationship of what turned out to be the two dominant forces in the anti-apartheid struggle: the African National Congress and the South African Communist Party.

African National Congress and South African Communist Party

Founded in 1912, the early ANC was led by "those aspirant members of the African proto-middle classes—doctors, lawyers, ministers, landowners and traders—who stood to lose most" from the Anglo-Boer unity around a white supremacist Union of South Africa. Embracing "modernizing ambitions" and "social conservatism," they were, as historian Saul Dubrow puts it, "informed by Christian and liberal conceptions of justice and humanity," and "while proud of their African identity, they eagerly embraced the universal qualities of Western civilization in the belief that its principles were color-blind and potentially of value to all." Although initially seeking equal rights for Blacks as loyal subjects of the British Empire, as time went on the ANC became committed to the end of colonialism altogether. Fluctuations of moderation and radicalism in the ANC, as well as competing personalities, affected the organization's fortunes over the next few decades. Among the ideological influences were some emanating from the United States—the racial coexistence and self-help approach of Booker T. Washington, the Pan-Africanism and left-liberal elitism of the young W. E. B. DuBois, and the militant Black nationalism of Marcus Garvey. Overall, however, ANC perspectives tended to envision an independent South Africa that would include all races.[6]

One new, powerful ideological influence on the ANC was the Russian Revolution of 1917 and the rise of the Communist movement. It was out of the white working class that South African Communism first arose (both Afrikaners and British, but also a smattering of other groups—not least being Eastern European and Jewish immigrants). While it was rooted in a tradition of class struggle in which "white capital and white labor quarreled over the division of profits largely obtained from black labor," as an early Communist, Edward Roux, later put it, by the early-to-mid-1920s some of the most perceptive Communist leaders were "trying to persuade an almost exclusively white party that its main task was to organize the non-whites for revolution." The earlier influence of prominent British socialists who toured South Africa, Keir Hardie and Tom Mann, had helped to challenge racist assumptions of some South African labor socialists, whose left wing (led by future Communists David Ivor Jones and Sidney Percival Bunting) predicted that the Black workers of South Africa would soon take their places among "the iron battalions of the proletariat" in a global struggle against capitalism.[7]

It took some time for the South African Communists to find their way. Some "radical" white workers—during a militant strike wave of 1922 supported by the Communists—had carried a banner proclaiming "Workers of the World Unite for a White South Africa!" By 1928, however, 1,600 of South Africa's 1,750 Communists were Black. Not all of these early Black Communists were by any means well versed in Marxist theory. More knowledgeable than many was Albert Nzula, a teacher at an A.M.E. Mission School and later the first Black African to hold the position of general secretary of the Communist Party, who declared: "I have come to the conclusion that every right-minded person ought to be a Communist." He cited the works of neither Marx nor Lenin to make his case but instead the book *Communism and Christianism* by defrocked Episcopal bishop William H. Brown from the United States, who blended the teachings of Jesus, Charles Darwin, and Karl Marx. Initially, Nzula represented the minority view among ANC members, but within a few years, James La Guma, a "colored" trade unionist and party leader, was able to play a decisive role in developing (in consultation with Nikolai Bukharin and others in the Communist International) the slogan of "an independent Native republic, as a stage towards a workers' and peasants' government." He also helped win the SACP to the notion that the way forward to socialism was through African majority rule.[8]

In the same period, ANC president Josiah Gumede had concluded that "of all political parties, the Communist Party is the only one that honestly and sincerely fights for the oppressed people." Yet the radical perspective represented by Gumede was soon shunted aside by the ANC's more moderate elements, whose disinclination to engage in serious struggle resulted in the organization's precipitous decline. At the same time, more authoritarian, rigid, and sectarian forces in the Communist International, largely through the influence of Stalinism, resulted in "a harshly intolerant, ultra-left period . . . which cost the Party untold damage in membership and influence," according to Communist historian Michael Harmel. Throughout the 1930s, therefore, neither the ANC nor the Communist Party was able to provide central leadership in the liberation struggle.[9]

By the 1940s, however, and into the early 1950s, both organizations recovered—and the ANC, under a succession of more activist-oriented presidents (Alfred Xuma, James Moroka, Albert Luthuli), opened its ranks to members of the Communist Party. A number of militant youth leaders influenced by a Pan-Africanist Black nationalism—the most famous being Nelson Mandela—initially opposed this opening to the Communists. Mandela soon changed his mind, however, and thoroughly described the evolution of his own ideological perspective:

> I acquired the complete works of Marx and Engels, Lenin, Stalin, Mao Tse-tung, and others and probed into the philosophy of dialectical and historical materialism. I had little time to study these works properly. While I was stimulated by the *Communist Manifesto,* I was exhausted by *Das Kapital.* But I found myself strongly drawn to the idea of a classless society, which, to my mind, was similar to traditional African culture where life was shared and communal. I subscribed to Marx's basic dictum, which has the simplicity and generosity of the Golden Rule: "From each according to his ability; to each according to his needs."
>
> Dialectical materialism seemed to offer both a searchlight illuminating the dark night of racial oppression and a tool that could be used to end it. It helped me to see the situation other than through the prism of black and white relations, for if our struggle was to succeed, we had to transcend black and white. I was attracted to the scientific underpinnings of dialectical materialism, for I am always inclined to trust what I can verify. Its materialistic analysis of economics rang true to me. The idea that the value of goods was based on the amount of labor that went into them seemed particularly appropriate for South Africa. The ruling class paid African labor a subsistence wage and then added value to the cost of the goods, which they retained for themselves.
>
> Marxism's call to revolutionary action was music to the ears of a freedom fighter. The idea that history progresses through struggle and change occurs in revolutionary jumps was similarly appealing. In my reading of Marxist works I found a great deal of information that bore on the type of problems that face a practical politician. Marxists gave serious attention to national liberation move-

ments and the Soviet Union in particular supported the national struggles of many colonial peoples. This was another reason why I amended my view of Communists and accepted the ANC position of welcoming Marxists into its ranks.[10]

The closely allied ANC and SACP were united with other groups in which Communists played a role: the South African Indian Congress, the Colored People's Congress, and the white anti-racist Congress of Democrats, as well as trade unions that were largely Black (which had mobilized strikes of bus drivers, mine workers, and others in the 1940s). In addition to mass strikes that were savagely repressed by the government, there were defiance campaigns and boycotts that targeted the increasingly repressive policies of segregation and apartheid. According to Edward Roux, such protests were commonly the result of "a spontaneous mass movement, unprepared and owing little or nothing to political leadership."[11]

Yet the Communist-influenced organizations, nonetheless, played a central role in channeling and giving focus to such spontaneous upsurges. This political focus was shaped by theoretical and strategic perspectives that had developed within the world Communist movement during the latter phases of the Stalinist period from the mid-1930s, and those perspectives endured through the Second World War, into the early 1950s, and long afterward. This was the "popular front" orientation, which held that the struggle for capitalist democracy—in the face of fascism and colonialism—must be won before there could be any thought of socialist revolution. This called for a broad alliance of workers, farmers, shopkeepers, liberal business interests, and others. In the South African context, this meant that the ANC, as well as the SACP, was struggling for the victory of a "national democratic revolution," with the goal of a democratic republic based on a capitalist economy—for the SACP, socialism being the goal of a later stage of the struggle.[12]

This approach is consistent with the point emphasized by Nelson Mandela in 1964, that (despite Marxism's influence on his own thinking) "the ANC has never at any period of its history advocated a revolutionary change in the economic structure of the country, nor has it, to the best of [his] recollection, ever condemned capitalist society," and that far from emphasizing class distinctions, "the ANC seeks to harmonize them." Another ANC activist, Albertina Sisulu (wife of Walter Sisulu, the organization's former secretary general who was imprisoned for 26 years), put it this way: "We have never objected to the idea of a ruling class. We just want a government which has the interest of all South Africans at heart." Far from creating a barrier either against support from South African Communists or against substantial material aid from the

Soviet Union, this perspective dovetailed with the self-conception of the government of the Soviet Union. Beginning with the triumph of the Stalin dictatorship, it was committed to creating "socialism in one country" (the USSR), with, accordingly, a primary foreign policy goal to seek "progressive" capitalist allies to help establish a "peaceful coexistence." Loyal comrades in the mainstream of the world Communist movement were expected to shape political strategies in their own countries to harmonize with considerations "dictated by the ever-changing tactics of Soviet foreign policy," in the bitter words of George Padmore, onetime architect of Communist policy in Africa and later a theorist of Pan-Africanism.[13]

Some analysts see all of this reflected in what became the central document of the ANC and its allies, the 1955 Freedom Charter, which Communists played an important role in helping to draft. Historian Saul Dubow notes that the democratic and humanistic affirmations of the Freedom Charter were "relatively uncontroversial" but that two "studiedly ambiguous" provisions—couched in ambiguous formulations—were "rather more problematic."[14] They were

> the statement that "South Africa belongs to all who live in it, black and white," and the provisions to transfer into common ownership the country's mineral wealth, banks and monopoly industries. The Africanist element within the ANC resented the implication that Africans did not have prior and superior rights to the country (though this was often dressed up in a confusing discourse about the difference between multiracialism and non-racism); on the question of economic nationalization, liberals and Marxists and Africanists engaged in extended polemics as to whether the wealth clause amounted to a pseudo-communist manifesto.[15]

Writing from Ghana, George Padmore dismissed the Freedom Charter as "a Stalinist maneuver." South African sociologist Thomas Ranuga later described it as being permeated by "the philosophy of liberal-reformism."[16]

Pan-Africanism and Black Consciousness

The Africanists were particularly influenced by the radicalism of George Padmore, who explained in 1956 that "Pan-Africanism sets out to fulfill the socio-economic mission of Communism under a libertarian political system," and to do so independently of the USSR, elaborating:

> Politically, Pan-Africanism seeks the attainment of the government of Africans by Africans, with respect for racial and religious minorities who desire to live in Africa on a basis of equality with the black majority. Economically and socially, Pan-Africanism subscribes to the fundamental objectives of Democratic Socialism, with state control of the basic means of production and

distribution. It stands for the liberty of the subject within the law and condones the Fundamental Declaration of Human Rights, with emphasis upon the Four Freedoms.[17]

Under the leadership of Robert Sobukwe, a number of ANC dissidents who were influenced by Padmore's Pan-Africanism and critical of white political influence in the organization broke away to form the Pan-Africanist Congress (PAC) in 1959. The PAC immediately launched a militant campaign of nonviolent action aimed at breaking the passbook system through massive disobedience, mass demonstrations, and mass arrests in order to clog the jails and overturn apartheid. On March 21, 1960, ten thousand men, women, and children surrounded a police station in Sharpeville near Johannesburg, proclaiming that they were proudly in violation of apartheid laws and demanded to be arrested. The police opened fire on the peaceful crowd, resulting in 69 demonstrators killed and 186 wounded. Violence also flared in Langa near Cape Town. More than a quarter of a century afterward, this bloody day remained a central reference point in the consciousness of South African freedom fighters.[18] Dennis Brutus poetically expressed this collective sentiment:

> As the seasons turn
> And Summer droops to Autumn
> The dyings continue
> And resistance grows:
> There are still those willing to give their lives:
> Sharpeville, Langa
> You are sacred names:
> In the center of our brains
> The flame of desire for freedom
> Fiercely burns.[19]

The government banned the PAC as well as the ANC. Both of the outlawed organizations decided to abandon nonviolence and initiate armed struggle. The change in strategy led not to the end of the apartheid regime but the intensified clampdown on both the ANC and PAC in South Africa, with dramatic arrests of both Mandala and Sobukwe, along with many of their comrades, who ended up with life sentences on the notorious Robben Island. Those not arrested were driven either deep underground or into exile.

Yet by the 1970s the oppressiveness of the regime seemed to have generated even deeper resistance than ever before. A radical student leader, Steve Biko, influenced not only by Pan-Africanism but also by the ideas of Frantz Fanon, as well as the Black Power currents in the US civil rights movement, helped to propel the all-Black South African Students Organization into the national limelight, which helped to generate organization in the townships of the broad-based Black Consciousness Movement. Biko insisted on the necessity of Black South Africans overcoming the "inferiority and superiority complexes" built into the South African reality and into the psychology of Blacks and whites alike. This required building a Black liberation struggle independently of whites—both the apartheid oppressors and the well-meaning white liberals and leftists who sought to influence and control the Black struggle. "The call for Back Consciousness," he explained, "is more than just a reactionary rejection of whites by blacks. The quintessence of it is the realization by the blacks that, in order to feature well in this game of power politics, they have to use the concept of group power and to build a strong foundation for this." For Biko and his followers, this orientation had increasingly radical implications:

> It will not be long before the blacks relate their poverty to their blackness in concrete terms. Because of the tradition forced onto the country, the poor people shall always be black people. It is not surprising, therefore, that the blacks should wish to rid themselves of a system that locks up the wealth of the country in the hands of a few. No doubt Rick Turner was thinking of this when he declared that "any black government is likely to be socialist." . . .
>
> The Black Consciousness movement does not want to accept the dilemma of capitalism versus communism. It opts for a socialist solution that is an authentic expression of black communalism. . . . In our writings we at times speak of collective enterprises because we reject the individualistic and capitalist type of enterprises. But we are not taking over the Russian models.[20]

In both urban and rural areas, the Black Consciousness Movement sought to organize at the grassroots level to establish, in the words of its own literature, "health clinics, publishing ventures, cooperative building schemes, political prisoner relief funds and leadership training programs," as well as programs concerned with "welfare, culture, black theology, education, literacy, black arts, self-help and other relevant projects." The goals of such efforts were (1) "to help the black community become aware of its own identity," and (2) "to help the black community to create a sense of its own power."[21]

All of this reflected a ferment within—and also had an impact on—the Black townships, particularly among the youth. The culmination was an uprising in Soweto near Johannesburg on June 16, 1976. Independently of all existing anti-apartheid organizations, a crowd of more than fifteen thousand Black students, twelve to twenty years old, gathered in what has been termed a "jovial" mood to protest against being forced to learn Afrikaans in school. "Afrikaans Is the Oppressors' Language" read one of the placards. Another asserted "Viva Azania!" (Azania being the name that many Pan-Africanists gave to South Africa). The protesters sang the anthem "Nkosi Sikele'iAfrica," and shouted "Amandla!" (Power!) with clenched-fist salutes. Ten police vans arrived, with units sporting batons, tear gas, semiautomatic rifles, and sub-machine guns. In retaliation to the teargassing, the crowd threw stones—and then the shooting began. Street battles and attacks on symbols of apartheid were met with extreme violence by security forces. "When evening arrived," Ernest Harsch recounts, "workers returning from their jobs in Johannesburg joined their children in the streets. By nightfall the township was ablaze." The protests spread to other townships and neighborhoods, with some white students joining in—and facing police brutality as well. By June 19, the official death toll was put at 109, although some estimates put it as high as 700. Strikes, marches, and rallies continued over the next several months, but they were more than matched by violent repression and mass arrests. The uprising "was not a revolutionary movement," comments historian Nigel Worden. "It lacked clear organization and leadership. Despite some contact with workers, the students had no formal links with worker organizations. As some writers have stressed in this regard, the events of 1976 were a missed opportunity." Yet Soweto shook both South Africa and the world, becoming yet another powerful symbol of resistance."

In the following year, Steve Biko was beaten to death while in police custody. The Black Consciousness Movement did not have the means to with-stand the intense wave of repression, nor did the PAC succeed in building a significant organization capable of capitalizing on the upsurge. AZAPO—a new organization blending Black Consciousness, Pan-Africanist thought, and Marxist ideology—proved similarly unable to build itself into an organization to continue to lead the struggle. Many young activists involved in the Soweto uprising fled the country, a significant number ending up under the banner of the ANC. The fact that the ANC and SACP were primary beneficiaries of the Soweto aftermath—enabling them to play the central role of revolution-ary vanguard in the 1980s and early 1990s—can be related to several factors, which I discuss below.

"Scrambled Egg"

The relatively durable combination of the ANC and the SACP created a pow-erful dynamic. Nationalist Party leader F. W. de Klerk, scoffing at the assertion that there was an alliance between the ANC and SACP, once quipped, "It is not an alliance, it is a scrambled egg." There is truth to this. By the early

1990s, knowledgeable US scholar Martin J. Murray observed that the twenty thousand members of the SACP were "as a matter of strict policy" all members of the ANC (whose membership by then numbered five hundred thousand). Not only was the SACP the strongest organized political current within the ANC, but SACP members held more than twenty-five seats on the ANC's ninety-person National Executive Committee and held ten out of twenty-five positions on the National Working Committee, which oversaw the daily functioning of the ANC.[23]

The interweaving of the ANC and SACP could be understood in quite different ways. Nathaniel Weyl, a US apologist for the South African apartheid regime, explained to his readers that the ANC was a "Communist-controlled organization" that quite simply served "as the Communist Party's main instrumentality among the Negroes." Weyl and his sources in the apartheid regime asserted that the key moment occurred in 1950, when the Communist Party was banned by the government and, "under such highly intelligent Communist leaders as Joe Slovo and his wife, Ruth First, the Johannesburg Party made an effective adjustment to the new conditions," covertly reorganizing itself within the ANC.[24]

But the truth was even more complex and interesting than what Weyl described—it entailed the development of a symbiotic relationship in which the larger group was definitely not digested by the smaller but rather one through which each was transformed. The Communist Party dissolved in 1950, and it was up to local handfuls of Communists to cautiously regroup—which they did by gravitating to and cautiously rebuilding within the ANC. "In the hour of [Communist Party] dissolution," according to SACP historians Jack and Ray Simons, "the class struggle had merged with the struggle for national liberation." Another prominent Communist, Brian Bunting, remembered many years later that the banning of the party "did more than anything to bring the ANC closer to the Communists: it transformed it from a hole-in-corner body [in the 1950s the SACP had perhaps 2500 members] to a national organization." Particularly important was the current of young ANC Pan-Africanists gathered around Nelson Mandela and Walter Sisulu—contributing, according to SACP member Rusty Bernstein, to South African Communists having "an understanding of race and nationalism which Communists did not have in other countries. . . . The unique gift the party brought to the struggle was its multiracialism and internationalism." Important aspects of this internationalism involved substantial solidarity from the world Communist movement and its allies, as well as valuable material aid from the USSR.[25]

Particularly in light of post-apartheid developments, one could speculate that perhaps the non-Communist component of this "scrambled egg" was predominant. The fortunes of the South African Communists seemed absolutely dependent on the fortunes of the ANC, and their prestige inseparable from that of the ANC (a point Mandela would later emphasize in the late 1990s). As the SACP reorganized itself in the 1950s, it remained true to its respectful and loyal relationship with the ANC. By the 1960s, according to Rusty Bernstein, it was "hard to tell who was in the Party and who was not."[26]

Yet its militants had earned immense respect within the ANC. "For many decades Communists were the only political group who were prepared to treat Africans as human beings and their equals; who were prepared to eat with us, talk with us, live with us and work with us," Mandela told the judge at his 1964 trial. In his autobiography, Mandela recalled that in the 1940s a Communist friend had invited him "to a number of parties where there was a mixture of whites, Africans, Indians, and Coloreds. The get togethers were arranged by the [Communist] party, and most of the guests were party members."[27]

Indeed, the diversity was clearly reflected in the SACP's impressive leadership. Moses Kotane, who fought against a left-sectarian affliction in the early 1930s, stressed that "the party must become more Africanized, pay special attention to South Africa, study the conditions in this country and concretize the demands of the toiling masses from first-hand experience." He not only helped forge close relations with the ANC but also assumed a prominent position in that organization. The charismatic African trade union leader J.B. Marks, for a number of years the Communist Party's chairperson, used to tell his comrades: "Leaders come and go, but the masses are always there." After Marks's death, the chairmanship was passed to the tall, pipe-smoking scholar Dr. Yusuf M. Dadoo, who had led the South African Indian Congress, and "whose role as a fighter for human rights," in Mandela's words, "had made him a hero to all groups." Militant activist Alex La Guma (son of "colored" SACP pioneer James La Guma) wrote novels "with the sharp realism characteristic of most black fiction," according to South African scholar Robert Ross. There was the brilliant lawyer Bram Fischer, who came from a well-to-do Afrikaner family and who led the party's underground apparatus before his capture and life imprisonment. Rachel (Ray) Alexander, a young immigrant from Latvia, became well known during the 1930s in union organizing efforts among multiracial constituencies—and in 1954, after the Communist Party was banned, she successfully ran for Parliament, which she was barred from entering by government security forces. She later married another prominent South African Communist, Jack Simons, a professor of African law and administration at Cape Town University.[28]

Among the younger layer of Communist leaders were such figures as Joe Slovo (an "open-minded and flexible thinker" who became "a theoretical and strategic trailblazer," according to his comrade Ronnie Kasrils), Slovo's wife, journalist Ruth First ("a striking figure, with her dark hair and flashing eyes," a woman "particularly critically minded," especially in regard to "the conventional wisdom of our Movement, such as the uncritical view of the Soviet Union"), and Chris Hani ("an inspirational force, an extremely warm and caring human being with . . . an infectious sense of humor" who "cherished the opportunity for reflection and to put views about complex problems under the microscope" and was particularly concerned about overcoming "a culture of intolerance" that had developed among ANC and Communist leaders in the military wing of the movement). Ruth First was assassinated in 1982 by South African security forces with a letter bomb in Mozambique. Hani was killed in 1993 in South Africa by a right-wing assassin in 1993. Many non-Communist freedom fighters, such as the poet Dennis Brutus, could not help but honor such Communists, with such words as he offered in his commemoration of Ruth First:

> They would come again
> You wrote
> You knew
> But what they did not know
> Was that your spirit would live on
> In thousands willing to fight for freedom
> In thousands willing to die for freedom
> That you might be gone
> But that you would come again
> They would come again
> You wrote
> Because you knew
> They could not rest
> And would not lest you rest
> —dear restless spirit—
> until, finally, shattered
> in a bomb-wrecked office in Maputo
> your bloodied corpse rested.[29]

Bishop Desmond Tutu would later celebrate what for him was the Christ-like meaning of Hani's life at the Communist leader's funeral:

Chris Hani died on the most sacred weekend of the Christian calendar. Christ died between Good Friday and Easter Sunday. Let us recall that God extracted out of the death of Jesus Christ a great victory, the victory of life over death, that God showed in the victory of Jesus that goodness is stronger than evil, that light is stronger than darkness, that life is stronger than death, that love is stronger than hate. God is telling us the same message in the horrible death of Chris Hani. His death is not a defeat. His death is our victory. His death is the victory of truth, the truth of liberation, that liberation is stronger than the lie of apartheid, that liberation is stronger than the injustice of apartheid, of its oppression and exploitation.[30]

Working Class, Resistance, Insurgency

The working-class focus of the Communist Party gave it special relevance as time went on. Author Ernest Harsch observed: "Black workers are everywhere: hanging on scaffoldings at Johannesburg construction sites, digging drainage ditches in Cape Town, hauling cargo on Durban's docks, harvesting Natal's sugar cane, drilling and breaking up rock in Witwatersrand gold mines, assembling auto engines in Port Elizabeth." He observed that, as of 1977, "there were more than 8 million Black workers in South Africa—7 million Africans, 1 million Coloreds, and 221,000 Asians," adding that "Black workers and their families constitute the overwhelming majority of the Black population."[31]

In the late 1970s, "highly capitalized manufacturing industry now dominated the economy, using complex technology and requiring semi-skilled permanent workers rather than unskilled migrant laborers. In these circumstances, segregation and apartheid, so crucial to the earlier development and growth of industry, were no longer appropriate to the needs of South African capitalism." Economic shifts also were fragmenting "the cross-class Afrikaner nationalist alliance," while "the labor and urban resistance of 1973–77 had caught the government unprepared." Added to this was "the unfavorable international response and the threat of sanctions in the aftermath of Soweto," as well as the victory of left-wing anticolonial revolutions on bordering countries (Mozambique, Angola, Zimbabwe).[32] Allister Sparks dramatically captures some of the sociocultural impact of this economic transformation:

When the year 1978 saw the black tide fail to turn as predicted, it offered a glimpse of a future trend that would not only sweep apartheid away but sweep in its alternative. The cities that were supposed to become white are becoming black instead. "White" South Africa is being Africanized. Instead of the townships withering away, they are colonizing the suburbs; the black tide is flowing more strongly every day, washing away the Group Areas Act, the Separate

Amenities Act, and all the other sand castles of white delusion. It is washing away the bitter-almond hedge itself, sluicing great gaps in it and throwing people together in a convergence of mutual discovery that is both traumatic and formative and that will change South Africa forever.[33]

Sparks provides a vivid sense of the powerful upsurge mass struggle that developed within this context, focusing on the United Democratic Front (UDF), which was created and sustained by the ANC and SACP:

A wider range of groups were brought together than ever before. Soweto '76 was a children's revolution, but this time the UDF spanned the generation gap. The generations of the old Defiance Campaign, of Sharpeville, of Soweto '76, and the angry new generation of the day came together with trade unionists and liberation theologists, educators and students as well as politicians—from exiled ANC leaders to former Black Consciousness leaders now incorporated into the UDF. And more than ever before white liberals and radicals were involved, substantial numbers of whom identified with the UDF. Several predominantly white organizations, including the National Union of South African students, for many years the main students' organization on the English campuses, became affiliates.

The 1984 insurrection was more intense and lasted longer than any previous one. For three years it raged, resulting in more than three thousand deaths, thirty thousand detentions, and untold damage to property and the national economy. The government had to mobilize the army and declare two states of emergency to bring it under control, and even then it was only partially repressed.

It also had more strategic shape and revolutionary thrust than any previous uprising. The participation of politically experienced adults and of a national organization of affiliates deeply rooted in the communities meant that militant young "comrades," the shock troops of the uprising, were subject to some measure of direction and discipline. Although events developed a momentum of their own, impromptu actions taken in one area could be evaluated and, if successful, repeated elsewhere. The result was that a variety of strategies were employed: consumer and rent boycotts, school boycotts, strikes and stayaways, rallies, protest demonstrations, and an intermix of street confrontation and public and private negotiation.[34]

A significant element in the anti-apartheid vanguard, however, gathered around a competing formation that crystallized in 1983—the National Forum (NF). "Both the NF and the UDF were loosely knit confederations of community, youth and trade union organizations that had proliferated across the country in the late 1970s and early 1980s," writes Nigel Worden. Yet behind the UDF were the ANC and SACP, while the NF involved a polyglot of Black Consciousness and AZAPO militants, dissident Marxists and Trotskyist–influenced radicals. One of the most prominent spokesmen was the noted educator Neville Alexander, a founder of the Workers Organization for Socialist Action, who emphasized: "The immediate goal of the national liberation movement now being waged in South Africa is the destruction of the system of racial capitalism. Apartheid is simply a particular socio-political expression of this system. Our opposition to apartheid is therefore only a starting point for our struggle against the structures and interests which are the real basis of apartheid." The NF therefore called for the "establishment of a democratic, anti-racist worker Republic in Azania where the interests of the workers shall be paramount through worker control of the means of production and exchange." It emphasized that "the working-class struggle against capitalist exploitation and the national struggle against racial oppression have become one struggle under the general control and direction of the Black working class."[35]

The UDF called, with much vaguer formulations, for "the creation of a true democracy in which all South Africans will participate in the government of the country," which would be "a single non-racial, unfragmented South Africa" that would eventually end "all forms of oppression and exploitation." UDF publicity secretary Patrick Lekota went further:

> The UDF is not a class organization. It doesn't claim to work in the interests of the working class, the capitalist class, or the peasantry. It is an alliance of these classes. All those who don't have political rights and who are willing to do battle, have a home in the Front. We have never claimed to be led by the working class.[36]

"Put loosely," Martin Murray commented in 1987, "the UDF resembles a multi-class popular front and the National Forum resembles a working-class dominated united front." Much of the National Forum's orientation resonated among poor, working-class, and radicalized South Africans, of whom there were many, but the NF was no match organizationally for the UDF. While it is true that both boasted "of followings of working-class people who were incorporated through community-based civic associations, sport/cultural clubs, student and youth groups, and so forth," the ANC/SACP connection, with the attendant organizational apparatus and resources, enabled the UDF to surpass its rival in most of South Africa. This was guaranteed particularly when the militant and radical Congress of South African Trade Unions (COSATU)—whose fourteen affiliates rose from 450,000 to 1.3 million members between its founding in 1985 and 1994—formed an alliance with the UDF in 1989 called the Mass Democratic Movement.[37]

Victory and Defeat

Under a complex of immense international and domestic pressures, and through a set of rather complicated permutations and maneuvers, the dominant force of South Africa, the National Party, chose to seek an alternative to revolution and civil war, which it would inevitably lose, and which could result in the ascendancy of the more radical elements in the liberation movement. The path of negotiated resolution—facilitated by the freeing of Nelson Mandela and other anti-apartheid fighters, and the legalization of anti-apartheid organizations (including the ANC and SACP)—was designed to bring about a South African transition that would preserve the capitalist system. One Anglo-American business executive warned the ANC: "We dare not allow the baby of free enterprise to be thrown out with the bathwater of apartheid." This warning was entirely in harmony, however, with the traditional ANC program of not calling for socialism, and also with the old SACP "popular front" position of favoring only a national democratic revolution, with socialism being on the agenda only at some point in the (more or less) distant future. Marxist analyst John Saul concluded: "There can be little doubt that, in the end, the relative ease of the political transition was principally guaranteed by the ANC's withdrawal from any form of genuine class struggles in the socioeconomic realm and the abandonment of any economic strategy that might have been expected directly to service the immediate material requirements of the vast mass of desperately impoverished South Africans."[38]

Mandela and other ANC and SACP leaders carried out complex negotiations that dismantled apartheid power and paved the way for free elections allowing for a form of Black majority rule—with the ANC swept into power under the charismatic leadership of President Nelson Mandela. His retirement in 1999 brought former SACP militant Thabo Mbeki into the leadership of the ANC and the country. "In partnership with the SACP and COSATU," writes Saul Dubow, "the ANC was the leading element in a tripartite alliance which encompassed long-standing traditions of non-racialism, African nationalism and socialism." Yet despite the old radical rhetoric, there was to be no socialism. While the electoral strategy of the ANC succeeded in marginalizing political forces to its right, its policies also succeeded in sidelining forces to its left. "Is this what people have sacrificed their lives for?" asked former Robben Island prisoner Dennis Brutus upon his return after decades in exile. "If we are supposed to have won, how is it that those who are supposed to have lost seem not to have lost anything?"[39]

ANC policy director Michael Sachs emphasized another key element—the collapse of the USSR and the Communist bloc and the creation of a "unipolar world." This had certainly been a factor in the thinking of the National Party, as well as in the thinking of US, British, and other foreign policy-makers, in accepting the ANC coming to power—that a "radicalization" of an ANC regime would be unlikely. "You can't just go and redistribute things in this era," the ANC spokesman argued. "Maybe if we had a Soviet Union to defend us we could do that but, frankly, you've got to play the game, you've got to ensure that you don't go on some adventure. You know you will be defeated. They were defeated in Chile [in 1973], they were defeated in Nicaragua." Sachs added: "Should we be out there condemning imperialism? If you do those things, how long will you last? There is no organizational alternative, no real policy alternative to what we're doing." As a South African banker commented, "The ANC are not fools. They know where the balance of economic power lies." John Saul noted: "Too smart to be ineffectual lefties, they expected to play the only game in town (capitalism) successfully." In fact, according to Saul, "many of the most rightwing figures in the ANC government are senior SACP leaders."[40]

Dale T. McKinley, a prominent activist forced out of the SACP in 2000, explains:

> Since coming to power in 1994, the ANC has dutifully followed the liberal bourgeois democratic formula of institutionalizing (through a constitutional dispensation) the combination of individual rights and capitalist market economics. . . . Now combined with the more recent global offensive of internationalized corporate and finance capital (otherwise known as neo-liberalism), liberal bourgeois democracy has taken on the mantle of a necessary and natural product of an equally necessary and natural economic order. Under such a scenario, democracy itself becomes synonymous with the capitalist "free market," and everything else is merely about degrees and emphases. . . .
>
> As Neville Alexander has cogently argued, such a "liberal, free-market" approach is "unlikely to satisfy the material needs of the oppressed and impoverished majorities" in places like South Africa, "even though the gains in political space and in (individual) freedoms and rights are by no means unimportant." South Africa's experience since 1994 bears this out. In relation to the stated programs and constituent interests of its Alliance allies, the ANC's pursuit of elite-led, liberal democratic and deracialized capitalism has created a breeding ground for serious ideological opposition, organizational/class confrontation and more general political debate and dissent inside its own ranks and those of its Alliance partners.[41]

In multiple ways, however, the ANC leadership (as well as some elements in both the SACP and COSATU) can be seen as seeking to close off debate and intimidate dissidents inside and outside Tripartite Alliance ranks. The "National Democratic Alliance" has functioned "to preserve and advance the personal careers and political futures of leaders across the Alliance spectrum," McKinley tells us.[42]

"The ending of segregation opened the way for the rapid growth of South Africa's hitherto small black middle class in business and the professions, encouraged by affirmative action policies," Nigel Worden has pointed out. "But granting everybody the vote could not remove apartheid's legacy of profound economic and social deprivation." Others have made similar observations. "In mining, publishing and electronic media, black South Africans are increasingly prominent," observes the South Africa travel guide put out by Insight Guides and the Discovery Channel. "A small but growing number of companies listed on the Johannesburg Stock Exchange are now controlled by black investors." At the same time, the Insight Guides writers note that "the unemployment rate is 37 percent, making this by far the most important source of poverty and inequality."[43]

Despite the "de-racialization" of South African capitalism with the fall of apartheid, "worsening class division and social segregation appear to be the inexorable outcome of South Africa's elite transition," according to Patrick Bond. Given the fact that the great majority of Blacks were stuck on the bottom in the previous racial setup, this has meant that—with the enactment of the ANC government's neoliberal policies—certain aspects of the old apartheid reality have even gotten worse. For example, the average Black household income declined 19 percent from 1995 to 2000, while the average white household income went up 15 percent. Between 1995 and 2000 the poorest half of the South African population's share of the national income fell from 11.4 percent to 9.7 percent, while the country's richest 20 percent enjoyed 65 percent of the national income. COSATU reported in 2003: "Far from us turning the corner, in 2003 the nightmare of unemployment and poverty got steadily worse . . . [with] at least 22 million people suffering in desperate poverty and 5.3 million South African children suffering from hunger." Not being able to pay for the costs of electricity and even of the increasingly privatized water supplies, roughly ten million South Africans have had these essential utilities cut off.[44]

Chris Hani had warned that "having failed to smash the ANC-led movement, big capital would seek to undermine and transform our liberation movement, through corruption, influence and class accommodation with a new elite." With a formulation that seemed consistent with Trotsky's theory of permanent revolution, connecting victory against apartheid with victory over capitalism, Joe Slovo had emphasized that there was "no Chinese Wall between the national democratic revolution and socialism." The SACP leadership stressed in early 1995 that such views of its recently deceased leaders were "surely more relevant than ever before." Prominent party theorist Jeremy Cronin, viewing the SACP as the embodiment of revolutionary principles, observed that "the neo-liberal economic agenda poses a grave threat to the prospects of consolidating democracy and of beginning to address the social and economic crisis in which the majority of our people find themselves," and asserted that "we need to unleash a major effort at economic restructuring and democratization." Cronin emphasized "the critical need to wage class struggle for effective redistribution, and for the reconstruction and democratization of the economy."[45]

Remaining true to such perspectives would have required a separation from the ANC "scrambled egg"—which didn't happen. It is estimated that SACP membership was twenty thousand in 1991 and more than doubled in 1994—then suffered a remarkable decline. Far from dominating the ANC, the SACP now seemed ineffectual in its self-proclaimed role as "praetorian guard of ideological correctness within the ANC," and "its activists had no clear sense of what to do as party members" that they could not do as members of the ANC, COSATU, or other mass organizations. "In response to the government's economic policies, Communist politicians left the SACP in droves, to become staunch capitalists," observes Leonard Thompson. "SACP documents revealed that its membership declined from 80,000 a few years earlier to a mere 13,803 in 2000."[46]

What Will the Future Bring?

Not all of the old fighters have abandoned the struggle, however. In the left wing of the SACP and COSATU, dissident voices can be heard. There are some, like the leading ANC militant Trevor Ngwane, who have openly broken with and organized against the neoliberal policies of the ANC government. He has been prominent in anti-privatization campaigns and other struggles based in communities and workplaces, as well as anti-imperialist and antiwar movements. Of the other activists with whom he works, Ngwane says "these are ordinary people, like millions of other ordinary working people in South Africa. They have rescued a word which is disappearing into history or being lost in books and discussions of a few people from the middle class: socialism."[47]

Arundhati Roy, has aptly commented on the dynamics of de-radicalization (hardly unique to South Africa) in eloquent remarks to the 2004 World Social Forum:

> No individual nation can stand up to the project of corporate globalization on its own. Time and again we have seen that when it comes to the neo-liberal project, the heroes of our times are suddenly diminished. Extraordinary, charismatic men, giants in the opposition, when they seize power and become heads of state, are rendered powerless on the global stage. I'm thinking here of President Lula of Brazil. Lula was the hero of the World Social Forum last year. This year he's busy implementing IMF guidelines, reducing pension benefits and purging radicals from the Workers' Party. I'm thinking also of the former president of South Africa, Nelson Mandela. Within two years of taking office in 1994, his government genuflected with hardly a caveat to the Market God. It instituted a massive program of privatization and structural adjustment that has left millions of people homeless, jobless and without water and electricity.
>
> Why does this happen? There's little point in beating our breasts and feeling betrayed. Lula and Mandela are, by any reckoning, magnificent men. But the moment they cross the floor from the opposition into government they become hostage to a spectrum of threats—most malevolent among them the threat of capital flight, which can destroy any government overnight. To imagine that a leader's personal charisma and a c.v. of struggle will dent the corporate cartel is to have no understanding of how capitalism works or, for that matter, how power works. Radical change cannot be negotiated by governments, it can only be enforced by people.[48]

Some South African analysts have described the neoliberal globalization as global apartheid—"an international system of minority rule whose attributes include differential access to basic human rights, wealth and power." According to Patrick Bond, "if gender, race and class all contributed to apartheid's super-profits, then these factors are also crucial to global apartheid's uneven prosperity." Bond then draws our attention to "key insights into an earlier version of global apartheid—simply called 'imperialism'—[that] came from the German revolutionary Rosa Luxemburg." He notes that "Luxemburg considered polarization between the developed and developing worlds to be functional, not irrational, just as apartheid polarization between white cities and black rural areas was functional to South African capitalism." This—plus the fact that Luxemburg was a revolutionary struggling against the bureaucratic de-radicalization of the powerful German socialist movement, which was accommodating to imperialism and engaging in class collaboration—has generated growing interest in Luxemburg among South African activists.[49]

The revolutionary dynamic of the ANC/SACP vanguard formation—which had been so heroic in leading the anti-apartheid struggle—seemed to have exhausted itself by the end of the twentieth century. A vanguard social layer, capable of leading the working class and its allies in an effective struggle against the pernicious economic residues of apartheid and the "normal" tyranny of de-radicalized capitalism, had yet to find organizational expression in post-apartheid South Africa.

Sources

"Explorations in Plain Marxism" first appeared in the online journal *Links: International Journal of Socialist Renewal*, January 15, 2015, http://links.org. au/node/4251.

"Uneven and Combined Development and the Sweep of History" was presented at the 27th annual North American Labor History Conference, held at Wayne State University in Detroit, October 20–22, 2005. It appeared in the online journal *International Viewpoint*, September 21, 2006, www .internationalviewpoint.org/spip.php?article1125.

"Radical Labor Subculture: Key to Past and Future Insurgencies" was presented at the Historical Materialism Conference, New York University, January 14–16, 2010, and first appeared in *WorkingUSA* 13, no. 3 (2010): 367–85.

"Class and Identities" first appeared as an entry in *The International Encyclopedia of Revolution and Protest*, Immanuel Ness et al., eds. (Malden, MA: Wiley-Blackwell, 2009).

"Democracy" was written as a talk, "What Do Socialists Say about Democracy?," for the educational conference Socialism 2010, held in Chicago, June 18–20, and was published in the *International Socialist Review*, no. 74 (2010): 20–27.

"Making Sense of Postrevolutionary Russia" first appeared in *Against the Current*, no. 143, November/December 2009, under the title "Theories of Stalinism."

"The Darker the Night the Brighter the Star" was written for the educational conference Socialism 2016, held in Chicago, July 4, and first appeared in the online journal *Links: International Journal of Socialist Renewal*, July 18, 2016, http://links.org.au/node/4759.

"Origins and Trajectory of the Cuban Revolution" first appeared in *Against the Current*, no. 126, January/February 2007, under the title "On the Origins of the Cuban Revolution."

"Nicaragua: Revolution Permanent or Impermanent?" is published here for the first time, with a second portion composed especially for this volume.

The first portion, for the most part, is based on and summarizes a considerable amount of work ranging from my booklet *Permanent Revolution in Nicaragua* (New York: Fourth Internationalist Tendency, 1984) down to a doctoral dissertation at the University of Pittsburgh—"Workers and Revolution: A Comparative Study of Bolshevik Russia and Sandinist Nicaragua" (Ann Arbor, MI: University Microfilms International, 1990). The second portion was developed in consultation with Jonah McAllister-Erickson, who has an intimate sense of the current scene in Nicaragua, with last-minute input from veteran Sandinista militant Silvia Torres.

"South Africa: Race, Class, Vanguard" first appeared on the website Europe Solidaire Sans Frontières, January 2006 (www.europe-solidaire.org/spip .php?article4253), overseen by Pierre Rousset.

Notes

1: Explorations in Plain Marxism

1. C. Wright Mills, *The Marxists* (New York: New York: Dell Publishing, 1962), 34, 35.
2. Ibid., 96.
3. Ibid., 99.
4. Charles Post, *The American Road to Capitalism: Studies in Class Structure, Economic Development and Political Conflict, 1620–1877* (Chicago: Haymarket Books, 2011), 40; David Gordon, Richard Edwards, and Michael Reich, *Segmented Work, Divided Workers* (Cambridge: Cambridge University Press, 1982), 18. Terminological differences aside, I consider each of these to be extremely valuable contributions to the understanding of US capitalism.
5. For Marx and Engels on US capitalism, including in relation to the Civil War, see Karl Marx and Frederick Engels, *Marx and Engels on the United States*, Nelly Rumyantseva, ed. (Moscow: Progress Publishers, 1979); August H. Nimtz Jr., *Marx, Tocqueville, and Race in America: The "Absolute Democracy" or "Defiled Republic"* (Lanham, MD: Lexington Books, 2003); Robin Blackburn, *An Unfinished Revolution: Karl Marx and Abraham Lincoln* (London: Verso, 2011). On social composition of the International Workingmen's Association and the Paris Commune, see E. J. Hobsbawm, *The Age of Capital, 1848–1875* (New York: New American Library, 1979), 184; Stewart Edwards, ed., *The Communards of Paris, 1871* (Ithaca: Cornell University Press, 1973), 28–29. On the nineteenth-century European working class, see Geoff Eley, *Forging Democracy: The History of the Left in Europe, 1850–2000* (New York: Oxford University Press, 2002); Ira Katznelson and Aristide R. Zolberg, eds., *Working Class Formation: Nineteenth-Century Patterns in Western Europe and the United States* (Princeton: Princeton University Press, 1986). On the political orientation of Marx and Engels, see David Riazanov, *Karl Marx and Friedrich Engels: An Introduction to Their Lives and Work* (New York: Monthly Review Press, 1973); August H. Nimtz Jr., *Marx and Engels: Their Contribution to the Democratic Breakthrough* (Albany: State University Press of New York, 2000).
6. For a history of the US working class written from this standpoint, see Paul Le Blanc, *A Short History of the U.S. Working Class: From Colonial Times to the Twenty-First Century* (Amherst, NY: Humanity Books, 1999). For an application of Trotsky's theory to European history, see Paul Le Blanc, "Uneven and Combined

Development and the Sweep of History: Focus on Europe," *International Viewpoint*, September 21, 2006, www.internationalviewpoint.org/spip.php ?article1125.

7. Kim Moody, *Workers in a Lean World: Unions in the International Economy* (London: Verso, 1997), 178. Also see Paul Mason, *Live Working, Die Fighting: How the Working Class Went Global* (Chicago: Haymarket Books, 2010).

8. Hal Draper, *Karl Marx's Theory of Revolution*, vol. 2, *The Politics of Social Classes* (New York: Monthly Review Press, 1978), 34–38; Nicos Poulantzas, "On Social Classes," in *The Poulantzas Reader: Marxism, Law, and the State*, James Martin, ed. (London: Verso, 2008), 186–219; Erik Olin Wright, *Class, Crisis and the State* (London: Verso, 1979), 30–110. "Petty bourgeoisie" has traditionally meant small capitalists—owners of small businesses, independent artisans and professionals selling products and services, and independent small farmers. For some it has been common to include government employees, many or most "white collar" employees, etc. Sometimes it has also been conflated with the incredibly fuzzy term "middle class."

9. Phil Gasper, ed., *The Communist Manifesto: A Roadmap to History's Most Important Political Document* (Chicago: Haymarket Books, 2005), 39.

10. Francis G. Couvares, *The Remaking of Pittsburgh: Class and Culture in an Industrializing City, 1877–1919* (Albany: State University of New York, 1984). On the Paris Commune, see note 5 above.

11. This discussion draws substantially from my essay "Class and Identity," in Immanuel Ness et al., eds., *The International Encyclopedia of Revolution and Protest*, vol. 2 (Malden, MA: Blackwell Publishing/John Wiley and Sons, 2009), 776–83 (reproduced in the present volume). Weber's theorizations that correspond to aspects of identity conceptualizations can be found in H. H. Gerth and C. Wright Mills, eds., *From Max Weber: Essays in Sociology* (New York: Oxford University Press, 1958), 180–95.

12. This point is made in Roger Lancaster's brilliant anthropological study, *Life is Hard: Machismo, Danger, and the Intimacy of Power in Nicaragua* (Berkeley: University of California Press, 1992), 282.

13. David Roediger, "The Crisis in Labor History: Race, Gender and the Replotting of the Working Class Past in the United States," in *Towards the Abolition of Whiteness: Essays on Race, Politics, and Working Class History* (London: Verso, 1994), 76. Also see Sharon Smith, "Black Feminism and Intersectionality," *International Socialist Review*, 91 (Winter 2013): 6–24. This way of understanding the working class also owes much to Herbert G. Gutman, *Work, Culture and Society in Industrializing America* (New York: Vintage Books, 1977), 3–78; *Power and Culture: Essays on the American Working Class*, Ira Berlin, ed. (New York: Pantheon Books, 1987), 380–94.

14. See Jorge Larrain, "Ideology" in Tom Bottomore et al., eds., *A Dictionary of Marxist Thought*, 2nd ed. (Cambridge, MA: Basil Blackwell, 1991), 242–52.

15. This draws from Paul Le Blanc, "Spider and Fly: The Leninist Philosophy of Georg Lukács," *Historical Materialism* 21, no. 2 (2013): 47–75. More on class

consciousness can be found in Paul Le Blanc, *Lenin and the Revolutionary Party*, new edition (Chicago: Haymarket Books, 2015), 22–24, 27–33, 38–42, 52–61.

16. Charles Post, "Exploring Working-Class Consciousness: A Critique of the Theory of the 'Labour-Aristocracy,'" *Historical Materialism* 18, no. 4 (2010): 6, 25. See also the exposition in one of Post's targets, Max Elbaum and Robert Seltzer, *The Labour Aristocracy: The Material Basis for Opportunism in the Labour Movement* (Chippendale, NSW, Australia: Resistance Books, 2004). A criticism similar to that expressed here can be found in Alan Shandro, *Lenin and the Logic of Hegemony: Political Practice and Theory in the Class Struggle* (Leiden/Boston: Brill, 2014), 265.

17. This is drawn from Le Blanc, *Lenin and the Revolutionary Party*, 32, 262.

18. Ibid., 262. On the "pure and simple" ideology and practice that became dominant in the American Federation of Labor, see Philip S. Foner, *History of the Labor Movement in the United States,* vol. 2, *From the Founding of the American Federation of Labor to the Emergence of American Imperialism* (New York: International Publishers, 1955); *History of the Labor Movement in the United States,* vol. 3, *The Policies and Practices of the American Federation of Labor, 1900–1909* (New York: International Publishers, 1964); *History of the Labor Movement in the United States,* vol. 5, *The AFL in the Progressive Era, 1910–1915* (New York: International Publishers, 1980). Also see Paul Le Blanc, *Work and Struggle: Voices from U.S. Labor Radicalism* (New York: Routledge, 2011).

19. V. I. Lenin, "What Is to Be Done?" (1902), in *Revolution, Democracy, Socialism: Selected Writings*, Paul Le Blanc, ed. (London: Pluto Press, 2008), 143.

20. Lenin, "The Revolutionary Proletariat and the Right of Nations to Self-Determination" (1915), in Le Blanc, *Revolution, Democracy, Socialism*, 233–34. For discussion of "cutting-edge" aspects of Lenin's approach, also see Shandro (cited in note 17 above); Kevin Anderson, *Lenin, Hegel, and Western Marxism: A Critical Study* (Urbana: University of Illinois Press, 1995).

3: Radical Labor Subculture

1. My thanks to Michael Yates and Anthony Arnove for helpful feedback on earlier drafts of this paper. The paper was first presented at Historical Materialism conference, New York City, January 14–16, 2010. The present essay draws substantially from Paul Le Blanc, "Culture, Consciousness, and Class Struggle: Further Notes on the Relevance of Leninism," *Bulletin in Defense of Marxism*, no. 115, April 1994. Aspects of the analysis can also be found in Paul Le Blanc, "A Comment on Mary Scully's Polemic," *Bulletin in Defense of Marxism*, no. 113, February 1994; Paul Le Blanc, *Lenin and the Revolutionary Party* (Atlantic Highlands, NJ: Humanities Press, 1993), 354–60; Paul Le Blanc, "Notes on Building a Revolutionary Party in the United States," *Bulletin in Defense of Marxism*, no. 107, June 1993, and no. 109, July–August 1993; Paul Le Blanc, "Leninism in the United States and the Decline of the Socialist Workers Party," in George Breitman, Paul Le Blanc, and Alan Wald, *Trotskyism in the United States: Historical Essays and Reconsiderations*, 2nd ed. (Chicago: Haymarket Books, 2016), 195–279; Paul Le Blanc, *Marx, Lenin, and the Revolutionary Experience: Studies*

of Communism and Radicalism in the Age of Globalization (New York: Routledge, 2006), 148–51; Paul Le Blanc, "Introduction: Ten Reasons for Not Reading Lenin," in V. I. Lenin, *Revolution, Democracy, Socialism: Selected Writings*, Paul Le Blanc, ed. (London: Pluto Press, 2008), 62–65.

2.   Raymond Williams, *Keywords: A Vocabulary of Culture and Society* (New York: Oxford University Press, 1983), 87–93.

3.   Clyde Kluckhohn and W. H. Kelly, "The Concept of Culture" (1945), cited in A. L. Kroeber and Clyde Kluckhohn, *Culture: A Critical Review of Concepts and Definitions* (New York: Vintage Books, n.d.), 82, 83, 84, 112, 141.

4.   Eleanor Leacock, "Marxism and Anthropology," in Bertell Ollman and Edward Vernoff, eds., *The Left Academy: Marxist Scholarship on American Campuses* (New York: McGraw-Hill, 1992), 267–68.

5.   V. I. Lenin, "Critical Remarks on the National Question," in *Collected Works*, vol. 20 (Moscow: Progress Publishers, 1972), 23–24.

6.   Leon Trotsky, *Problems of Everyday Life, and Other Writings on Culture and Science* (New York: Monad/Pathfinder Press, 1973), 19; Phil Gasper, ed., *The Communist Manifesto: A Roadmap to History's Most Important Political Document* (Chicago: Haymarket Books, 2005), 58–59.

7.   Karl Marx, *The Eighteenth Brumaire of Louis Bonaparte*, in Karl Marx and Frederick Engels, *Selected Works*, vol. 1 (Moscow: Progress Publishers, 1973), 398.

8.   E. P. Thompson, *Customs in Common: Studies in Traditional Popular Culture* (New York: The New Press, 1993), 12, 13, 16; E. P. Thompson, *The Making of the English Working Class* (New York: Vintage Books, 1966), 9–10, 11.

9.   Herbert Gutman, *Work, Culture and Society in Industrializing America* (New York: Vintage Books, 1977), 15, 18; Herbert Gutman, *Power and Culture: Essays on the American Working Class*, Ira Berlin, ed. (New York: Pantheon Books, 1987), 381.

10.   Eleanor Marx and Edward Aveling, *The Working-Class Movement in America*, Paul Le Blanc, ed. (Amherst, NY: Humanity Books, 2000), 70–72, 76, 77, 78, 79, 143, 146, 151.

11.   Quoted in Le Blanc, *A Short History of the U.S. Working Class*, 48.

12.   V. I. Lenin, "Draft and Explanation for the Social Democratic Party" (1895), cited in Le Blanc, *Lenin and the Revolutionary Party*, 26.

13.   There are ample materials demonstrating the historical phenomenon of this labor-radical subculture in the United States; for example, Philip S. Foner, *History of the Labor Movement in the United States*, 10 vols. (New York: International Publishers, 1947–94); Mari Jo Buhle, Paul Buhle, and Dan Georgakas, eds., *Encyclopedia of the American Left*, 2nd ed. (New York: Oxford University Press, 1998); Nicholas Coles and Janet Zandy, eds., *American Working-Class Literature: An Anthology* (New York: Oxford University Press, 2006); Laura Hapke, *Labor's Text: The Worker in American Fiction* (New Brunswick, NJ: Rutgers University Press, 2001); Edith Fowke and Joe Glazer, eds., *Songs of Work and Freedom* (New York: Dover, 1973); David Montgomery, *Beyond Equality: Labor and the Radical Republicans, 1862–1872* (New York: Alfred A. Knopf, 1967); Franklin Rosemont and David Roediger, eds., *The Haymarket Scrapbook* (Chicago: Charles

H. Kerr, 1986); Joyce Kornbluh, ed., *Rebel Voices: An IWW Anthology*, rev. ed. (Chicago: Charles H. Kerr, 1988); John Graham, ed., *"Yours for the Revolution": The Appeal to Reason, 1895–1922* (Lincoln, NE: University of Nebraska Press, 1990); Oscar Ameringer, *If You Don't Weaken* (New York: Henry Holt, 1940); James Weinstein, *The Decline of Socialism in America, 1912–1925* (New York: Vintage Books, 1969); Bryan D. Palmer, *James P. Cannon and the Origins of the American Revolutionary Left, 1890–1928* (Urbana: University of Illinois Press, 2007); Michael Denning, *The Cultural Front* (London: Verso, 1998).

14. On the struggles of the decade (which actually spilled over into the first half of the following decade), see Art Preis, *Labor's Giant Step: Twenty Years of the CIO* (New York: Pathfinder Press, 1972), 3–283; these struggles are connected to the labor-radical subculture in Le Blanc, *Marx, Lenin, and the Revolutionary Experience*, 153–98.

15. On the labor-radical subculture of the German working class, see Evelyn Anderson, *Hammer or Anvil: The Story of the German Working-Class Movement* (Alameda, CA: Center for Socialist History, 2007); Vernon L. Lidtke, *The Alternative Culture: Socialist Labor in Imperial Germany* (New York: Oxford University Press, 1985); Eric D. Weitz, *Creating German Communism, 1890–1990* (Princeton, NJ: Princeton University Press, 1997). Also see Pierre Broué, *The German Revolution, 1917–1923* (Leiden, The Netherlands/Boston, MA: Brill, 2005), 14–16, 627–46.

16. Antonio Gramsci, *Selections from the Prison Notebooks*, Quintin Hoare and Geoffrey Nowell-Smith, eds. (New York: International Publishers, 1973), 16, 199, 204–5, 232–33, 340.

17. Leon Trotsky, "The United Front for Defense" (February 23, 1933), in Leon Trotsky, *The Struggle against Fascism in Germany*, George Breitman and Merry Maisel, eds. (New York: Pathfinder Press, 1971), 367.

18. Antonio Gramsci, "On Fascism 1921" and "Democracy and Fascism," in David Beetham, ed., *Marxists in the Face of Fascism* (Manchester, UK: Manchester University Press, 1983), 83, 84, 85, 121.

19. Frank Lovell, "The Socialist Purpose: To Educate the Working Class," in Paul Le Blanc and Thomas Barrett, eds., *Revolutionary Labor Socialist: The Life, Ideas, and Comrades of Frank Lovell* (Union City, NJ: Smyrna Press, 2000), 133; Ernest Mandel, *The Meaning of the Second World War* (London: Verso, 1986), 45, 159–68, 169.

20. Frank Lovell, "The Cataclysm: World War II and the History of American Trotskyism," in Le Blanc and Barrett, *Revolutionary Labor Socialist*, 135; Michael D. Yates, *In and Out of the Working Class* (Winnipeg, MB: Arbeiter Ring Publishing, 2009), 45.

21. Steve Nelson, with James R. Barrett and Robert Ruck, *Steve Nelson, American Radical* (Pittsburgh: University of Pittsburgh Press, 1981), 284–85.

22. A variety of informative and stimulating works provide information and insights on what is described here: Harry Braverman, *Labor and Monopoly Capital: The Degradation of Work in the Twentieth Century* (New York: Monthly Review Press, 2003); Lizabeth Cohen, *A Consumers' Republic: The Politics of Mass Consumption in Post-War America* (New York: Vintage, 2003); Mike Davis, *Prisoners of the*

American Dream: Politics and Economy in the History of the U.S. Working Class, 2nd ed. (New York: W. W. Norton, 2000); David M. Gordon, Richard Edwards, and Michael Reich, *Segmented Work, Divided Workers: The Historical Transformation of Labor in the United States* (Cambridge: Cambridge University Press, 1882); George Lipsitz, *Rainbow at Midnight: Labor and Culture in the 1940s* (Urbana: University of Illinois Press, 1994); Kim Moody, *An Injury to All: The Decline of American Unionism* (London: Verso, 1988).

23. James P. Cannon, "Trade Unionists and Revolutionists," in *Speeches to the Party* (New York: Pathfinder Press, 1973), 57, 58.

24. John C. Leggett, *Race, Class and Political Consciousness: Working-Class Consciousness in Detroit* (New York: Oxford University Press, 1968), 52, 53.

25. Stanley Aronowitz, *False Promises: The Shaping of American Working-Class Consciousness,* rev. ed. (Durham: Duke University Press, 1992), 95; James Boggs, *American Revolution: Pages from a Negro Worker's Notebook* (New York: Monthly Review Press, 1963), 15, 16.

26. Sol Chick Chaikin, *A Labor Viewpoint: Another Opinion* (Monroe, NY: Library Research Associates, 1980), 220; Archie Robinson, *George Meany and His Times: A Biography* (New York: Simon & Schuster, 1981), 294.

27. V. I. Lenin, *Left-Wing Communism, an Infantile Disorder,* in Lenin, *Revolution, Democracy, Socialism,* 306.

28. Warren R. Van Tine, *The Making of the Labor Bureaucrat: Union Leadership in the United States, 1870–1920* (Amherst, MA: University of Massachusetts Press, 1973), 33, 56.

29. The triumphant, several decades-long campaign is beautifully described and documented in Kim Phillips-Fein, *Invisible Hands: The Making of the Conservative Movement from the New Deal to Reagan* (New York: W. W. Norton, 2009). Its impact is capably analyzed in Patricia Cayo Sexton, *The War on Labor and the Left: Understanding America's Unique Conservatism* (Boulder, CO: Westview Press, 1991).

30. Kim Moody, *U.S. Labor in Trouble and Transition: The Failure of Reform from Above, the Promise of Revival from Below* (London: Verso, 2007), 11.

31. Ibid., 246–47; Michael D. Yates, *Why Unions Matter,* 2nd ed. (New York: Monthly Review Press, 2009), 205; Dan Clawson, *The Next Upsurge: Labor and the New Social Movements* (Ithaca, NY: ILR/Cornell University Press, 2003), 196; Bill Fletcher Jr. and Fernando Gapasin, *Solidarity Divided: The Crisis in Organized Labor and a New Path Toward Social Justice* (Berkeley: University of California Press, 2008), 198.

5: Democracy

1. See *The People Speak,* directed by Anthony Arnove, Chris Moore, and Howard Zinn (2009; New York: A&E Home Video, 2010); Howard Zinn, *A People's History of the United States* (New York: HarperCollins, 2004).

2. C. L. R. James (with Raya Dunayevskaya and Grace Lee Boggs), "The Invading Socialist Society," in Noel Ignatiev, ed., *A New Notion: Two Works by C. L. R. James* (Oakland, CA: PM Press, 2010), 28. Also see David Forgacs, ed. *An Antonio*

Gramsci Reader (New York: Schocken Books, 1988); Gregor Benton, ed., *Chen Duxiu's Last Articles and Letters, 1937–1942* (Honolulu: University of Hawaii Press, 1998); Michael Pearlman, ed., *The Heroic and Creative Meaning of Socialism: Selected Essays of José Carlos Mariátegui* (Amherst, NY: Humanity Books, 1996).

3.   James P. Cannon, "Socialism and Democracy," in *Speeches for Socialism* (New York: Pathfinder Press, 1971), 356, 361. Also see Jean Tussey, ed., *Eugene V. Debs Speaks* (New York: Pathfinder Press, 197) and Paul Le Blanc, *From Marx to Gramsci: A Reader in Revolutionary Marxist Politics* (Amherst, NY: Humanity Books, 1996).

4.   The controversial conception of *bourgeois revolution* is discussed and defended intelligently in Colin Mooers, *The Making of Bourgeois Europe* (London: Verso, 1991) and Henry Heller, *The Bourgeois Revolution in France, 1789–1815* (New York: Berghahan Books, 2006).

5.   See Pauline Maier, *American Scripture: Making the Declaration of Independence* (New York: Vintage Books, 1998).

6.   I had to look up the definitions of some of Morris's words. *Vernal* means "spring-time," and "casting off one's winter slough" is what snakes and other reptiles do—shedding their dead skin. For the quotes, see Gary B. Nash, *The Unknown American Revolution. The Unruly Birth of Democracy and the Struggle to Create America* (New York: Penguin Books, 2005), 100, 203, 206, 278–79, 367; Sean Wilentz, *The Rise of American Democracy, Jefferson to Lincoln* (New York: W. W. Norton, 2005), 32.

7.   Knox quoted in Diego Rivera and Bertram D. Wolfe, *Portrait of America* (New York: Covici Friede, 1934), 104; Wilentz, 27–28. Also see Edward Countryman, *The American Revolution*, rev. ed. (New York: Hill and Wang, 2003).

8.   M. I. Finley, *Democracy Ancient and Modern*, rev. ed. (Rutgers, NJ: Rutgers University Press, 1985), 13; Ellen Meiksins Wood, "Demos Versus 'We the People': Freedom and Democracy Ancient and Modern," in *Dēmokratia: A Conversation on Democracies, Ancient and Modern*, Josiah Ober and Charles Hedrick, eds. (Princeton, NJ: Princeton University Press, 1996), 122–23, 132; Alexander Hamilton, James Madison, and John Jay, *The Federalist Papers*, Clinton Rossiter, ed. (New York: New American Library, 1961), 214, 215.

9.   *Federalist Papers*, 79, 81, 322–25.

10.   Dietrich Rueschemeyer, Evelyne Huber Stephens, and John D. Stephens, *Capitalist Development and Democracy* (Chicago: University of Chicago Press, 1992), 40, 44, 122–32.

11.   Ibid., 141, 140. Also see Göran Therborn, "The Rule of Capital and the Rise of Democracy," *New Left Review* 103 (1977): 3–41; and Geoff Eley, *Forging Democracy: The History of the Left in Europe, 1850–2000* (New York: Oxford University Press, 2002).

12.   August H. Nimtz Jr., *Marx and Engels: Their Contribution to the Democratic Breakthrough* (Albany, NY: State University of New York Press, 2000), vii; also see my review of the book, "Marx and Engels: Democratic Revolutionaries," *International Viewpoint*, September 2002, www.internationalviewpoint.org/spip .php?article381.

13.   Karl Marx and Frederick Engels, The *Communist Manifesto: A Road Map to*

History's Most Important Documents, Phil Gasper, ed. (Chicago: Haymarket Books, 2005), 42–43, 53, 56, 59, 69. On "true democracy" being the same as communism, see Richard N. Hunt, *The Political Ideas of Marx and Engels*, vol. 1 (Pittsburgh: University of Pittsburgh Press, 1974), 74–75; Michael Löwy, *The Theory of Revolution in the Young Marx* (Chicago: Haymarket Books, 2005), 41–43.

14.   Karl Marx, "The Civil War in France," in *The First International and After: Political Writings*, vol. 3, David Fernbach, ed. (Harmondsworth, UK: Penguin Books, 1974), 210; Karl Marx and Frederick Engels, *Selected Correspondence*, rev. ed, S. Ryzanskaya, ed. (Moscow: Progress Publishers, 1965), 452.

15.   "Practical Politics," *Alarm*, October 11, 1884, 1 (microfilm).

16.   Albert Einstein, "Why Socialism?," *Monthly Review*, May 1949, www.monthlyreview.org/598einstein.php.

17.   Sheldon Wolin, "Transgression, Equality, and Voice," in *Dēmokratia*, Ober and Hedrick, eds., 87.

18.   Paul Goodman, "Getting Into Power," in *Seeds of Liberation*, Paul Goodman, ed. (New York: George Braziller, 1964), 433.

19.   On the profoundly democratic nature of the 1917 revolution, and on the horrors of its aftermath see Rex A. Wade, *The Russian Revolution, 1917* (New York: Cambridge University Press, 2000); William Henry Chamberlin, *The Russian Revolution, 1917–1921* (Princeton: Princeton University Press, 1987). On the faulty theoretical justifications, see Hal Draper, *The "Dictatorship of the Proletariat" from Marx to Lenin* (New York: Monthly Review Press, 1987). On the Stalinist dictatorship, see Leon Trotsky, *The Revolution Betrayed* (New York: Doubleday, Doran, 1937); Roy Medvedev, *Let History Judge: The Origins and Consequences of Stalinism* (New York: Columbia University Press, 1989).

20.   V. I. Lenin, "The Revolutionary Proletariat and the Right of Nations to Self-Determination," in *Revolution, Democracy, Socialism: Selected Writings*, Paul Le Blanc, ed. (London: Pluto Press, 2006), 233–34.

21.   Trotsky, "The United Front for Defense," 367–68.

6: Making Sense of Postrevolutionary Russia

1.   Kunal Chattopadhyay, *The Marxism of Leon Trotsky* (Kolkata: Progress Publishers, 2006).

2.   See Isaac Deutscher, *The Prophet: The Life of Leon Trotsky* (London: Verso, 2015); Pierre Broué, *Trotsky* (Paris: Fayard, 1988); Tony Cliff, *Trotsky*, 4 vols. (London: Bookmarks, 1989–94).

3.   See Ernest Mandel, *Trotsky as Alternative* (London: Verso, 1995); Michael Löwy, *The Politics of Combined and Uneven Development: Trotsky's Theory of Permanent Revolution* (London: Verso, 1981); Duncan Hallas, *Trotsky's Marxism and Other Essays* (Chicago: Haymarket Books, 2003); and John Molyneux, *Leon Trotsky's Theory of Revolution* (New York: St. Martin's Press, 1981).

4.   Baruch Knei-Paz, *The Social and Political Thought of Leon Trotsky* (Oxford: Oxford University Press, 1978).

5. Chattopadhyay, *The Marxism of Leon Trotsky*, 359.
6. Ibid., 398.
7. Ibid., 537.
8. Ibid., 515.
9. Ibid., 436.
10. Ibid., 440.
11. Ibid., 447.
12. For an impressive challenge to the gist of Trotsky's 1904 criticism of Lenin and thus of Chattopadhyay's characterization, see Lars Lih's splendid *Lenin Rediscovered* (Chicago: Haymarket Books, 2008).
13. Chattopadhyay, *The Marxism of Leon Trotsky*, 220.
14. Marcel van der Linden, *Western Marxism and the Soviet Union* (Chicago: Haymarket Books, 2009). Hereafter, page numbers for this book are cited in parentheses.
15. Lenin, "The Party Crisis," in *Revolution, Democracy, Socialism*, 336.

7: The Darker the Night the Brighter the Star

1. Tony Cliff, *Trotsky: The Darker the Night the Brighter the Star 1927–1940*, vol. 4 (London: Bookmarks, 1993). A more succinct account is offered in Paul Le Blanc, *Leon Trotsky* (London: Reaktion Books, 2015), from which some elements in this presentation are drawn. Also see an intimately knowledgeable account in Victor Serge and Natalia Sedova, *The Life and Death of Leon Trotsky* (Chicago: Haymarket Books, 2016), and Isaac Deutscher's massive classic, *The Prophet: The Life of Leon Trotsky* (London: Verso, 2015).
2. Friedrich Schlotterbeck, *The Darker the Night, the Brighter the Stars* (London: Victor Gollancz, 1947). For more on this, see Allan Merson, *Communist Resistance in Nazi Germany* (London: Lawrence and Wishart, 1986), and Donny Gluckstein, *The Nazis, Capitalism, and the Working Class* (Chicago: Haymarket Books, 2012).
3. Leon Trotsky, "The Beginning of the End," *Writings of Leon Trotsky, 1936–37*, Naomi Allen and George Breitman, eds. (New York: Pathfinder Press, 1978), 328–29.
4. Roy Medvedev, *Let History Judge: The Origins and Consequences of Stalinism* (New York: Columbia University Press, 1989); Mikhail Baitalsky, *Notebooks for the Grandchildren: Recollections of a Trotskyist Who Survived the Stalin Terror* (Atlantic Highlands, NJ: Humanities Press, 1995).
5. Maria Joffe, *One Long Night: A Tale of Truth* (London: New Park, 1978), 162, 190.
6. Nadezhda Joffe, *Back in Time: My Life, My Fate, My Epoch* (Oak Park, MI: Mehring Books, 1995), 84.
7. George Saunders, ed., *Samizdat: Voices of the Soviet Opposition* (New York, 1974), 141.
8. Joseph Berger, *Shipwreck of a Generation* (London: Haverill, 1971), 94–95.
9. Saunders, ed., *Samizdat*, 206, 210–11.
10. Joffe, *Back in Time*, 40–41.
11. Berger, *Shipwreck of a Generation*, 96–98; Saunders, ed., *Samizdat*, 215, 216.
12. Joffe, *Back in Time*, 190; Moshe Lewin, *The Soviet Century* (London: Verso, 2005),

106–7; Vadim M. Rogovin, *Stalin's Terror of 1937–1938* (Oak Park, MI: Mehring Books, 2009), 446–47. Also see Oleg V. Khlevniuk, *The History of the Gulag: From Collectivization to the Great Terror* (New Haven, CT: Yale University Press, 2004).

13. Thomas M. Twiss, *Trotsky and the Problem of Soviet Bureaucracy* (Chicago: Haymarket Books, 2015). Trotsky's analysis is capably compared with others' in Marcel van der Linden, *Western Marxism and the Soviet Union* (Chicago: Haymarket Books, 2009).

14. Leon Trotsky, *The Revolution Betrayed* (New York: Pathfinder Press, 1972), 56; Karl Marx, "The German Ideology," in *Writings of the Young Marx on Philosophy and Society*, Loyd Easton and Kurt H. Guddat, eds. (Garden City, NY: Doubleday, 1967), 427. A more substantial summary of the revolutionary Marxist orientation can be found in Paul Le Blanc, *From Marx to Gramsci* (Chicago: Haymarket Books, 2016), 3–145.

15. Leon Trotsky, *The Permanent Revolution and Results and Prospects* (London: Resistance Books, 2007); Michael Löwy, *The Politics of Combined and Uneven Development: Trotsky's Theory of Permanent Revolution* (Chicago: Haymarket Books, 2014).

16. Trotsky, *The Revolution Betrayed*, 112.

17. E. H. Carr, *The Russian Revolution from Lenin to Stalin, 1917–1929* (New York: Palgrave Macmillan, 2004); Victor Serge, *From Lenin to Stalin* (New York: Pathfinder Press, 1973); Michal Reiman, *The Birth of Stalinism* (Bloomington: Indiana University Press, 1987). Reference to "skinflint reactionary utopia" is from Leon Trotsky, *The Third International after Lenin* (New York: Pathfinder Press, 1970), 45–46.

18. Robert C. Tucker, *Stalin in Power: The Revolution from Above, 1928–1941* (New York: W. W. Norton, 1992).

19. See Stephen F. Cohen, *Bukharin and the Bolshevik Revolution* (New York: Vintage Books, 1975); Moshe Lewin, *Russian Peasants and Soviet Power: A Study of Collectivization* (New York: W. W. Norton, 1975).

20. Trotsky, *The Revolution Betrayed*, 120.

21. David Dallin, *The Real Soviet Russia*, 2nd ed. (New Haven, CT: Yale University Press, 1947), 121. Naturally, those at the top of the bureaucratic pyramid lived a variant of the "good life" much closer to that of our own top 1 percent—see Ernest Mandel, *Power and Money: A Marxist Theory of Bureaucracy* (London: Verso, 1992), 72–74. A comparative analysis of ruling elites and inequality under capitalism and Stalinism is offered in Paul Le Blanc, *Marx, Lenin, and the Revolutionary Experience: Studies of Communism and Radicalism in the Age of Globalization* (New York: Routledge, 2006), 15–48.

22. Trotsky, *The Revolution Betrayed*, 281–90.

8: Origins and Trajectory of the Cuban Revolution

1. Samuel Farber, *The Origins of the Cuban Revolution Reconsidered* (Chapel Hill: University of North Carolina Press, 2006).

2. Tom Gjelten, "Cuba's Castro an Inspiration, Not a Role Model," NPR, September 15, 2006, www.npr.org/templates/story/story.php?storyId=6083227.

3. Jorge Castañeda, *Utopia Unarmed: The Latin American Left after the Cold War* (New York: Vintage Books, 1994).

4. Farber, *Origins of the Cuban Revolution*, 49,

5. Ibid., 57, 58, 59.

6. Ibid., 61, 63.

7. Among the useful accounts of the revolution are Robert Taber, *M-26: The Biography of a Revolution* (New York: Lyle Stuart, 1961); Carlos Franqui, *Diary of the Cuban Revolution* (New York: Viking Press, 1980); K. S. Karol, *Guerrillas in Power: The Course of the Cuban Revolution* (New York: Hill and Wang, 1970); Marta Harnecker, *Fidel Castro's Political Strategy: From Moncada to Victory* (New York: Pathfinder Press, 1987). A valuable general source can be found in Aviva Chomsky, Barry Carr, and Pamela Maria Smorkaloff, eds., *The Cuba Reader: History, Culture, Politics* (Durham, NC: Duke University Press, 2003).

8. Franqui, *Diary of the Cuban Revolution*, vi.

9. Farber, *Origins*, 133; emphasis added.

10. Ibid., 40, 178–179.

11. Ibid., 137, 179.

12. Ibid., 134, 135, 138.

13. Ibid., 63, 67, 127.

14. Ibid., 64–65.

15. Ibid., 39.

16. Harnecker, *Fidel Castro's Political Strategy*, 102–3.

17. Farber, *Origins*, 49–50.

18. Ibid., 65.

19. Ibid., 4–5.

20. Carlos Franqui, *Family Portrait with Fidel* (New York: Vintage Books, 1985), 23, 24, 58, 158–159; Farber, *Origins*, 60–61, 114, 125–26.

21. Farber, *Origins*, 63.

22. Ibid., 120, 133, 135, 136.

23. Ibid., 70.

24. Ibid., 70, 71, 76.

25. Ibid., 144, , 147, 152.

26. Ibid., 137.

27. Ibid., 5, 168.

28. Ibid., 68, 168.

29. Leo Huberman and Paul Sweezy, *Socialism in Cuba* (New York: Monthly Review Press, 1969), 204.

30. Janette Habel, *Cuba: The Revolution in Peril* (London: Verso, 1991); Frank T. Fitzgerald. *The Cuban Revolution in Crisis: From Managing Socialism to Managing Survival* (New York: Monthly Review Press, 1994).

31. Celia Hart, "Fidel and Trotsky," *International Viewpoint*, May 2006, www .internationalviewpoint.org/spip.php?article1052, and "'Welcome' . . . Trotsky," *International Viewpoint*, November 2005, www.internationalviewpoint.org/spip .php?article898. Unfortunately, Celia Hart and her brother died in a car accident

in 2008. Some of her writings can be found online at www.marxists.org/archive /celia-hart.

32. Hart, "'Welcome'. . . Trotsky."

33. Farber, *Origins*, 172.

9: Nicaragua

1. Thomas W. Walker, *Nicaragua, Land of Sandino*, 3rd ed. (Boulder, CO: Westview Press, 1991), in expanded incarnations, has long served as a useful broad entry point to Nicaraguan history. A regional contextualization and explicitly Marxist analysis are provided in James Dunkerley, *Power in the Isthmus: A Political History of Modern Central America* (London: Verso, 1988).

2. Richard Millet, *Guardians of the Dynasty: A History of the U.S. Created Guardia Nacional de Nicaragua* (Maryknoll, NY: Orbis Books, 1977), and Walter LaFeber's more broadly conceived *Inevitable Revolutions: The United States in Central America* (New York: W. W. Norton, 1984) provide essential background on US policy in regard to Nicaragua.

3. Gregorio Selser, *Sandino* (New York: Monthly Review Press, 1981), 89, 93; Donald Clark Hodges, *Intellectual Foundations of the Nicaraguan Revolution* (Austin: University of Texas Press, 1986), 9.

4. See Jaime Biderman, "The Development of Capitalism in Nicaragua: A Political Economic History," *Latin American Perspectives* 10, no. 1 (1983): 7–32.

5. George Black, *Triumph of the People: The Sandinista Revolution in Nicaragua* (London: Zed Books, 1981), 174. Black's informative account and that of Henri Weber, *Nicaragua: The Sandinist Revolution* (London: Verso, 1981), provide an early blend of eyewitness accounts, valuable background information, and sympathetic yet critical analysis by sophisticated radical journalists.

6. Bernard Diederich, *Somoza and the Legacy of U.S. Involvement in Central America* (New York: E. P. Dutton, 1981), 33.

7. Carlos Vilas, *The Sandinista Revolution: National Liberation and Social Transformation in Central America* (New York: Monthly Review Press 1986), 15, 105; Paul Le Blanc, *Workers and Revolution: A Comparative Study of Bolshevik Russia and Sandinist Nicaragua* (doctoral dissertation, University of Pittsburgh; Ann Arbor, MI: University Microfilms International), 143–79.

8. Information on conditions of the Nicaraguan population is drawn from Joseph Collins, with Frances Moore Lappé, Nick Allen, and Paul Rice, *Nicaragua: What Difference Could A Revolution Make? Food and Farming in the New Nicaragua*, 2nd ed. (San Francisco: Institute for Food Development Policy, 1985), 252; Bob Gibson, "A Structural Overview of the Nicaraguan Economy," in *The Political Economy of Revolutionary Nicaragua*, Rose J. Spalding, ed. (Boston: Unwin & Allen, 1987), 30, 31; Thomas John Bossert, "Health Care in Revolutionary Nicaragua," in *Nicaragua in Revolution*, Thomas W. Walker, ed. (New York: Praeger, 1982), 261–63; Reinaldo Antonio Téfel, Humberto Mendoza López, and Jorge Flores Castillo, "Social Welfare," in *Nicaragua: The First Five Years*, Thomas W. Walker, ed. (New York: Praeger, 1985), 366.

9. Among the valuable reminiscences of participants in the Sandinista struggle are Gioconda Belli, *The Country under My Skin: A Memoir of Love and War* (New York: Alfred A. Knopf, 2002); Omar Cabezas, *Fire from the Mountain: The Making of a Sandinista* (New York: Crown Publishers, 1985); Tomás Borge, *Carlos, the Dawn Is No Longer Beyond Our Reach* (Vancouver: New Star Books, 1984). A detailed exploration of the FSLN's martyred founder is provided in Matilde Zimmermann, *Sandinista: Carlos Fonseca and the Nicaraguan Revolution* (Durham, NC: Duke University Press, 2001), and a series of rich reflections by women who played an important role can be found in Margaret Randall, *Sandino's Daughters* (Vancouver: New Star Books, 1981).

10. Randall, *Sandino's Daughters*, 52.

11. Bruce Marcus, ed., *Sandinistas Speak* (New York: Pathfinder Press, 1982), 82.

12. Orlando Nuñez, "The Third Force in National Liberation Struggles," *Latin American Perspectives* 8, no. 2 (1981): 11–14.

13. Jiri Valenta and Esperanza Duran, eds., *Conflict in Nicaragua: A Multidimensional Perspective* (Boston: Allen and Unwin, 1987), 14.

14. Black, *Triumph of the People*, 267; Bruce Marcus, ed., *Nicaragua: The Sandinista People's Revolution* (New York: Pathfinder Press, 1985), 174.

15. Central American Historical Institute, "Analysis of Electoral Results," *Envío*, November 1984, 3a–6c; Harry E. Vanden and Gary Prevost, *Democracy and Socialism in Sandinista Nicaragua* (Boulder, CO: Lynne Rienner Publishers, 1993), 75–88.

16. Arnold Berthau, "Ten Years after the Nicaraguan Revolution," *International Viewpoint*, September 18, 1989, 26.

17. Omar Cabezas, "Our Revolution Will Not Be Destroyed," *Socialist Action*, April 1986, 7.

18. Thomas W. Walker, ed., *Reagan versus the Sandinistas: The Undeclared War on Nicaragua* (Boulder, CO: Westview Press, 1987), 67–72.

19. Cynthia Brown, ed., *With Friends Like These: Americas Watch Report on Human Rights and U.S. Policy in Latin America* (New York: Pantheon, 1985), 160; Catholic Institute for International Relations, *Right to Survive: Human Rights in Nicaragua* (London: CIIR, 1987), 34–40.

20. Thomas W. Walker, ed., *Revolution and Counterrevolution in Nicaragua* (Boulder, CO: Westview Press, 1991), 305, 345.

21. Ibid., 333.

22. Walker, *Reagan versus the Sandinistas*, 23.

23. Vanden and Prevost, *Democracy and Socialism in Sandinista Nicaragua*, 82–83.

24. Ibid., 142.

25. Vanden and Prevost, *Democracy and Socialism in Sandinista Nicaragua*, 129–51.

26. Ilja A. Luciak, *The Sandinista Legacy: Lessons from a Political Economy in Transition* (Gainesville: University Press of Florida, 1995), 44, 45.

27. Pierre La Ramée and Erica G. Polakoff, "The Evolution of Popular Organizations in Nicaragua," in *The Undermining of the Sandinista Revolution*, Harry E. Vanden and Gary Prevost, eds. (New York: Macmillan, 1997), 191, 196.

28. Stephen Kinzer, *Blood of Brothers: Life and War in Nicaragua* (New York: G. P.

Putnam's Sons, 1991), 394.

29. Roger Burbach, "Et Tu, Daniel? The Sandinista Revolution Betrayed," Global Alternatives, March 2009, http://globalalternatives.org/node/102; Maurice Lemoine, "Why Nicaragua Chose Ortega," Le Monde diplomatique, June 2012, http://mondediplo.com/2012/06/11nicaragua; Victor Figueroa-Clark, "21st Century Sandinismo—or Losing the Revolution?," Red Pepper, August 8, 2012, www.redpepper.org.uk/central-america-21st-century-sandinismo-or-losing-the-revolution/; Dan Kovalik, "Nicaragua: The Sandinista Revolution Continues!," Huffington Post, February 9, 2012, www.huffingtonpost.com/dan-kovalik/sandinista-revolution_b_1265367.html; Stephen Kinzer, "Daniel Ortega Is a Sandinista in Name Only," Al Jazeera, April 2015, http://america.aljazeera.com/opinions/2015/4/daniel-ortega-is-a-sandinista-in-name-only.html.

30. Alberto Cortés-Ramos and Martha Isabel Cranshaw, "Winning Elections, Losing the Revolution," Red Pepper, August 2012, www.redpepper.org.uk/central-america-21st-century-sandinismo-or-losing-the-revolution; "Bold and Light Interview with Mónica Baltodano," by pachakuti, Kaos en la Red, November 10, 2012, http://2014.kaosenlared.net/component/k2/37000-entrevista-intr%C3%A9pida-y-liviana-a-m%C3%B3nica-baltodano.html; Augusto Zamora, "Some Reflections on the Piñata," Envío, July, 1996, www.envio.org.ni/articulo/3019; Tim Rodgers, "Nicaragua's Newest Tycoon? 'Socialist' President Daniel Ortega," Christian Science Monitor, October 14, 2009, www.csmonitor.com/World/Americas/2009/1014/p06s01-woam.html.

31. Burbach, "Et Tu, Daniel?"; Chuck Kaufman, "Nicaragua Will NOT Have the Next Coup," Alliance for Global Justice, April 22, 2010, http://afgj.org/nicaragua-will-not-have-the-next-coup; Lemoine, "Why Nicaragua Chose Ortega."

32. Mónica Baltodano, "What Mutations Have Turned the FSLN into What It Is Today?," Envío, January 2014, www.envio.org.ni/articulo/4804.

33. Jon Lee Anderson, "The Comandante's Canal," New Yorker, March 10, 2014, www.newyorker.com/magazine/2014/03/10/the-comandantes-canal.

34. Chuck Kaufman, "Nicaragua Vive! 35 Years since the Triumph of the Sandinista Revolution," Truthout, July 25, 2014, www.truth-out.org/opinion/item/25170-nicaragua-vive-35-years-since-the-triumph-of-the-sandinista-revolution; Lemoine, "Why Nicaragua Chose Ortega"; Figueroa-Clark, "21st Century Sandinismo"; Rory Carroll, "Second Coming of the Sandinistas Turns Sour," Guardian, January 10, 2009, www.theguardian.com/world/2009/jan/11/nicaragua-world-ortega 2009; Hector Tobar, "Old Rivals Unite in New Nicaragua," Los Angeles Times, October 24, 2006, http://articles.latimes.com/2006/oct/24/world/fg-ortega24.

35. Belli, The Country under My Skin; Andrew Anthony, "From Comandante to Caudillo," Guardian, November 7, 2006, www.theguardian.com/commentisfree/2006/nov/07/thecomandantewhobecameaca; Lemoine, "Why Nicaragua Chose Ortega"; Cortés-Ramos and Cranshaw, "Winning Elections"; Anderson, "The Comandante's Canal"; Kinzer, Daniel Ortega Is a Sandinista."

36. Alejandro Gutiérrez, "The Disconcerting 'Success' of Nicaragua's 'Anti-Poverty' Programs," NACLA, February 2010, https://nacla.org/news/disconcerting-%E2%80

%98success%E2%80%99-nicaragua%E2%80%99s-anti-poverty-programs; Katherine Hoyt, "Report from a Fact-Finding Trip to Nicaragua: Anti-Poverty Programs Make a Difference," NACLA, December 2009, https://nacla.org/node/6313; Kovalik, "Nicaragua"; Figueroa-Clark, "21st Century Sandinismo."

37. Lemoine, "Why Nicaragua Chose Ortega"; Hoyt, "Report from a Fact-Finding Trip"; Kovalik, "Nicaragua"; Kaufman, "Nicaragua Will NOT Have the Next Coup"; John Hollis, "Election Night in Nicaragua," *Counterpunch*, November 8, 2011, www.counterpunch.org/2011/11/08/election-night-in-nicaragua/; Figueroa-Clark, "21st Century Sandinismo."

38. Anderson, "The Comandante's Canal."

39. Ibid.; Lemoine, "Why Nicaragua Chose Ortega."

40. Rodgers, "Nicaragua's Newest Tycoon?"; Tim Johnson, "Despite Nicaragua's Constitution, Ortega Headed for Re-election," *Miami Herald*, November 2, 2011, www.miamiherald.com/news/nation-world/world/americas/article1938939.html; Anderson, "The Comandante's Canal."

41. Kinzer, "Daniel Ortega Is a Sandinista."

42. Baltodano, "What Mutations Have Turned the FSLN."

43. Rodgers, "Nicaragua's Newest Tycoon?"; Cortés-Ramos and Cranshaw, "Winning Elections"; Lemoine, "Why Nicaragua Chose Ortega"; Baltodano, "What Mutations Have Turned the FSLN."

44. Tobar, "Old Rivals Unite in New Nicaragua"; Anthony, "From Comandante to Caudillo"; Anderson, "The Comandante's Canal."

45. Cortés-Ramos and Cranshaw, "Winning Elections"; Baltodano, "What Mutations Have Turned the FSLN"; Rodgers, "Nicaragua's Newest Tycoon?"; Gutiérrez, "The Disconcerting 'Success' of Nicaragua's 'Anti-Poverty' Programs."

46. Baltodano, "What Mutations Have Turned the FSLN."

47. Diego Cupolo, "Construction of Nicaraguan Canal to Begin in Late 2014," *Upside Down World*, January 17, 2014, http://upsidedownworld.org/main/nicaragua-archives-62/4653-construction-of-nicaraguan-canal-to-begin-in-late-2014; Anderson, "The Comandante's Canal"; James S. Henry, "Nicaraguan Ortega's Power Grab," The Real News, October 3, 2014, http://therealnews.com/t2/index.php?option=com_content&task=view&id=31&Itemid=74&jumival=11058; Mark Burton and Chuck Kaufman, "Nicaragua's Grand Canal: The Other Side of the Story," *Liberation*, December 26, 2014, www.liberationnews.org/nicaraguas-grand-canal-side-story/.

48. Anderson, "The Comandante's Canal."

49. Ibid.

50. Baltodano, "What Mutations Have Turned the FSLN."

51. Anderson, "The Comandante's Canal"; Baltodano, "What Mutations Have Turned the FSLN."

52. Baltodano, "What Mutations Have Turned the FSLN."

53. *Envío* Team, "Notes Written beneath the Trees of Life," *Envío*, August, 2013, www.envio.org.ni/articulo/4733; Henry, "Nicaraguan Ortega's Power Grab"; Anderson, "The Comandante's Canal"; Rodgers, "Nicaragua's Newest Tycoon?"

54. Dora Maria Tellez, interview by Arlen Cerda, July 18, 2010, www.laprensa.com
    .ni/2010/07/18/politica/431030-ortega-fue-reclutado-por-el-somocismo.
55. Rodgers, "Nicaragua's Newest Tycoon?"
56. Tellez, interview.
57. Kinzer, "Daniel Ortega Is a Sandinista"; Rodgers, "Nicaragua's Newest Ty-
    coon?"; Baltodano, "What Mutations Have Turned the FSLN."
58. Baltodano, "What Mutations Have Turned the FSLN."
59. Email communication to author from Silvia Torres, August 30, 2017.
60. Baltodano, "What Mutations Have Turned the FSLN."
61. "Bold and Light Interview with Mónica Baltodano"; Baltodano, "What Muta-
    tions Have Turned the FSLN."
62. Baltodano, "What Mutations Have Turned the FSLN."
63. Ibid.
64. Ibid.
65. Ibid.; Rodgers, "Nicaragua's Newest Tycoon?"

10: South Africa

1. Melissa de Villiers et al., *South Africa* (London: Insight Guides, 2004), 21–23,
   52; John Hoffman and Nxumalo Mzala, "'Non-Historic Nations': A South African Perspective," *Science and Society* 54, no. 4 (1990): 408–26; Allister Sparks, *The
   Mind of South Africa* (New York: Ballantine Books, 1991), 121.
2. A useful synthesis is found in Nigel Worden, *The Making of Modern South Africa*,
   3rd ed. (Oxford: Blackwell, 2000). See also Robert Ross, *A Concise History of
   South Africa* (Cambridge: Cambridge University Press, 1999).
3. Rosa Luxemburg, *The Accumulation of Capital* (London: Routledge and Kegan
   Paul, 1951), 411–16; Worden, *The Making of Modern South Africa*, 86, 98–106.
4. Harold Wolpe, "Capitalism and Cheap Labor Power in South Africa: From
   Segregation to Apartheid," in *Segregation and Apartheid in Twentieth-Century
   South Africa*, William Beinart and Saul Dubow, eds. (London: Routledge, 1995),
   88; Ernest Harsch, *South Africa: White Rule, Black Revolt*, 2nd ed. (New York:
   Pathfinder Press, 1983), 14.
5. Kevin Danaher, *In Whose Interest? A Guide to U.S.-South Africa Relations* (Washington, DC: Institute for Policy Studies, 1985), 45; Sparks, *The Mind of South
   Africa*, 121.
6. Saul Dubow, *The African National Congress* (Johannesburg: Jonathan Ball Publishers, 2000), 3, 4, 9, 11.
7. Edward Roux, *Time Longer than Rope: A History of the Black Man's Struggle
   for Freedom in South Africa*, 2nd ed. (Madison: University of Wisconsin Press,
   1964), ix, 125, 126, 129.
8. Ibid., 198–217. A. Lerumo [Michael Harmel], *Fifty Fighting Years: The Communist Party of South Africa, 1921–1971* (London: Inkululenko, 1971), 63; Thomas
   K. Ranuga, *The New South Africa and the Socialist Vision: Positions and Perspectives
   toward a Post-Apartheid Society* (Atlantic Highlands, NJ: Humanities Press,
   1996), 23.

9. Lerumo, *Fifty Fighting Years*, 63, 67, 72; Dubow, *The African National Congress*, 12–19; Ranuga, *The New South Africa*, 25–31.

10. *Long Walk to Freedom: The Autobiography of Nelson Mandela* (Boston: Little, Brown, 1995), 120–21.

11. Lerumo, *Fifty Fighting Years*, 98–102; Roux, *Time Longer than Rope*, 319.

12. Roux, *Time Longer than Rope*, 308; Lerumo, *Fifty Fighting Years*, 159; Martin J. Murray, *Revolution Deferred: The Painful Birth of Post-Apartheid South Africa* (London: Verso, 2000), 126; Dubow, *The African National Congress*, 31; Steven Mufson, *Fighting Years: Black Resistance and the Struggle for a New South Africa* (Boston: Beacon Press, 1990), 223; Stephan Ellis and Tsepo Sechaba, *Comrades against Apartheid: The ANC and the South African Communist Party in Exile* (Bloomington: Indiana University Press, 1992), 22, 37; George Padmore, *Pan-Africanism or Communism* (Garden City, NY: Anchor Books, 1972), 126.

13. Nelson Mandela, *The Struggle Is My Life* (New York: Pathfinder Press, 1986), 173, 174; Mufson, *Fighting Years*, 142; Padmore, *Pan-Africanism or Communism*, 268; Ranuga, *The New South Africa*, 55–62.

14. Mandela, *The Struggle Is My Life*, 50–54; Dubow, *The African National Congress*, 50–52; Ellis and Sechaba, *Comrades against Apartheid*, 28; Mufson, *Fighting Years*, 224; Ranuga, *The New South Africa*, 46–52.

15. Dubow, *The African National Congress*, 51.

16. Padmore, *Pan-Africanism or Communism*, 339–40.

17. Padmore, *Pan-Africanism or Communism*, xix. The Four Freedoms are 1) freedom of thought and religion, 2) freedom of speech and expression, 3) freedom from fear, and 4) freedom from want.

18. Ranuga, *The New South Africa*, 77–87; Roux, *Time Longer than Rope*, 402–14.

19. Dennis Brutus, "March 21, 1987," *Airs and Tributes*, Gil Ott, ed. (Camden, NJ: Whirlwind Press, 1990), 2.

20. Donald Woods, *Biko*, rev. ed. (New York: Henry Holt, 1987), 57, 59, 122.

21. Black Communities Programs document, quoted in Ranuga, *The New South Africa*, 98.

22. John Kane-Berman, *South Africa: The Method in the Madness* (London: Pluto Press, 1979); Mufson, *Fighting Years*, 13–19; Ellis and Sechaba, *Comrades against Apartheid*, 80–86; Ranuga, *The New South Africa*, 103–7; Harsch, *South Africa*, 281–84; Worden, *The Making of Modern South Africa*, 135.

23. Murray, *Revolution Deferred*, 119, 124, 125.

24. Nathaniel Weyl, *Traitors' End: The Rise and Fall of the Communist Movement in Southern Africa* (New Rochelle, NY: Arlington House, 1970), 89, 131.

25. Anthony Sampson, *Mandela: The Authorized Biography* (New York: Alfred A. Knopf, 1999), 64; Sebastian Mallaby, *After Apartheid: The Future of South Africa* (New York: Random House, 1993), 233; Ellis and Sechaba, *Comrades against Apartheid*, 24, 25; Ranuga, *The New South Africa*, 55–56.

26. Sampson, *Mandela*, 136, 564–65.

27. Mallaby, *After Apartheid*, 233; Mandela, *Long Walk to Freedom*, 74–75.

28. Ronnie Kasrils, *"Armed and Dangerous": My Undercover Struggle against Apartheid*

(Cambridge, UK: Heinemann, 1994), 368; Ross, *A Concise History of South Africa*, 184–85; Lerumo, *Five Fighting Years*, 133; Mandela, *Long Walk to Freedom*, 102, 120; Ellis and Sechaba, *Comrades against Apartheid*, 21; Roux, *Time Longer than Rope*, 330, 383.

29. Brutus, "For Ruth First," *Airs and Tributes*, 13.
30. Desmond Tutu, *The Rainbow People of God*, John Allen, ed. (New York: Doubleday, 1994), 253.
31. Harsch, *South Africa*, 13, 80.
32. Worden, *The Making of Modern South Africa*, 138.
33. Sparks, *The Mind of South Africa*, 373.
34. Ibid., 337.
35. Worden, *The Making of Modern South Africa*, 145; Martin Murray, *South Africa: Time of Agony, Time of Destiny* (London: Verso, 1987), 221, 229–30.
36. Murray, *South Africa*, 229; Worden, *The Making of Modern South Africa*, 154.
37. Dubow, *The African National Congress*, 106; Leonard Thompson, *A History of South Africa* (New Haven, CT: Yale University Press, 2000), 225, 236; Murray, *Revolution Deferred*, 121–22, 128, 143–46.
38. John S. Saul, "Cry for the Beloved Country: The Post-Apartheid Denouement," *Monthly Review*, January 2001, 12, 14.
39. Dubow, *The African National Congress*, 109; Murray, *Revolution Deferred*, 5.
40. Patrick Bond, *Talk Left, Walk Right: South Africa's Frustrated Global Reforms* (Scottsville, SA: University of KwaZulu-Natal Press, 2004), 180; Saul, "Cry for the Beloved Country," 28, 29, 43.
41. Dale T. McKinley, "Debate and Opposition within the ANC and the Tripartite Alliance since 1994," *Links*, no. 16 (2000): 55, 56.
42. Ibid., 71. Also see Bond, *Talk Left, Walk Right*, 179–90.
43. Worden, *The Making of Modern South Africa*, 164; de Villiers et al., *South Africa*, 71, 73;
44. Bond, *Talk Left, Walk Right*, 14, 15.
45. "The 9th SACP Congress—a Key Strategic Challenge," and Jeremy Cronin, "Challenging the Neo-Liberal Agenda in South Africa," *South African Communist*, no. 139/140, First Quarter (1995): 3, 38, 49.
46. Thompson, *A History of South Africa*, 290; Murray, *Revolution Deferred*, 124, 128.
47. Bond, *Talk Left, Walk Right*, 231.
48. Roy quoted in Paul Le Blanc, "The World Social Forum, 2004," *Against the Current*, no. 109, March/April 2004, http://solidarity-us.org/site/node/414.
49. Bond, *Talk Left, Walk Right*, 4, 192; the quote by the South African analysts comes from "Report of the Anti-War Coalition/Rosa Luxemburg Foundation Seminar, May 20–22, 2004, at the Workers' Library and Museum, Newtown Precinct, Johannesburg," Rosa Luxemburg Foundation, 2004.

Index

About Haymarket Books

Haymarket Books is a radical, independent, nonprofit book publisher based in Chicago.

Our mission is to publish books that contribute to struggles for social and economic justice. We strive to make our books a vibrant and organic part of social movements and the education and development of a critical, engaged, international left.

We take inspiration and courage from our namesakes, the Haymarket martyrs, who gave their lives fighting for a better world. Their 1886 struggle for the eight-hour day—which gave us May Day, the international workers' holiday—reminds workers around the world that ordinary people can organize and struggle for their own liberation. These struggles continue today across the globe—struggles against oppression, exploitation, poverty, and war.

Since our founding in 2001, Haymarket Books has published more than five hundred titles. Radically independent, we seek to drive a wedge into the risk-averse world of corporate book publishing. Our authors include Noam Chomsky, Arundhati Roy, Rebecca Solnit, Angela Davis, Howard Zinn, Amy Goodman, Wallace Shawn, Mike Davis, Winona LaDuke, Ilan Pappé, Richard Wolff, Dave Zirin, Keeanga-Yamahtta Taylor, Nick Turse, Dahr Jamail, David Barsamian, Elizabeth Laird, Amira Hass, Mark Steel, Avi Lewis, Naomi Klein, and Neil Davidson. We are also the trade publishers of the acclaimed Historical Materialism Book Series and of Dispatch Books.

Also Available from Haymarket Books

Black Liberation and the American Dream:
The Struggle for Racial and Economic Justice
Edited by Paul Le Blanc

C. L. R. James and Revolutionary Marxism:
Selected Writings of C.L.R. James 1939–1949
Edited by Paul Le Blanc and Scott McLemee

Left Americana: The Radical Heart of US History
Paul Le Blanc

Lenin and the Revolutionary Party
Paul Le Blanc

Leon Trotsky and the Organizational Principles of the Revolutionary Party
Dianne Feeley, Paul Le Blanc, and Thomas Twiss
Introduction by George Breitman

A Short History of the U.S. Working Class:
From Colonial Times to the Twenty-First Century
Paul Le Blanc

Trotskyism in the United States: Historical Essays and Reconsiderations
Edited by George Breitman, Paul Le Blanc, and Alan Wald

Unfinished Leninism: The Rise and Return of a Revolutionary Doctrine
Paul Le Blanc

About the Author

Paul Le Blanc is a professor of history at La Roche College, has written on and participated in the US labor, radical, and civil rights movements, and is author of such books as *Marx, Lenin, and the Revolutionary Experience*, *A Short History of the U.S. Working Class*, and *Work and Struggle: Voices from U.S. Labor Radicalism*. In addition, he has coauthored, with economist Michael Yates, the highly acclaimed *A Freedom Budget for All Americans: Recapturing the Promise of the Civil Rights Movement in the Struggle for Economic Justice Today*.